THINKING skills

PITTEUCHAR EAST PRIMARY SCHOOL

ages 5-7

CREDITS

Author
Georgie Beasley

Editor
Christine Harvey

Assistant Editor
Roanne Charles

Series Designers
Rachael Hammond
Joy Monkhouse

Designer
Rachael Hammond

Illustrations
Martin Aston

Cover image
© Digital Vision and © Dynamic Graphics

Published by Scholastic Ltd,
Villiers House,
Clarendon Avenue,
Leamington Spa,
Warwickshire CV32 5PR

www.scholastic.co.uk

Text © 2004 Georgie Beasley
© 2004 Scholastic Ltd

Designed using Adobe Indesign

Printed by Bell & Bain Ltd, Glasgow

2 3 4 5 6 7 8 9 0   4 5 6 7 8 9 0 1 2 3

British Library Cataloguing-in-Publication Data
A catalogue record for this book is available from the
British Library.

ISBN 0-439-98339-8

Material from The National Curriculum © Crown
copyright. Reproduced with the permission of the
Controller of HMSO and the Queen's Printer for Scotland.

Material from the National Literacy Strategy *Framework
for Teaching* and the National Numeracy Strategy
Framework for Teaching Mathematics © Crown copyright.
Reproduced under the terms or HMSO Guidance Note 8.

CONTENTS

INTRODUCTION

Thinking Skills is a series of books which outlines detailed lesson plans for developing children's thinking and helping them to develop key skills of learning. The series gives ideas on how to incorporate the teaching of thinking skills into current curriculum teaching by making changes to the way activities are presented and, in particular, matching tasks to the different ways that children learn.

There are five thinking skills identified in the National Curriculum 2000 document:
- information-processing skills
- reasoning skills
- enquiry skills
- creative thinking skills
- evaluation skills.

Teachers are probably most familiar with information-processing skills and are used to planning activities to develop these skills in maths and science. Similarly, evaluative thinking skills are usually developed well in gymnastics, dance, music and design and technology lessons, when children are encouraged to evaluate the quality of their own and other's performances, or the quality of their models and other artefacts and to consider ways to make any improvements. The aim of this series of books is to find contexts in all subjects in which to develop all types of thinking skills.

ABOUT THE BOOK
Where appropriate, this book follows the National Literacy and Numeracy strategy objectives and the QCA Schemes of Work for all National Curriculum subjects.

The activities in this book identify exactly how to develop each thinking skill within specific units of work. They also show how to adapt familiar activities to make sure that suitable emphasis is given to developing children's thinking. Sometimes an activity which follows one identified in a QCA unit of work is planned with a specific focus on its organisation so that it will support the development of children's thinking. Sometimes activities rely on specific questions which will encourage the children to identify why a particular activity is being done.

There are many specific learning styles and strategies that encourage children's thinking, including those to develop memory, thought sharing, concept mapping and exchanging ideas. Very often a lesson activity can be organised in a different way to allow children to organise their own thoughts and work. This will encourage thinking rather than having knowledge over-directed. For example, the activity in the Information-processing skills chapter 'Finding information quickly' (page 18) asks children to decide for themselves the best way to present data in order to answer a set of questions quickly and draw relevant conclusions more systematically. This is an example of how children can be encouraged to think for themselves about why we record information in graphical form. Too often children are told how to present their findings with too little opportunity to understand why.

QUESTIONING
Asking questions of very young children is a dangerous sport. We all think in a different way and the first thing to remember about asking questions is that children of the 5–7 age group are most definitely not thinking the same things, or in the same way, as the teacher. Questions which encourage children to guess what the teacher is thinking are the worst kind to ask. Instead, open-ended questions not only help the teacher to find out what the children are thinking, but also what they already know. This helps the teacher to understand where the children are in their thinking processes and to gain an insight into their conceptual understanding. This early assessment will help the teacher form the next set of questions to challenge and build on the children's understanding.

There are different kinds of questions that can be asked to encourage and actively develop children's thinking. The skill of questioning isn't always getting the question right but being able to respond to the children's answers with another suitable question. This way the teacher is not giving the children a right or wrong answer but using questioning to direct their thinking to the correct answer. This will enable the children to think their way to the correct answer by themselves and iron out any misconceptions that they may have. There are suggestions to get teachers started on this process and these can be used as prompts to help you direct the children's thinking towards the required answer for the purpose of the activity.

THE ORGANISATION OF THE BOOK

There are six chapters in this book. The first five focus on developing each of the five types of thinking. Chapter 6 includes two thinking-skills projects. The first, 'Oh, we do like to be beside the seaside', is planned to suit older children in Key Stage 1, while the second, 'Hansel and Gretel', is linked to the work on traditional tales in the National Literacy Strategy and is more suitable for younger or less able children. These projects are intended to develop all the thinking skills in a themed cross-curricular way. Teachers may wish to save these projects to the last half-term, but in order to complete the project children will be required to work over a longer period of time than is required for the other activities in the book. The first project can extend over the whole half-term, while the activities in 'Hansel and Gretel' are planned to be completed over a week or a fortnight.

Each chapter begins with a short explanation of the thinking skill being focused on and is followed by two sections of activities – to introduce then extend skills – each section covering most if not all of the curriculum subjects. Each section includes a quick-reference grid for teachers to see what the activities contain and quickly evaluate which fit easily into their own schemes of work.

The first section introduces thinking in short activities. These contain a learning objective specific to the activity and related to QCA Schemes of Work or the Literacy or Numeracy Strategies. A 'Thinking objective' outlines the particular thinking skill that the children will be developing in the course of the activity. This is expanded under 'Thinking skills', which detail how the activity will bring out the particular thinking skills in line with the learning objective. A useful resource list is provided, along with a detailed explanation of how to conduct the activity. These detailed activities have been designed to encourage and develop the children's thinking skills through practical investigation and enquiry. They are structured to encourage the children to ask why that particular activity is being carried out. Particular emphasis is placed on 'how' the children will learn – the way the learning is organised and the involvement of the children in this process – rather than the 'what'. Suggestions for questions to spark discussion and encourage the children to pose questions for investigation themselves are a focus of the activities.

The second section contains extended activities which, in addition to those sections outlined above, also contain a differentiation section with suggestions for how lower attaining children can be supported and the thinking of higher attaining children can be extended. The 'Where next' section gives ideas on how teachers can consolidate, practise, reintroduce or extend the particular activity and thinking skill. There is assessment advice on how to gauge the children's success in thinking through a problem or planning an investigation. 'Learning outcomes' relate to the 'Thinking objectives', expanding on them to describe what the children have achieved and can now do.

INFORMATION-PROCESSING SKILLS

INTRODUCTION

Information processing is about being able to collect, sort, organise and interpret a range of information to support learning in all subjects. By learning to process information in different ways, children are beginning to make sense of the world in which they live. The process is more than presenting data in different forms. It also involves deciding whether information is useful for a particular purpose. Organising information in certain ways can support memory development, and help to make links and define relationships between different parts of information.

Information can be found in the form of data, facts and knowledge. Data is collected in maths, science, history, geography, ICT and design and technology. Most data is recorded in graphical form through tables, pictograms, bar charts and sets. Facts are found to support work in most subjects, including history, geography, music, art and design and RE. In history, for instance, timelines are a useful way to organise facts and knowledge to allow interpretation of information, and in geography, finding a possible route to the local park on a large-scale map of the local area is useful for sequencing routes and directions. Knowledge is collected to support work in English, maths and PE. Information and communication technology is used throughout to present data in a range of different forms, as well as being used as a source for a variety of research activities. The activities in this chapter show how computers and other ICT equipment can be used to support learning in a range of subjects.

Information processing helps children to develop the learning process and equips them with skills which can be applied throughout their school career. By allowing the children to process information more and more independently, you enable thinking to be developed.

The key to information processing is opening the children's inquisitive minds. *What are we trying to find out and for what purpose?* is the usual question, but we need to take the children beyond that for them to realise that information will often give us more than one answer, and often raises further questions. By adjusting the organisation of existing lessons and planned activities, and identifying suitable questions which will require the children to consider carefully what they are doing and why, the children will process the information as a natural part of learning. This means that as teachers we must learn to step back and give the children time to organise their learning themselves, let them develop their ideas, and refrain from directing them towards the lessons' objectives. By allowing the children this freedom, we encourage them to begin noticing when they can use the processes in other learning. This will accelerate their learning in the long term.

The lessons in this chapter require you to let the children explain what they doing so that their thinking can be assessed. You can then move things forward by asking relevant and open questions to shift the direction of the work or consolidate the children's ideas.

Skills in the following areas all form part of information processing:
- sequencing
- pattern and relationship
- sorting and classifying
- matching
- locating and collecting
- comparing and measuring
- analysing.

INTRODUCING INFORMATION-PROCESSING SKILLS

Subject and QCA unit, NLS or NNS objective	Activity title	Thinking objective	Activity	Page
English NLS objective: To recognise words by common spelling patterns	Word spotters	To locate and collect relevant information	Locating and collecting words that contain smaller words	9
Maths NNS objective: To describe and extend simple number sequences	What comes next?	To sequence numbers in an identified order	Predicting what number comes next in a sequence, giving reasons for their choices	9
Science QCA unit: 1C Sorting and using materials	Odd one out	To make comparisons and notice pattern and relationship	Sorting a set of objects, choosing whether they have different or similar characteristics as other given objects	10
History QCA unit: 1 How are our toys different from those in the past?	Toys timeline	To sequence items chronologically	Sequencing toys in order of age as a three-dimensional timeline	10
Geography QCA unit: 24 Passport to the world	What's the weather like today?	To measure and compare; to analyse information	Collecting and recording information about the weather and comparing this to other places around the world	11
Design and technology QCA unit: 2A Vehicles	Wheels	To collect and analyse information	Looking at different types of wheels and analysing how they are attached and used	12
ICT QCA unit: 1E Representing information graphically	Fruit flavours	To sort and classify information	Using computer software to present data in graphical form	12
Art and design QCA unit: 2B Mother Nature, designer	Paintbox	To collect and sort objects; to match colours	Copying colour from observation of the natural environment	13
Music QCA unit: 1 Ongoing skills	Musical casserole	To identify pattern and sequence	Learning a song's structure to help remember the words and the tune	14
RE QCA unit: 1E How do Jewish people express their beliefs in practice?	Hanukkah	To identify objects	Matching artefacts from the Jewish celebration of Hannukah to learn about the festival	14
PE QCA unit: Gymnastic activities unit 1	Rolling around	To look at pattern and relationships	Putting together a sequence of rolling movements	15

WORD SPOTTERS

SUBJECT: ENGLISH. NLS OBJECTIVE: TO RECOGNISE WORDS BY COMMON SPELLING PATTERNS.

LEARNING OBJECTIVE
To find small words within larger ones in order to recognise critical features of words.

THINKING OBJECTIVE
To locate and collect relevant information.

THINKING SKILLS
Here, the purpose is for the children to learn how to use the skills of locating and collecting to help them find new words using words they already know. They may well develop this skill later to help them with more difficult spellings. This activity can be employed in different contexts so the children can practise these thinking skills when reading to parents and carers at home.

WHAT YOU NEED
Any large-format story or non-fiction text with which the children are familiar (it must contain a lot of smaller words within larger words); board or flip chart; photocopied extracts from different texts suitable for the children to read (pages from local newspapers are often good sources, but check for content first); highlighter pens, or paper and writing materials.

WHAT TO DO
Identify the words and associated page references you intend to use from the large-format book before the lesson begins. Read an extract with the children and together find all the times *it*, for example, is written on a particular page. Repeat the activity using different small words. Then allow the children to start locating small words themselves.

Write the word *outstanding* on the board. Read the word to the class and talk briefly about what it means. Ask the children to find all the smaller words that they can in it, such as *out*, *and* and *in*. Highlight these so that they can see them clearly. Repeat this activity using other words, such as *interesting*, *comfortable* or *consonant*.

Then start to extend the children's locating and collecting skills by giving them the photocopied text extracts. Ask them to find a given small word, such as *in*, contained within other words in the text. Match the level of work to the children's different abilities by choosing differentiated texts that contain different words inside larger ones. Then allow the children to think of their own small word to locate.

Ask the children to write down the small word they are searching for and either write a list underneath or highlight on their text the collection of larger words they find it in. (Children think highlighter pens are fun to use.) With lower attaining children collate, or ask an additional adult to collate, lists of words containing *am, an, and, at, if, in, it, on, or, up.*

WHAT COMES NEXT?

SUBJECT: MATHS. NNS OBJECTIVE: TO DESCRIBE AND EXTEND SIMPLE NUMBER SEQUENCES.

LEARNING OBJECTIVE
To use knowledge of number patterns to predict the next number in a sequence.

THINKING OBJECTIVE
To sequence numbers in an identified order.

THINKING SKILLS
The children will learn to sequence numbers and apply a rule for processing information about numbers. This will help them begin to understand that numbers can be sequenced in different steps according to the pattern and relationships between them.

WHAT YOU NEED
Number tiles or cards; pegs and a length of string or washing line, or Blu-Tack; a variety of different number patterns.

WHAT TO DO
Begin with a mental–oral starter – counting in ones, twos, doubling up to 20 and adding 1 then 2 then 3, and so on.

Then place number cards, with the numbers 1, 2 and 4 on them, face away, either on a washing line or attached with Blu-Tack to a board or wall. Turn the card with number 1 on it round and ask the children to name the number. Do the same with the number 2 card. Then ask the children to say which number they think will come next in the sequence and why. (This could be 3 and the children should be praised if they think of this and are able to give a reason for their choice.) Turn round the number 4 card. Ask the children what the rule must be for this number in the sequence to be correct? (It is to double the number. It can't be to add 2 if we are starting at 1 – the sequence would need to start at 0 for the rule to be to add 2.) Ask the children to predict the next number in the sequence. Repeat with other sequences until you are sure the children understand what to do. Sequences to try could be even numbers, odd numbers, adding 5 or 10, starting from 0 for most children or any other number to challenge the higher attainers.

Extend this work in groups, by giving the children a series of numbers and asking them to predict what number they think comes next, with reasons for their choice. Match the number sequences to the children's abilities by using large and small number patterns accordingly. Use table sequences, doubling, halving, counting forwards and backwards in tens from any number, counting forwards and backwards in fives from any number, and so on. Ask higher attainers to think of their own number sequence to present to the class. Challenge them to use some that use addition and subtraction, for example 'add 2, take away 1'.

ODD ONE OUT

SUBJECT: SCIENCE. QCA UNIT: 1C SORTING AND USING MATERIALS.

LEARNING OBJECTIVE
To learn that objects have different properties and we can find out about these using our senses.

THINKING OBJECTIVE
To make comparisons and notice pattern and relationship in a set of objects.

THINKING SKILLS
The children will use their knowledge and understanding of similarities and differences between materials to give reasons for any comparisons they can make and any patterns and relationships they have noticed. Young children find it easier to identify differences and may need focused support to find similarities. This activity will, in fact, help all children develop the more difficult understanding of similarities. They can then learn to develop their skills to classify materials into groupings according to observable similarities and differences at a later date.

WHAT YOU NEED
A collection of objects, some that are different (in texture, colour, shape, use) and some that share the same characteristics; two large hoops; paper; writing materials.

WHAT TO DO
Take two objects from the collection you have made and show them to the class. Ask the children to suggest all the things that are the same and different about them. Focus on all their observable characteristics, such as texture, colour, use and shape, encouraging the children to handle the objects

and to use vocabulary such as *smooth, transparent, bendy*.

Place two large hoops on the floor labelled *the same* and *different* (or you could use two arrows with the words written on them pointing in opposite directions). Show the children the collection of objects and place one object in between the hoops/ arrows. Ask the children to find an object from the collection that is the same as it in some way. Place this object in the hoop marked *the same*. Now ask the children to identify an object which is different to it in some way and place this in the hoop marked *different*. Ask the class to continue to sort all the objects in the same way, noting the similarities and differences each time. Encourage them to pass the objects around so that texture and material can be taken into account.

Choose three objects from either of the hoops at random and encourage the children to talk about their characteristics. Ask, *Which is the odd one out? Why?* (One or all may be the odd one out depending on the reasons given by the children.)

In groups of three, give the children three objects, for example a sheet of red cellophane, a red stickle brick and a red scourer, and ask them to agree which is the odd one out. Tell them they should record their thinking and think of three clues to help the rest of the class work out which is the odd one out, such as *The odd one out is not rigid, is not transparent, is not smooth.* (The odd one out must, therefore, be rough, flexible and not transparent, which is the scourer.) Any of the objects could be the odd one out depending on the criteria used.

Ask each group to present their three objects and challenge the class to say which is the odd one out. They can present the clues they have written if necessary. When a classmate makes a suggestion, explain that it can only be accepted if they give a reason for their choice. The group presenting must decide whether the suggestion is acceptable or not. Ask, *Could a different object be the odd one out from that thought of by the presenting group? Why?*

TOYS TIMELINE

SUBJECT: HISTORY. QCA UNIT: 1 HOW ARE OUR TOYS DIFFERENT FROM THOSE IN THE PAST?

LEARNING OBJECTIVE
To order toys from the past by age.

THINKING OBJECTIVE
To sequence items chronologically.

THINKING SKILLS

Sequencing in time order is an important skill to help children gain a sense of time in history. This will develop into an understanding of chronology as they repeat similar activities.

WHAT YOU NEED

A collection of toys or pictures of toys from different post-war decades; card labels of decades: *1940s, 1950s, 1960s* and so on, and *oldest, old, modern, most modern*.

WHAT TO DO

Different

Show some of the toys in your class collection and ask the children to talk about their features and how they are played with. For each toy ask the children:

◉ Is the toy suitable for a boy or a girl, or is it suitable for both?

◉ Is the toy old or new?

◉ How old is the toy?

◉ What feature of the toy gives us the clue to its age?

◉ Is it a toy that would have been played with by your parents or by your grandparents? How do you know?

◉ Is it a toy from a popular TV show of a particular time?

Show the children the labels and talk them through each one if necessary. Then ask them to organise the labels in a line from oldest to newest. When they have done this ask them to match each toy with an appropriate label for its era. Use this labelling of the toys as a three-dimensional timeline display, further labelling the decades *oldest, old, modern, most modern* depending on the ability of the children.

Give the children other toys to add to the correct sections of the display, asking them to give reasons why they have added toys to a particular decade.

WHAT'S THE WEATHER LIKE TODAY?

SUBJECT: GEOGRAPHY. QCA UNIT: 24 PASSPORT TO THE WORLD.

LEARNING OBJECTIVE

To collect and record evidence about a place and to link this information with other places around the world.

THINKING OBJECTIVES

To measure and compare; to analyse information.

THINKING SKILLS

Through the collection of weather statistics in both their local area and in other places, children will learn how to compare, measure and analyse information. These skills will help them to look carefully at information and begin to draw conclusions about what it actually tells them. It would be helpful if you relate the different types of weather to the clothes they might wear, or whether the place would be good for a holiday.

WHAT YOU NEED

Thermometer, rain gauge; board or flip chart; computer with a graphing package and Internet access; paper and writing materials.

WHAT TO DO

Tell the class that they are going to collect information about the weather each day for at least a week. Tell them they need to observe the type of weather, such as sunny, windy, wet, foggy, snowing. Make a list of the days of the week on the board. Put the date at the top, for example *Week beginning 1st December*. For each day, record what the weather is like from the children's suggestions, either by drawing a picture or writing a label. Record the temperature also. With higher attaining children, if it has been raining, get them to use the rain gauge to find out how much water has fallen. Record this alongside the other information.

Once you have data for a week's weather ask the children if they can suggest a good way to present the information. Encourage them to think of charts, bar charts or line graphs, depending on the information. As a class activity, collate the information onto a pictogram or bar chart.

Extend the activity by recording weather information for a month. Higher attaining children could record the temperature in a line graph and the amount of rainfall in a simple bar chart. Other children can begin to keep individual or group charts for the month. Use a monthly calendar type of presentation and, depending on the children's ability, at the end of the month collate the information into a class pictogram or bar chart to show the different weather types. Use a data-handling computer package if you wish.

Ask the children to work in groups to count up the number of sunny days, windy days and so on from the data collected. Ask them questions about the rainfall levels over the month and which were the warmest and coolest days. Ask, *What does this tell us about the weather? Is it usual for this time of year? Has the weather been the same for the whole month or different over the weeks?*

Get the groups to compare their weather data with that of a different area in the country, or an area in another country. The weather pages of the BBC website, www.bbc.co.uk/weather, provides this information. The children should note the things that are the same and the things that are different and think of reasons why.

Discuss with the children the features of different areas around the world and look at their weather types, for example deserts in dry areas; rainforests in wet, hot areas; high mountains with snow-covered peaks.

WHEELS

SUBJECT: DESIGN AND TECHNOLOGY. QCA UNIT: 2A VEHICLES.

LEARNING OBJECTIVE
To understand that wheels can be used in two different ways.

THINKING OBJECTIVE
To collect and analyse information.

THINKING SKILLS
The children will be finding wheels in the classroom and the immediate area to understand how they work and move. Through collecting and analysing this information on wheels they will discover for themselves that wheels are always joined to an axle and that sometimes the wheel moves freely and sometimes it is the axle that moves, depending on the wheel's job.

WHAT YOU NEED
Models, toys and photographs of vehicles that have wheels; a bicycle; a fishing rod; construction kits which have wheels and axles; a digital camera and display space; small sticky circles; paper and drawing materials.

WHAT TO DO
Look together at the wheels on the vehicles and toys in your collection. Explain to the children that wheels help things to move. Talk about how the wheels make your particular models move. Ask, *Which part moves? Is it the wheels or the bit that the wheels are attached to?*

Look at the bicycle wheels. Describe how the wheel is attached to the axle. Make the wheel go round and talk about what is happening to the axle. Do the children think the axle is attached to anything else? Draw their attention to the chain cogs. Make sure they watch as the wheel goes round and see that the axle moves with it because it is firmly attached to the wheel.

Next show the children the fishing rod. Look at the wheel and talk about what it does. Note that it is joined to an axle. Ask, *Does the axle go round when the wheel turns? Why not?* Make the distinction between a wheel that makes things travel, and a wheel that does a winding job.

Get the children to work in groups to build models with the construction kits, and ask them to say whether the wheels or the axle are moving round. Make sure the children understand that wheels are always connected to an axle. Take photographs of the children's models.

Finish by taking the children on a walk around the school and asking them to identify the wheels that they find. They could add small sticky circles to them. Can any children suggest where there might be wheels even though they are not visible? (Cogs in clocks and door knobs.) Ask the children to draw pictures of some of the objects they notice and display these with the collection of toys and the photographs of their models.

FRUIT FLAVOURS

SUBJECT: ICT. QCA UNIT: 1E REPRESENTING INFORMATION GRAPHICALLY.

LEARNING OBJECTIVE
To learn how to represent data using a pictogram.

THINKING OBJECTIVE
To sort and classify information in order to interpret data.

THINKING SKILLS
The children will learn how to sort and classify information, and then to interpret it by presenting it in graphical form. They will sort and classify information in three different ways, sorting, tallying and presenting the data in graphical form, to reinforce their knowledge and understanding of how information can be presented. They will begin to understand that the way information is presented helps with how easily we can use it and answer questions about it.

WHAT YOU NEED
Computer with a graphing program (to make pictograms); board or flip chart; paper and writing materials.

WHAT TO DO

Tell the children that you want to know which kind of fruit to buy for their playtime snack the next day. Give three or four examples of fruit, such as bananas, apples, oranges, and ask them to indicate which they like best.

Draw three or four large circles on the board. Use them to record the number of children who voted for each fruit and then count up how many votes you have in total. Ask the class, *Is it the correct number? How do we know?*

Explain that you are going to present the information as a pictogram and/or bar chart, to allow you to see more quickly how many votes each fruit received. Transfer the information into a graphing package on the computer, deciding with the children which icon will be used for each fruit to produce the pictogram.

When the pictogram is finished ask the children questions about the information, for example, *Which is the class's favourite fruit and how can you tell? Which is the least favourite fruit?* Ask the children to think of questions of their own which will help them interpret the data. For example, 'Are there more bananas than apples?' 'How many more oranges than bananas are there?' These should get them to show the difference between the totals of each kind of fruit.

Let the children repeat the activity in groups, using their choices of, for example, vegetables or books.

PAINTBOX

SUBJECT: ART AND DESIGN. QCA UNIT: 2B MOTHER NATURE, DESIGNER.

LEARNING OBJECTIVE

To copy colour from first-hand observation of natural objects in the local environment.

THINKING OBJECTIVES

To collect and sort objects; to match colours.

THINKING SKILLS

The children will look at objects in the local environment to collect, identify and sort colours by tones and tints. They will then produce paint mixes to match the colours of natural objects they have collected. This will help them develop an understanding of which colours to mix to make different hues, for example, that hues of orange are made with yellow and red, hues of turquoise with blue and green, and to gain a deeper understanding of colour mixing.

WHAT YOU NEED

Small palettes half covered in double-sided tape for the children to stick small samples of natural materials to (one for each group); paper, pencils and a clipboard (for each group), or a digital camera; paints in a range of colours, mixing palettes and brushes; a range of collage materials with different textures; large containers with separate compartments; PVA glue.

WHAT TO DO

Go out into the local environment with the class and look for natural objects. This could just be in the playground, or in a local park. Tell the children that you want them to find objects that have tints and tones of the same colour, such as brown leaves, twigs, conkers and bark.

Split the class into groups and tell each group to concentrate on one colour only and to collect small pieces of natural objects of that colour to stick on their palette. Tell them to be particularly careful if they are looking at insects, such as slugs or woodlice. Stress that they shouldn't move or touch them, but should draw them instead and colour them the correct colour when they return to the classroom, or they could photograph them if you want to include this option.

Return to the classroom and ask the groups questions about their finds, for example, *Which colour have you collected? Which is the darkest tone on your palette? Are all the leaves the same shade of green?* Ask the children to sort their finds into shades of colour, from light to dark. Then ask them to mix paint and also find collage materials to match the different shades of the natural colour samples they have collected. Ask them to sort the shades of paint and collage materials into a large container with separate compartments, or in consecutive trays, in order from light to dark.

The children can use the colours, the collage materials and the natural objects to create a section of a landscape picture of the area where they found their natural objects. When all the groups have finished, put together their sections to form a large picture and talk about the different colours and shades included.

MUSICAL CASSEROLE

SUBJECT: MUSIC. QCA UNIT: 1 ONGOING SKILLS.

LEARNING OBJECTIVE
To learn that songs have a structure, which help us remember the words and tune.

THINKING OBJECTIVE
To identify pattern and sequence.

THINKING SKILLS
This activity can be repeated with different songs to reinforce the children's understanding of structure and pattern in music. In the activity, they will learn to identify suitable words and phrases to use as a basis for repeating rhythmic patterns. When learning a new song, encourage the children to identify the structure for themselves as part of a natural learning style.

WHAT YOU NEED
'Paint-box' by HC Mitchell and VP Mitchell, from the songbook *Harlequin* (A&C Black); the words of the song written on a board or interactive whiteboard; percussion instruments; broad bean pods.

WHAT TO DO
Teach the children the song. Talk about the words and how the composer has expressed where each vegetable and fruit is found and what it looks and tastes like. Ask, *What does 'broad beans are sleeping in a blankety bed' mean?* Show the children a broad bean and let them feel the inside of the pod to help them understand.

Focus on introducing the children to the pattern of the song by getting them to sing the first verse and chorus again. On the board with the words on it, ask the children to identify which section is the verse and which is the chorus. Ask them to find the chorus, and verses 2 and 3 and to mark these on the board.

Let the children compose a repeating rhythmic percussion accompaniment (ostinato) in groups, based on phrases from the song, for example *blankety bed* or *cauliflowers fluffy* using drum, tambourine, woodblock or claves. Can they note places where a single sound may depict a particular fruit or vegetable? (For example, a triangle beat when *strawberries sweeter* is sung.) Extend the activity for higher attaining children by discussing how to vary the sound by making the percussion accompaniment louder, quieter, faster or slower.

Compose a class percussion piece by asking each of the groups to play their rhythms in parts to produce a percussive introduction to the song.

HANUKKAH

SUBJECT: RE. QCA UNIT: 1E HOW DO JEWISH PEOPLE EXPRESS THEIR BELIEFS IN PRACTICE?

LEARNING OBJECTIVE
To learn details about the Jewish festival of Hanukkah.

THINKING OBJECTIVE
To identify objects.

THINKING SKILLS
The children will identify and learn about a range of artefacts and customs surrounding the festival of Hanukkah.

WHAT YOU NEED
The story behind the celebration of Hanukkah; a menorah and candles; potato cakes (latkes); dough balls; dreidels; card and pencil, or spinner; counters and small bowl; a selection of artefacts from different religions.

WHAT TO DO
Read the story of Hanukkah to the children. Draw their attention to the menorah, dreidels, candles and items of food from your collection, talking about each one and what each is used for in the celebration.

Cauliflowers fluffy and cabbage
Strawberries sweeter than any
Beetroot purple and onions wh
All grow steadily day and nigh

The apples are ripe, the plums
Broad beans are sleeping in a

Blackberries juicy and rhuba
Marrows fattening hour by h
Gooseberries hairy and lettu
Radishes round and runner

The apples are ripe, the plu
Broad beans are sleeping i

Orangey carrots and turnip
Reddening tomatoes that
Brown potatoes in little h
Down in the darkness whe

The apples are ripe, the
Broad beans are sleeping

Look with the children at the order in which Jewish people light the candles on the menorah during Hanukkah. You could do this in the classroom over a number of days for the children to fully appreciate the length of time of the festival, or to support the Jewish children in the class.

If possible bring in or make some potato cakes (latkes) and enjoy tasting these together.

Play a game in small groups using your own dreidels. You can make a dreidel by decorating a 6cm square of thin card and putting a pencil through the centre to allow you to spin it. Alternatively, stick symbols to a spinner you already have in the classroom to make a dreidel. Draw a different symbol or instruction on each corner of the dreidel, such as *Take one*, *Put one back* and *Do nothing*. Place a number of counters into a bowl in the centre of a group of children. When the dreidel stops spinning the group should follow the instruction given on the appropriate side. Continue until all the counters have been taken and counted up. The winner is the person with the most counters at the end of the game.

Place the menorah and candles, latkes and dreidel, and other objects associated with Hanukkah, on a table with a number of artefacts from different religions. Ask the children to identify which objects they think Jewish people use to help them celebrate Hanukkah.

ROLLING AROUND
SUBJECT: PE. QCA UNIT: GYMNASTIC ACTIVITIES UNIT 1

LEARNING OBJECTIVE
To execute a range of gymnastic rolling movements.

THINKING OBJECTIVE
To look at pattern and relationship.

THINKING SKILLS
The children will learn a number of individual rolling movements, which will form the basis for a pattern of movements, linking the movements into relationship with one another.

WHAT YOU NEED
Enough mats for the children to work in groups no larger than three; a range of tables and benches.

WHAT TO DO
Conduct the usual warm up activities with the children. Explain that they are going to explore different rolls that can be incorporated into gymnastic sequences.

Explain to the children the different rolls you would like them to try, such as forward, backward, curled in a circle, sideways in a long straight shape. Encourage the children to begin with a still start or balance; perform the roll in a controlled way and then demonstrate a good finish. This will prevent the children throwing themselves into the roll and injuring themselves.

Split the class into eight or nine groups and give the children the opportunity to explore a range of rolls in their groups. Give the observers the job of identifying good execution or an interesting variation of a roll. Tell them to look for whether the demonstrator started with a suitable balance or moment of stillness, whether the roll was controlled, and how the demonstrator controlled the speed and kept the shape of the roll. Observe a few rolls yourself and help the children to improve upon the quality of their performance.

Then ask the children to put two rolls together, merging the finish of one into another controlled start. If they cope well with this challenge you could ask them to put a sequence of rolls together, asking the observers in each group to comment and correct the movements each time.

Talk about what the children have learned from both performing and looking at the rolls. Explain that by starting with a basic movement they have been able to link movements into a pattern and increase the number of rolls in the pattern.

EXTENDING INFORMATION-PROCESSING SKILLS

Subject and QCA unit, NLS or NNS objective	Activity title	Thinking objective	Activity	Page
English NLS objective: To use rhymes, patterned stories and poems as models for writing	What will they say next?	To identify sequences	Noting and following the pattern to a familiar story	17
Maths NNS objective: To solve a given problem by collecting, sorting and organising information	Finding information quickly	To collect information and analyse results	Collecting information and sorting and presenting it in different ways to answer questions quickly	18
Science QCA Unit: 2D Grouping and changing materials	Remembering objects	To match and classify objects	Identifying similarities and differences between materials	20
History QCA unit: 2 What were homes like a long time ago?	Home entertainment	To compare and sequence objects	Looking at different ways people entertained themselves during Victorian times and comparing this with the range of home entertainment today	21
Geography QCA unit: 25 Geography and numbers	How far to the park?	To analyse information	Reading and using information on signposts	22
Design and technology QCA unit: 2B Puppets	How did we do that?	To sequence a series of actions	Making a sock puppet and writing instructions on how to do so	24
ICT QCA unit: 2C Finding information; Music QCA unit: 6 What's the score?	Orchestral manoeuvres	To sort and classify musical instruments	Exploring a CD-ROM about musical instruments and sorting the instruments into sets	25
Art and design QCA unit: 2C Can buildings speak?	Line safari	To locate and collect lines and patterns	Finding different line patterns in the local environment	26
Music QCA unit: 5 Taking off	What comes first?	To compare and sequence sounds	Exploring and sequencing the sounds of different instruments	28
RE QCA unit: 1F What can we learn from visiting a church?	Church furniture	To match labels and pictures	Learning about some of the important features of a church	29

What will they say next?

SUBJECT: ENGLISH. NLS OBJECTIVES: TO USE RHYMES AND PATTERNED STORIES AS MODELS FOR THEIR OWN WRITING; TO USE STRUCTURES FROM POEMS AS A BASIS FOR WRITING.

LEARNING OBJECTIVE
To understand that stories and poems have structures that are sometimes based on repetition.

THINKING OBJECTIVE
To identify sequences.

THINKING SKILLS
Being able to identify pattern in literacy can be helpful in that it enables children to predict what the words will say in the next part of the story. By recognising sequences, children can begin to examine the structure of a story as it aids their memory of the story content. Encourage the children to use this knowledge of story structure to support their individual reading and writing.

WHAT YOU NEED
Not Now, Bernard by David McKee (Red Fox) or a similar story which follows an easily recognisable pattern (for example *We're Going on a Bear Hunt* by Michael Rosen, Walker Books), or traditional tales such as 'Little Red Riding Hood', 'The Gingerbread Man', 'The Enormous Turnip' or 'The Three Little Pigs'; board or flip chart.

WHAT TO DO
Read the first part of *Not Now, Bernard* (or your chosen story) to the children and talk about the characters. For example, ask the children how old they think Bernard is, or why Dad says, 'Not now, Bernard.'

Read the next bit of the story, but this time don't relay Dad's speech. When you get to this part ask the children to say what they think Dad is going to say. How do they know this? (Have the children successfully processed the information provided by the story sequence to allow them to make an informed prediction?) As the story progresses keep asking the children to predict Mum and Dad's speech and write down these suggestions for the children to see. Then write down what the characters actually say, to reinforce the pattern.

At the end of the story ask the children to say how it is structured. Ask, *How is it put together? Which bits are repeated? Is each page different? What usually happens when Bernard tells Dad or Mum something?* Note the things that the children notice are the same and different.

Talk about the children writing a story of their own like this one. Some children will be happy to write an additional part for this story, while others will come up with their own ideas entirely. Invite each child to complete a page of story to share with the rest of the class at the end of the lesson. Pose some questions to get the children thinking about what might happen in their story, such as *Do you think that Bernard is always telling 'stories' about things that are not really happening? Do you think Dad and Mum always say 'Not Now, Bernard' or do they sometimes listen?*

In subsequent lessons talk about other stories, such as *We're Going on a Bear Hunt* and 'The Three Little Pigs', which follow the same kind of pattern and use speech as a repeating form. Look with the children at what information we gain from the structure. (It helps us remember what is happening in the stories.)

DIFFERENTIATION
Give lower attaining children pictures from *Not Now, Bernard* and ask them to add the speech pattern that is repeated throughout. Ask higher attaining children to work together to rewrite a traditional tale with a repeated sequence of speech. Give each child the task of rewriting one page of a familiar story. They should be encouraged to work together as a group, deciding who will complete which page and then to retell the story during a lesson.

WHERE NEXT
Make a wall story of 'The Three Billy Goats Gruff' or 'Goldilocks and the Three Bears', or any of the stories which follow a structural pattern.

ASSESSMENT
Ask a classroom assistant to note the children who are able to use the pattern of *Not Now, Bernard* to make up a new part for Bernard or to make up their own story. Assess how well the higher attaining children are able to work together to produce their own version of a familiar story. Have they identified the structure and pattern, and used this successfully in their own writing?

LEARNING OUTCOMES
Most children will be able to predict patterns in a story and use them to write their own story with a repetitive structure. They will also be able to recognise such structures in other reading.

FURTHER ENGLISH CHALLENGES
A repetitive poem
Read the rhyme 'The House that Jack Built' to the class. Talk about the structure and how the poem

adds a new part and goes back to each part that has come before it before reaching the end. Other stories that can be used include the Hairy Maclary stories by Lynley Dodd. Develop the children's understanding of sequencing information by asking them to write the ending of a poem that you have begun for them. Start with a simple idea that can be expanded. For example *This is the car that Jane owned. This is the window left open and wide in the front of the car that Jane owned. This is the dog that got off his lead that climbed in the window left open and wide in the front of the car that Jane owned...*

Filling in a repetitive poem

Give the children a copy of 'The House that Jack Built', or part of it, with some of the words missing. Ask the children to read the poem and to fill in the missing words as a cloze procedure. The children will need to have identified the pattern of the poem before completing their own version. This will also develop spelling.

FINDING INFORMATION QUICKLY

SUBJECT: MATHS. NNS OBJECTIVE: TO SOLVE A GIVEN PROBLEM BY COLLECTING, SORTING AND ORGANISING INFORMATION IN SIMPLE WAYS.

LEARNING OBJECTIVE

To sort and present information in different ways in order to find answers to questions.

THINKING OBJECTIVE

To collect information and analyse results.

THINKING SKILLS

At some stage children learn about presenting information as a list, table, set or graph. Often they are directed towards using a particular presentation and lose touch with the learning of when and why a list, table, set or graph is suitable. The activity here allows the children to make decisions about the way that information is presented and also to consider why a particular format is best suited to particular information. The activity is an example of how, by organising familiar types of exercises in a different way, children's thinking can be developed effectively.

WHAT YOU NEED

A large sheet of paper with a list of the children's names on; coloured pencils; large sheets of paper with sorting rings on them, coloured sticky squares or circles; a tally sheet; a bar chart with colours written along the x-axis and a scale on the y-axis; board or flip chart.

WHAT TO DO

Tell the children that you are going to collect data to find out which is the class's favourite colour. You can link this exercise to a particular context, such as the different coloured cars seen on the road, or the different colours of front door the children have on their homes. Talk to the children about why we collect such data. Explain that there has to be a purpose, for example to find answers to questions, or to find out what people want. Ask the children to think of reasons why they might want to collect information about their favourite colours. Perhaps it is to make sure that if they buy a present for someone that they buy the right colour, or perhaps to decorate the classroom using the children's collective favourite colours.

Explain that they are going to collect this information in different ways, so that they can decide for themselves which is the best way to present it. Tell the children of the four different ways that you want them to collect the information:

1. Show them a sheet containing a list of all the children's names in the class. Tell them that you want them to find their own name and to colour a square in their favourite colour next to their name.

2. Show them the sheets containing rings and how to stick a coloured square in their favourite colour inside one of the rings.

3. Show them the tally chart and explain how to record their favourite colour by tallying. (Depending on the ability of your group, you may want to use this as a tick sheet.) Check that the children are using their knowledge of adding 5 to find the totals.

4. Show them the bar graph. Explain that you want them to find the column showing their favourite colour and to colour the next square on the bar, or add a new column if their favourite colour isn't shown.

You could let the children do this as a class activity, with the children moving around the classroom to complete the information. If you wish to monitor more closely what the children do, you could organise them into groups, asking each group to complete one of the recording methods one at a time. It will depend on your class and whether they are able to complete the recordings independently. It may be that you will want to collect the information over two or three days, or do the activity when you have additional adult support.

When all the groups have recorded their information, gather the children together. Ask them to think of a number of questions that will help them to find out the children's and the class's favourite colours. Start by prompting them with obvious questions, such as *Which children like red most? Which is the colour liked by the most/the least children?* Then move on to more difficult questions that will require the children to make comparisons and find differences. Include questions like *Do more children like red than green? How many more children like blue than orange?* Record the questions you have decided on together on the board.

Look first at the list on which the children recorded their favourite colours next to their names. Ask the children the questions you agreed upon, letting them answer based on the information recorded on the list. Afterwards, ask the children, *Did you find the questions easy to answer? Why? Could you think of a better way to present the information?*

Then look at the sheet where the colours are recorded in rings. Ask the class to answer the questions again. Ask if they think it was easier to understand the information presented in this way.

Look at the tally chart and again ask the class the questions. Ask if it is easier to see the totals recorded in each column using this method of collecting the information.

Finally, look at the bar chart and if they don't know, show the children how to read the scale at the side of the graph to find the answers to the questions. Ask how they found this way of reading the information.

Ask the class to tell you what their collective favourite colour is and which way of presenting the data they found was the best to find out this information.

DIFFERENTIATION

Explain to higher attainers how each square on the bar chart can represent two, three, four, five or any number of people. Ask them to transfer the data in the bar chart onto another one where the gradations represent 2, 5 or 10. Let the children decide which is the best way to represent the information.

Support those who require it by using cubes of colour. Put cubes of the same colour into towers and make comparisons by measuring them against each other. Children can see and feel the difference in the heights of each tower. This will support the children's understanding of what *difference* means when analysing information.

WHERE NEXT

Give the children some graphs already completed and invite them to ask questions and to find the answers by reading the graphs.

Repeat the activity and collect information about favourite things relevant to the current interests and age of the children, for example television and book characters, favourite foods and games.

ASSESSMENT

Use a tick chart to note the children who are able to find the answers to the questions quickly. Set up a similar activity for the children to complete independently and keep this example in a portfolio of their work.

LEARNING OUTCOMES

The children will understand how to collect information and experiment on presenting it in a way which helps them find answers to questions easily and quickly.

FURTHER MATHS CHALLENGES

What does this tell us?

Give each child a chart which shows the distance cars travelled when rolled down a ramp. For example, list the cars down the left-hand column and write the distance they travelled in the right-hand column. Ask the children to write 1 by the car that travelled the furthest distance, 2 by the car that travelled the second furthest distance, and so on. When the children have finished this, ask them a series of questions and to quickly find the answers, for example *Which car travelled the shortest distance? Which car travelled the fifth furthest distance? How do you know?* Can the children think of a better way to organise the information to help them answer these questions more quickly?

Minibeasts

Make a database or a list of information about minibeasts. Include information about the number of legs each creature has, its colour, how it moves and whether it has a pattern on its body. Give the children the list, or access to the database, and ask them to present the information in a chart. Then ask them to use their chart to answer a series of questions about the minibeasts. For example, *How many of the creatures have six legs? How many have a pattern? How many fly?* Did the children find it easy to answer the questions from the way that their information was presented? Challenge higher attaining children to make bar charts to present the information collected on the various minibeasts' attributes.

REMEMBERING OBJECTS

SUBJECT: SCIENCE. QCA UNIT: 2D GROUPING AND CHANGING MATERIALS.

LEARNING OBJECTIVE

To identify similarities and differences between materials.

THINKING OBJECTIVE

To match and classify objects.

THINKING SKILLS

The children will learn to use matching and classification skills to aid their memories, as well as to reinforce their knowledge and understanding of materials. This will also help the children to structure their thinking when trying to remember facts and figures in other subjects.

WHAT YOU NEED

A tray, and cloth to cover it; board or flip chart; four different collections of objects:
1. two each of wooden, plastic, metal, fabric and paper objects
2. a different set of objects with the same characteristics and materials as above
3. two each of objects which have different textures, such as smooth, rough, fluffy, soft, silky, bumpy and hard
4. five objects or materials which change shape by twisting, bending, stretching or squashing, and five that do not.

WHAT TO DO

Ask the children to sit on the carpet in a circle. Put the first collection of objects on a tray and place it in the centre of the circle so everyone can see it clearly. Invite the children to look closely at the objects. After one minute, ask them to close their eyes. Remove one object from the tray. When they open their eyes, ask the children to say which object has been removed. Repeat this a few times. Then cover the tray with a cloth and ask the children to name all the objects on the tray. List these on the board if appropriate, then see how many the children remembered.

Get out the second collection of objects. Ask the children to say what they can see. They will possibly name the objects, which is fine, but encourage them afterwards to also describe the texture, colour, shape and size of the objects. If they are able, ask them to name the materials the objects are made from too. Ask the children if they can organise the objects in a way that will help them to remember what they are when covered. Then suggest that they try to match objects made from the same material and place them together. Record the objects that they match up. Then cover the tray (and the recording) and ask the children to name the objects they can remember. Afterwards, ask if they found it easier to remember the objects this time.

Bring out the objects in collection 3 and this time ask the children to match objects according to their texture. Give the children pointers, such as *smooth*, *rough*, and so on, if they need it. Record their matched objects if you wish and cover the tray again, asking the children to name the objects from memory.

Finally, repeat the activity with collection 4. This time the children need to match the objects according to the properties of the materials in terms of whether they change their shape by twisting, stretching, squashing, bending, and any that do not change shape. Carry out the recording, covering up and memory game again to finish.

DIFFERENTIATION

Include in collection 4 a set of objects the state of which can be changed and then reversed, for example by heating and cooling, for higher attaining children to consider.

Use a smaller number of objects each time for lower attaining children. Support those who still find it difficult by playing the opening activity more often until you are able to see that children are beginning to use classification to support their memory recall.

WHERE NEXT

Repeat the activity, using different sets of objects for the children to match and classify, depending on your particular current topic or learning theme, for example fruits, coins, shapes, objects beginning with *pl-* and so on.

ASSESSMENT

Note the children whose memories have improved due to the use of matching and classification techniques, and set up interactive displays with a range of different objects to keep their skills sharp. Invite the children to organise these in some kind of logical groupings, which will help them remember what is there.

LEARNING OUTCOMES

All children should be able to identify which object has been removed from a set of objects. Most will be able to classify by material properties to support their memory recall. Some may be able to use more sophisticated criteria to sort and classify the sets of objects to help their memory recall.

FURTHER SCIENCE CHALLENGES

The conveyor belt game

Set up a series of objects, or pictures of objects, for the children to recall in a particular order. The children will need to decide for themselves how to classify the objects before trying to memorise them in the correct order. The sets could include, for example, which room of the house objects belong in, whether objects are from a particular country or religious culture.

Find the material

Write a precise description on a board or flip chart, which will only fit one material of those used in a collection of objects. Challenge the children to find an object with the same material and to say how it fits the description by indicating the different properties described. Follow this up by asking the children to write descriptions of the range of materials in the collection during a guided writing session. Read some of the children's descriptions to the class.

HOME ENTERTAINMENT

SUBJECT: HISTORY. QCA UNIT: 2 WHAT WERE HOMES LIKE A LONG TIME AGO?

LEARNING OBJECTIVE

To make comparisons between features of household objects from the past and present.

THINKING OBJECTIVE

To compare and sequence objects.

THINKING SKILLS

The children will be comparing how people entertained themselves in the past and the present, and sequencing objects from old to new. Sequencing objects will help develop the children's sense of chronology. The children will need to compare methods of entertainment from Victorian times to the present day.

WHAT YOU NEED

Pictures of people entertaining themselves during Victorian and Edwardian times, such as playing the piano, singing to family members, listening to a steam organ or a wind-up record player; a collection of pictures of, or actual, radios, records and a record player, tapes and a tape player, CDs and a CD player, DVDs and a DVD player, videos and a video recorder, a television.

WHAT TO DO

Talk to the children about all the things they do to entertain themselves. If they are struggling, suggest favourite toys they play with and activities such as watching television, going to the park, and so on.

Focus on entertainment that is based on technology, such as watching television, and ask the children to talk about their favourite programmes. Then talk about the different music that the children listen to. Ask questions about their favourite bands or singers. How do the children play this music? Do they use a CD player or a tape player?

Show the children your collection of records and talk about the material from which they are made. Discuss whether the children's parents or grandparents would have listened to records when they were younger. Talk about your own experience. Talk about how records and CDs are played – with a needle or laser. If you have one, play the vinyl record on a record player, showing the children the needle and explaining how the sound is produced. Show them a CD player and explain how it plays the CDs. Ask the children, *Which is the most modern way to play music? How do you know?* Ask them to say whether they think the record player was invented before the television. What about the video and DVD – when were they invented and was it before the record player and television?

Ask the children to suggest how you should put the record player, tape player, radio, television, video player, CD and DVD players in the correct sequence from oldest to most modern, and how to match the records, CDs, DVDs and tapes to the correct player.

Go on to look at the pictures of how people during Victorian or Edwardian times entertained themselves. Ask the children, *How did these people listen to music or watch films?* Show the picture of an early record player and tell the children that it worked by winding it up. Do the children know why? Were there radios at that time? Did people go to the cinema? Tell the children about the role that live theatre played at that time. Talk about the fact that there was no electricity and people didn't know how to transfer sound mechanically or digitally. Relate this knowledge to the children's learning about other household items. Explain that the record player and early cinema film were invented before radio and television because they could be operated without electricity. Compare Victorian and Edwardian activities with those that the children enjoy today. Finish by asking the children to sort all the pictures and/or objects that have been used in the lesson into Victorian entertainment and modern entertainment.

DIFFERENTIATION

Ask higher attaining children to look at only radios, music players or televisions and get them to discuss which are the oldest and most modern, giving reasons. They should develop their time-related vocabulary including *new, older, oldest, old-fashioned, modern, more modern* and *most modern*.

With less able children concentrate on whether items were used a long time ago or whether they are used today. Ask the children to sort the objects into whether the items are operated by electricity or not as a measure. Concentrate on restricted words with them, such as *old-fashioned* and *modern*.

WHERE NEXT

Use photographs or pictures of the children as babies and young children, and of their parents and grandparents and produce a class timeline using the photographs rather than dates.

Look at a piano and electric keyboard, or pictures of these, and ask the children to note the similarities and differences between them. Ask the children to say which would only have been used in Victorian times. How many homes do they think have a keyboard today? How many have pianos? Which is the more popular instrument today?

ASSESSMENT

Make a timeline labelled *a long time ago, long ago, now* and ask the children to sequence pictures of radios and music players into the correct order on the timeline. Use pictures of children, parents and grandparents to help their decisions where they need it. Ask the children to give reasons for their decisions

during a plenary session. Which children agree and which disagree with the sequencing each time?

LEARNING OUTCOMES

The children will begin to develop a sense of time and chronology, and use language related to the past when comparing household entertainment systems. They will be able to sequence artefacts according to their age.

FURTHER HISTORY CHALLENGES

Lamplight

Give the children a collection, or pictures, of lights from different periods. Look at some that are powered by oil, flame, gas, battery and electricity. Include some from the same period, but of different styles. Ask the children to put the lights in order from the oldest to the most modern. Check the children's understanding of *old* and *old-fashioned* with any modern lamps in a reproduction style.

Tick, tock

Give the children different clocks and ask them to put these in order of age. Include a pendulum clock, wind-up clock, battery and electrically operated clocks, a digital clock and modern fun clocks. Ask the children to note the styles and the materials from which the clocks are made, as well as the way that they operate, to make their decisions.

HOW FAR TO THE PARK?

SUBJECT: GEOGRAPHY. QCA UNIT: 25 GEOGRAPHY AND NUMBERS.

LEARNING OBJECTIVE

To learn that signs give us information about the local area and enable us to answer geographical questions.

THINKING OBJECTIVE

To analyse information.

THINKING SKILLS

The children will locate information from signs and maps to learn about the local area. They will use the information given on signposts to find out information about places. This will help them to develop a sense of space, and to develop their mapping skills.

WHAT YOU NEED

Photographs of different signposts giving the distances to places, including both local signposts that show small distances of less than a mile (rural signposts often have signs with small numbers and familiar fractions on) and signposts with places further afield to enable a comparative study; photographs of signposts with symbols indicating local amenities (picnic areas, campsites, toilet facilities, telephone, café, car park and so on); road and Ordnance Survey maps of the local area; photographs and/or a large plan of a local attraction or theme park.

WHAT TO DO

Show the class some of the photographs of distance signposts, from the immediate and wider area, and ask the children what information the sign is giving us. *Is it telling us, for example, that we can buy petrol, eat a meal, make a telephone call or park our car? Does it tell us how far away a place is?* Ask questions about some of the signposts, such as, *How far is it to travel to this place? Is it more than or less than a mile?* If necessary go outside and walk one quarter of a mile with the children so that they have an idea of how far this is and how far a mile would be.

Compare the distances on the signposts with the class. Ask, *Which is the furthest place to travel to? Which is the closest?*

Visit, or show the children photographs and a large plan of, a familiar attraction in the local area. This could be a local park, a visitor attraction or an amusement park. Together locate, or look at photographs of, any signs which give information about facilities there and discuss how we can tell what facilities there are from the signs. Add signposts if there aren't enough on the plan. Ask questions, such as *If you wanted to make a telephone call in which direction would you go? If you want to have a picnic, is there a suitable place and how far away is it from the car park? What about if you need to use the toilet? Which symbols tell us there are telephone, picnic or toilet facilities?*

Choose any signpost on the plan. Ask the children to say how far it is to the facility to which it is pointing (for example, the toilets). Trace a path towards this facility until you reach another sign and ask, *Does the sign tell us how far away we are now? Are we closer or further away than where we started from? How do we know?* (Adding illustrations of additional facilities would be a good idea. Include toilets, a shop, a restaurant, a picnic area and telephone boxes. Add signs with quarter and half-mile measures at different points around the plan, pointing towards the facilities. For example, from one point include a sign indicating half a mile to the toilets and from a second point a sign reading a quarter of a mile.)

Look at road maps and OS maps of the local area with the children, and find different symbols showing tourist spots and interesting places to visit. Find out what the symbols mean as a class and revise the symbols representing facilities used earlier.

Ask the children to work in groups to make a visitors' information board showing the amenities available in an imaginary tourist attraction, using the symbols they have learned. Tell them they should consider things such as how far it is to get there from their locality and in which direction it can be found. They should make a map of the imaginary attraction and add signposts with information on distances to facilities and symbols showing the different facilities available.

DIFFERENTIATION

Look at signposts for places that are a long way away, measured in miles, with higher attaining children. Ask the children to choose one of the places named on a sign and to find out what they can about that place by using the Internet, maps and/or brochures. Use only signs that can be found in the immediate area with lower attaining children and ask them to plot these on a simple plan of the locality.

WHERE NEXT

Get the children to make signposts to help people find the school facilities, measuring the distances in metres to add to them.

When going out on a school visit get the children to look for symbols and signposts which tell them how far they have travelled and what facilities they are passing on the way.

ASSESSMENT

Make a note of the children who can read signposts in terms of their direction and distance. Note those who are beginning to relate this information to the length of time it takes to walk particular distances. Note the children who can analyse the signs to work out whether they are closer to facilities from different spots on the plan.

LEARNING OUTCOMES
Most children will be able to analyse the information given on signposts and through symbols. Some children will begin to take this further and understand distances.

FURTHER GEOGRAPHY CHALLENGES
Giving directions
Look at your plan or map of the local attraction and ask the children to say in which direction they would travel to get to a certain place. How many roads would they have to cross? Can they get there without crossing any roads by going a different way? What features would they pass on the way? Let one child pretend to 'walk' to a chosen spot by following instructions given by other children in the class.

Calculating routes
Using local maps, give groups of children two routes to a destination and ask them to analyse which of the two would be the best or safest route to take. They need to give reasons for their answer and be able to analyse which route will be the longest and which the shortest.

HOW DID WE DO THAT?

SUBJECT: DESIGN AND TECHNOLOGY. QCA UNIT: 2B PUPPETS.

LEARNING OBJECTIVE
To make a sock puppet and write a set of instructions recording how to do this.

THINKING OBJECTIVE
To sequence a series of actions.

THINKING SKILLS
The children will learn the importance of getting the order right when making models and other artefacts in design and technology lessons. Sometimes the order will not matter, but at other times it will be vital. For example, it doesn't matter which feature the children add to their sock puppet first, but they do need to design the puppet, decide what materials to use and how to fix them to the sock before starting to make the puppet. This ordering becomes more important as the children get older and start to make more complicated models. This activity makes sure that the sequencing process when making models is understood early.

WHAT YOU NEED
A sock puppet; materials for the children to make their own sock puppets; paper and writing/drawing materials; a selection of simple sets of instructions; board or flip chart; a camera (optional).

WHAT TO DO
Explain to the children that you want them each to make a sock puppet. Show them your sock puppet and tell a simple story, showing the children how you can manipulate the puppet to help convey the action and mood of the story. Tell the children that the first thing they need to do is decide what the puppet will look like when it is finished. Pose questions, such as *What will its character be like? Will it be an animal, a person or a cartoon character?* This part will not be easy for some Year 1 children who still like to decide what their finished puppets are going to be like only when they have started to create them. Give these children the chance to work like this if necessary, but return at frequent intervals, or work with them in a small group, to establish this learning as the puppet takes shape. Also, talk at this stage about the materials the children will need and how they are going to attach the features to the puppet.

Get the children to sketch a design for their puppets and then to make them. Admire the children's sock puppets when they have finished them, and point out that in order to make puppets like these again it would be useful to have a list of instructions detailing how they made them. Explain that you would like to create a class instruction list and that the list of instructions must be precise and in the right order. Show the class a number of different sets of instructions and look at different layouts. This will link well with literacy lessons on writing instructions. Focus on whether to use numbers, bullet points or time words, such as *first, second, third, next, then* and *finally*.

Perform this exercise as a shared writing activity, and start with a suitable title before talking about what the children did first. Did they start with a sock? Did they gather together all their resources? Did they consider the character of their puppet and decide what it would look like? Write down the first instruction on the board after taking suggestions from the children. Continue with the list, discussing what the children did at each stage of their puppet making. You may find that the children change their minds or want to add other things as you discuss the sequence of stages. These considerations should be included. The children may also disagree with the order, as they may have created their puppet in different ways, so you may have to come to a class agreement.

When you have finished the list on the board and the children are happy with it, type it out and give each child a copy, so they have their own list of instructions. Ask them to illustrate their lists, either with their own drawings or with photographs of their puppets.

DIFFERENTIATION
Work with less able children in a smaller group while they make their puppets, or get them to make their puppets in groups over a number of days. Help them to look at, read and analyse different ways of presenting lists of instructions while the other children copy out the class instructions.

WHERE NEXT
Repeat the activity using other types of puppets, including glove, pop-up, stick and finger puppets.

Present the sequence of instructions in an incorrect order in a text document on the computer. The children can learn how to use the cut and paste facility, and to understand that it is easier to edit using a computer than to write out by hand each time.

ASSESSMENT
Check if the children have learned the importance of sequencing when carrying out a design and technology task. Check also whether they understand

that this order of steps needs to be considered before they start to make a puppet or other model.

LEARNING OUTCOMES
The children will begin to appreciate the importance of performing tasks in a logical sequence to aid their making skills. They will see that recording a sequence of instructions is helpful when creating designs.

FURTHER DESIGN AND TECHNOLOGY CHALLENGES

Writing instructions
Challenge the children to write instructions independently for other tasks that involve following a precise sequence, for example planting seeds, a cooking recipe or a science activity.

Sort it out
Put a sequence of instructions in an incorrect order and ask the children to put them in the right order. These should include things that will go disastrously wrong if not in the correct order.

ORCHESTRAL MANOEUVRES

SUBJECT: ICT. QCA UNIT: 2C FINDING INFORMATION
SUBJECT: MUSIC. QCA UNIT: 6 WHAT'S THE SCORE?

LEARNING OBJECTIVES
To search a CD-ROM to find information; to identify different ways instruments make sounds.

THINKING OBJECTIVE
To sort and classify musical instruments.

THINKING SKILLS
The children will be required to think of the nature of different musical instruments in terms of the way the sound is produced and the way they are played. They will classify a range of instruments and physically sort them into different groups. This activity takes sorting to a higher level. It will develop the children's abilities to sort using unobservable differences, which is an extension to usual sorting activities where they sort according to what they can see, hear, feel, taste or smell.

WHAT YOU NEED
A collection of musical instruments which are played in different ways (or laminated pictures of such different instruments); a CD-ROM which contains pictures of different musical instruments which are played in different ways; a clip art package; computers (enough for groups of children to work at); board or flip chart.

WHAT TO DO

Show the children the musical instruments you have collected. Talk with them about how each instrument is played, focusing on how the sound is produced, and whether the instrument is blown, struck, scraped or shaken, for example. You could ask some of the children to demonstrate playing the instruments. Then ask the class to sort the instruments into sets according to this criteria.

Next, look at the CD-ROM and show the children how to navigate through the windows to find information about and pictures of different musical instruments. Remind the children how to search using menus, indexes and key words. Allow them time to explore the CD to find as many different instruments as they can. If possible, show the children how to save the pictures into a blank Word document, where they can then sort the instruments into groups that are played in the same way. Otherwise record on the board the children's ideas about how each instrument is played as you look at them on the screen and which groups they suggest the instruments should be sorted into.

Ask the children to work in groups to use a clip art package to set up a screen with a range of musical instruments which are played in different ways. Ask them to move the pictures around to sort the instruments into groups. Tell them that they should choose any criteria for sorting the instruments, as long as they can explain what these criteria are, for example all the stringed instruments could be grouped together, or all those whose sound is produced by blowing, and so on.

DIFFERENTIATION

Give higher attaining children more obscure musical instruments to sort, using real instruments or those on a CD-ROM or the Internet (follow the school's policy for Internet access and supervision). Expect higher attainers to resize their pictures before moving them together in sets so that they don't overlap.

WHERE NEXT

Repeat the activity using other items linked to a particular topic. Use this also as an assessment for the children's skills and knowledge of the processes involved in sorting and classifying.

ASSESSMENT

Note the children who work out that some instruments can be played in different ways and can therefore be put into more than one set. For example, a violin can be played by scraping (bowing) or plucking.

LEARNING OUTCOMES

The children will have had good practice in searching a CD-ROM to find information. They will understand how to classify information and objects to given criteria and how to organise knowledge of musical instruments by sorting them into groups.

FURTHER ICT AND MUSIC CHALLENGES

Sorting instruments on screen

Place labels according to the way that different instruments are played at intervals around a blank Word document. Form the class into groups working around different computers and show the children how to insert instruments from a clip art program next to the label that they think the instrument belongs to. (Ensure that the pictures are the correct size before the lesson, and resize and save them to a separate file for the children to use if necessary.) If an instrument can be played in more than one way tell the children they may need to copy it and attach it to more than one label. Save the children's work before printing a copy if relevant. Often it is just as easy to look at the work on screen to discuss why the children have put the instruments into a particular set.

LINE SAFARI

SUBJECT: ART AND DESIGN. QCA UNIT: 2C CAN BUILDINGS SPEAK?

LEARNING OBJECTIVE

To find different line patterns in local buildings and to record these to examine the way they make up shapes, pattern and decoration in buildings.

THINKING OBJECTIVE

Locating and collecting lines and patterns.

THINKING SKILLS

The children will identify a range of lines from buildings in the locality and think about how these combine to make shapes and patterns. They will use this analysis to collect a wide range of different types of lines and will start to describe these using their own language.

WHAT YOU NEED

For the outdoor activity: paper, wax crayons, sketchbooks, drawing materials, a digital camera. In the classroom: housing magazines; wall bricks, wheel trims, fencing trellis; board or flip chart.

WHAT TO DO

Explain to the children that they will be going outside to look for lines in the playground and/or around the school. Before you go out ask them to think of all the lines they are likely to find. Show them pictures in magazines, such as mortar lines between bricks, edges of roof tiles fitting together, the patterns in fencing and gates, lead windows and drain covers. Collect the children's ideas and record them in pictorial form on the board. Make sure a good variety of lines are included, such as curved, spiral, curled and wiggly, straight, horizontal, vertical, dashed and diagonal lines.

Go outside with the class, taking the resources for recording with you. Notice with the children all the lines that can be seen. Get them to collect these by making wax rubbings, drawing different kinds of lines in their sketchbooks and using the digital camera.

Return to the classroom and look at all the lines the children have made. Load the pictures from the digital camera onto the computer screen and point out the lines that can be seen. Ask the children questions to promote discussion, such as *What sort of line is this one? Can you describe which way the line travels? Does it go round in a circle or a straight line? Does it change direction? Does it meet a different line? Do any lines make a shape or picture?* Model the language to describe the size, shape and direction of lines if necessary. Make a large display of the lines the children recorded. Ask them to make enlarged pictures of the lines and patterns they found. Add objects with lines in them to the display, such as bricks built into a low-level wall, wheel trims and garden trellis.

DIFFERENTIATION

Keep a less able group with you whilst outdoors so that you can point out and prompt the children to see the lines that you want them to collect.

Help them to record these in their sketchbooks if necessary, making sure that they do some of the recording themselves! Higher attaining children should be challenged to locate unusual lines and shapes, and to relate this to their knowledge and understanding of the properties of shape.

WHERE NEXT

Look with the children at wall tiles and wallpaper patterns and ask them to locate the patterns that use lines. Get them to note whether the lines are straight or curved, whether they cross or not and in which direction they travel. Ask them to make up names to describe each different type of line they have located.

Ask the children to design wrapping paper and wallpaper using their knowledge about line patterns.

ASSESSMENT

Look at the children's collections of lines in their sketchbooks and count up the different types of line that they have located and collected. Which children have been able to use some or all of these ideas in their own work?

LEARNING OUTCOMES

The children will describe the shapes, patterns and decoration they can see in their school environment and how they are made up of different lines. They will begin to understand that the most complex of designs can actually be a collection of different types of lines.

FURTHER ART AND DESIGN CHALLENGES

Fabric designs

Look at fabric designs with the class and locate the lines the designer has used to create the patterns and shapes (African and Indian designs are interesting for this exercise). Ask the children to point out how often the pattern is repeated and the distances between each repeat. Ask them to copy the line patterns in the fabric and replicate the pattern in any way they wish. They could use a scanner, a photocopier or block printing, for example.

Modern art

Look with the class at paintings by artists who use lines prominently in their work. Kandinsky, Picasso, Miró and Mondrian are obvious choices. Ask the children to locate the line patterns in the artwork you show them, then get them to create paintings in the same style. When they have completed their painting ask the children to talk about the shapes and patterns they have created with their lines. Intersperse examples of these lines between their paintings in a class display.

WHAT COMES FIRST?

SUBJECT: MUSIC. QCA UNIT: 5 TAKING OFF.

LEARNING OBJECTIVE
To explore the pitch of different instruments.

THINKING OBJECTIVE
To compare and sequence sounds.

THINKING SKILLS
The children will need to link what they are seeing to what they are hearing when making decisions about pitch. Explore with the children the questions they are asking themselves about each sound as they hear it, such as *Is this one a higher sound?* Their comparison skills will be refined further when putting the instruments in order from those that make the lowest to the highest sound.

WHAT YOU NEED
Families of instruments at different pitches, for example a set of drums, triangles, cymbals and hand bells, which are different sizes and thus make differently pitched sounds; a set of chime bars, a xylophone or glockenspiel; a piano or keyboard.

WHAT TO DO
Look at a set of chime bars, or a xylophone or glockenspiel with the children. Slowly, play up and down the notes and invite the children to say what they notice about each of the sounds. Are they high or low? Play a conducting game by asking the children to indicate with their hands whether the sounds are going from low to high or high to low each time. Allow them to look at the instrument as you are playing the game so that they can link the range of the instrument with whether the sound is high or low in pitch.

Then go on to ask a variety of questions about the instruments you have, showing the instruments to the class as you ask the questions: *Which drum makes the lowest/highest sound? Can you put the drums in order?* Repeat this for all the instruments in your collection and then get the children to compare the instruments' range of pitches. Ask them, *Do you think the bell or triangle will make the highest sound? Do you think the cymbal or triangle will make the lowest sound? Which of these instruments makes the lowest sound?*

Look at a piano or keyboard with one group of children at a time. Play a very high note and then a very low note. Ask the children to say which is the higher and which the lower sound. Reduce the interval so that the sounds are not so high and low, and ask the children to say again which is the higher and lower sound. Continue like this until either you are playing two notes very close to each other in pitch, or the children are unable to tell the difference.

DIFFERENTIATION
Work with a restricted number of instruments with lower attaining children and make sure that they have a good understanding of pitch. Relate higher attaining children's knowledge and understanding to a context of how pitch is used to create effects, for example choosing a rising tune to depict suspense or a falling one to depict church bells.

WHERE NEXT
Set up games for the children to play which require them to order instruments according to their pitch. Give them challenges to work out, such as *Is the highest sound always the smallest instrument? Is the lowest sound always the biggest instrument?* Look at photographs of the instruments in an orchestra and ask the children to say whether they think each one gives high or low sounds, giving reasons for their answers.

ASSESSMENT
Note the children who can compare the sounds and put the instruments in the correct order according to pitch. Note those who can distinguish between very small intervals.

LEARNING OUTCOMES
The children will learn to compare and sequence differently pitched sounds and instruments. Some children will recognise how sounds of different pitch can create different effects and what these might be.

FURTHER MUSIC CHALLENGES
Water music
Fill bottles with different amounts of water and show the children how to make sounds from them. Ask the children to compare the sounds and put the bottles in order of pitch. Can the children explain how they made their decisions? How many ordered the sounds visually by the amount of water in the bottles, and how many by trial and error, comparing the sounds by tapping the bottles? Challenge the children to work

out how to play 'Twinkle, Twinkle Little Star' on the bottles once they know the pitch of each.

Can you hear the wind?

Investigate sets of wind chimes with the children. Challenge them to predict and then find out which wind chimes will make the lowest and highest sound. Ask the children what they based their predictions on. Did they use their knowledge and understanding of comparing other instruments in previous investigations?

Church furniture

SUBJECT: RE. QCA UNIT: 1F WHAT CAN WE LEARN FROM VISITING A CHURCH?

Learning objective

To learn about some of the important features of a church and their functions.

Thinking objective

To match labels and pictures.

Thinking skills

By matching labels to pictures children will reinforce their knowledge of Christian church furniture and artefacts. By matching pictures to religious ceremonies they will begin to establish links between their knowledge and their understanding.

What you need

Photographs of a cross, font, altar, lectern, pulpit, aisle and pews; labels for the photographs; pictures of the interiors of churches, christening and wedding ceremonies.

What to do

Talk to the children about the times that they, or people they know, have been to a Christian church. Was it for a family wedding or christening? Show the class the pictures you have of churches and ask questions such as *What shape are the insides laid out as? Are they all in the shape of a cross? Why is this?* Relate the shape of the cross to the symbol of the crucifixion and how Christians remember Jesus through the sign of the cross. Ask for a volunteer to pick out the photograph of the cross from your collection and match it to its corresponding label.

Then show the children a picture of a christening and talk briefly about what is happening in the picture. Explain that it is only Christians, those who believe that Jesus is the Son of God, who are

christened. Show the children the picture of the font and ask if they know what it is called. Ask, *How is it used? What is special about the water? What is the sign that is put on the person's head?* Then ask for someone else to come up and match the picture of the font with its label.

Repeat the matching and labelling activity with the altar, lectern, pulpit, aisle and pews, explaining what each one is used for each time. Finally, show the class the pictures of the wedding and christening services and ask the children to verbally match the artefacts with the ceremonies.

Differentiation

With higher attaining children talk about the significance of the altar area and some of the furniture there, such as the choir stalls and the cleric's seat, the cross and the candles. Use only the font, cross, aisle and alter with lower attaining children so they have the opportunity to both practise the matching skills and understand the religious learning.

Where next

Organise a visit to a church or cathedral for the children to recognise the artefacts at first hand. Act out a christening or wedding service in the classroom or local church, asking the local priest or vicar for advice and support.

Assessment

Notice the children's ideas when they are matching the artefacts to the correct ceremony to assess their knowledge of Christian artefacts and the link they have to religious services, as well as their matching abilities.

Learning outcomes

The children will be able to recognise some features and artefacts of a church and begin to talk about what they signify to Christians and how they fit into Christian ceremonies.

Further re challenges

Does it belong?

Give groups of children pictures of different features and artefacts from the places of worship and religions with which they are familiar (try to have mixed-faith groups if possible). Ask them to locate the ones which belong in a Christian church, and to match them to a corresponding label or picture.

Design a church

Give each child a large outline of a church and ask them to copy the pictures of the artefacts, drawing them into their correct places in the church.

REASONING SKILLS

INTRODUCTION

Reasoning skills enable children to make considered decisions and give explanations for those decisions. Asking the children to explain what they are thinking or to talk through how they reached a particular conclusion, for example, will develop their reasoning skills. Five- to seven-year-old children are usually just beginning to make links between different pieces of information and using these links to solve problems. This requires them to make judgements, interpret evidence and start to use inference and deduction skills to work out who carried out a particular action, how something happened or why. Identifying links and predicting what may happen, and giving reasons for their opinions, are at the basics of the children's abilities to solve a problem.

One strategy for developing children's emerging reasoning skills is concept mapping, as it allows you to identify whether children are beginning to make, or are already making, links between different ideas. Many teachers use this to establish children's current knowledge and understanding of a concept or a new process, before planning work matched at a suitable level for groups and individuals. A simplified version of this strategy is used in a science activity in this chapter, 'Noticing links' (page 33), which asks the children to match pairs of words and give reasons for their choices.

Although concept mapping is used especially effectively in science, where new scientific concepts can be explored with the children and used as a basis for discussion, the same idea can be used in other subjects to find out what the children already know and understand before you start planning a unit of work. It is also useful at the end of a unit to find out what they have learned. Making links between ideas allows you to assess the children's understanding of these ideas. An example of this is found in the art and design activity 'Construction links' on page 36.

As well as concept mapping, children will need to develop their reasoning skills using other strategies. For example, in English the children can be developing their reasoning skills when they are trying to find a solution for a character in a story, looking at pictures to try to predict the ending of a story or by explaining why something happened the way it did. In maths and PE, solving problems and explaining strategies used, in order to find an answer, immediately springs to mind, while in history, children are frequently asked to give opinions and to give reasons for these opinions. Art and design and design and technology require the children to overcome problems by colour mixing or joining materials. In ICT and music the children make choices and decide which element is most suitable to create a particular effect in developing their listening and appraising skills.

The following skills all form part of the reasoning process:
⊙ explaining
⊙ forming opinions
⊙ making judgements
⊙ making decisions
⊙ interpreting
⊙ inferring
⊙ deducing
⊙ giving reasons.

INTRODUCING REASONING SKILLS

Subject and QCA unit, NLS or NNS objective	Activity title	Thinking objective	Activity	Page
English NLS objective: To use graphic knowledge to make sense of what they read	Kipper's Toybox	To use inference and deduction skills	Discussing pictures to support understanding in a story	32
Maths NNS objective: To know by heart all addition and subtraction facts for each number to 10	Bingo	To make decisions	Recalling number facts of addition, subtraction and multiplication to at least 10	32
Science QCA unit: 2B Plants and animals in the local environment	Noticing links	To link and interpret information	Noticing features of common animals and plants	33
History QCA unit: 2 What were homes like a long time ago?	Washday	To interpret information and make inferences	Discussing how objects from the past would have been used	33
Geography QCA unit: 5 Where in the world is Barnaby Bear?	Around the world	To form opinions and make judgements	Finding out about different places in the world	34
Design and technology QCA unit: 2A Vehicles	Rolling vehicles	To deduce and give reasons	Setting up an investigation to find out whether a vehicle will travel further when rolled down a steeper ramp	35
ICT 2D Routes – controlling a floor turtle	Robot routes	To make decisions	Learning to give precise instructions to program a robot	35
Art and design QCA unit: 2C Can buildings speak?	Construction links	To explain and give reasons	Identifying links between line, shape and pattern	36
Music QCA unit: 7 Rain, rain, go away	Rainbow Fish	To make decisions and explain why they made them	Creating sound effects for different characters in a story	37
RE QCA unit: 1C Celebrations	What's in the box?	To form opinions	Thinking about the word *precious* and about the true value of possessions	37
PE QCA units: Gymnastic activities units 1 and 2	Gym trails	To make deductions	Linking movement phrases and improving work	38

KIPPER'S TOYBOX

SUBJECT: ENGLISH. NLS OBJECTIVE: TO USE GRAPHIC KNOWLEDGE TO MAKE SENSE OF WHAT THEY READ.

LEARNING OBJECTIVE
To use pictures to support understanding in a story.

THINKING OBJECTIVE
To use inference and deduction skills.

THINKING SKILLS
Using pictures whilst reading a story will support the development of the children's inference and deduction skills. This will aid their ability to understand what is happening in a story. In this story, the children will try to reason who could own the extra noses.

WHAT YOU NEED
Kipper's Toybox by Mick Inkpen (Hodder Children's Books).

WHAT TO DO
Read *Kipper's Toybox* to the children, up to the part where Kipper counts the noses. Talk about the story they have heard so far.

Discuss the part where Kipper counts too many noses. Talk to the children about who could own the extra nose. Ask the children a series of questions about this part of the story, showing them the picture to help them. For example, *Can you see the noses that Kipper is trying to count? How many can you see? Do they all belong to his toys or can you see another one?*

When the children realise that the noses do not all belong to the toys, ask them, *How many mice do you think are there? Is there another one hidden somewhere else? Where could one be hiding?* Ask the children to give reasons for their answers. This will help them use the clues in the pictures to infer and deduce what is happening in the story. Ask them, *Where are the clues in the pictures that tell us there is more than one mouse?*

BINGO

SUBJECT: MATHS. NNS OBJECTIVE: TO KNOW BY HEART ALL ADDITION AND SUBTRACTION FACTS FOR EACH NUMBER TO AT LEAST 10.

LEARNING OBJECTIVE
To recall quickly number facts of addition, subtraction and multiplication to at least 10, and some children to 25.

THINKING OBJECTIVE
To make decisions.

THINKING SKILLS
The children will be using their knowledge and understanding of numbers to make decisions about what the matching sum for a given total will be. This will reinforce their recall of number facts and give them the opportunity to make independent decisions.

WHAT YOU NEED
Make or buy a set of bingo cards on which there are between six and ten addition and subtraction calculations (use calculations to and from 10 for lower attaining children, for example have cards with 5+3, 7+2, 2+2, 9–6, 8–2, 5–1 on; to and from 20 and beyond and multiplications for the rest of the class; and a set of cards with higher totals and products for higher attaining children, some of whom may even manage division); a list of total numbers that the calculations on the bingo cards will make; water-based pens or squares of card big enough to cover the calculations.

WHAT TO DO
Give out the bingo cards, as appropriate to the levels in your class, and make sure the children understand how a game of bingo is played. Play an easy game first with the whole class. If you have an additional adult, you could ask him or her to play the easier version with the lower attaining children so you can play a more challenging version with the rest of the class.

Play by calling out a number within the range of answers that the calculations on the cards will make. Ask the children to find a matching calculation on their cards. Tell them they should cover each one as it matches the total you are reading out (they can either use water-based pens to mark the calculations, or cover them with squares of card). When the game is over (when the first child shouts out *House* because he or she has a full card) ask the children to explain how they found the match each time. What strategies did they use to make their decision? For example, did they use near doubles, know the answer or count on in ones?

Over a few days, play the game in smaller groups in a numeracy lesson. Once the children are familiar with the game, let them play it independently. Perhaps give those who are more able turns at the job of caller. They should call out the numbers, giving the other children an agreed amount of time to cover the matching calculation when they find it. The amount of time should vary from a few seconds to a quarter of a minute depending on the children's prior knowledge.

Once the children can play the game independently, you can change the totals during the year to include the concepts the children are currently learning. You could also take one of the totals and ask the class to find as many calculations as they can to match it, using all four operations if relevant.

NOTICING LINKS

SUBJECT: SCIENCE. QCA UNIT: 2B PLANTS AND ANIMALS IN THE LOCAL ENVIRONMENT.

LEARNING OBJECTIVES
To understand that plants and animals are found in certain places called their habitats; to notice some features of common plants and animals.

THINKING OBJECTIVE
To link and interpret information.

THINKING SKILLS
This activity will help draw the children's attention to the different habitats in which plants and animals are found. The children will interpret information collected in a previous lesson by converting it into a simple concept map, allowing them to consider carefully what the information tells them about the features and habitats of different creatures and plants. This idea can be extended into other scientific variation activities.

WHAT YOU NEED
Information collected in a survey of the local environment from a previous lesson; pictures of the plants and animals and the places where they were found; board or flip chart.

WHAT TO DO
Look with the children at the information collected in a survey of the local environment. On the left-hand side of the board, list all the plants that were found. List the places where the plants were found on the right (but not necessarily in order). For example, *buttercup, daisies* and *daffodil* on the left, and

flowerbed, field and *hedgerow* on the right. Discuss with the children where you would write the word *grass*. Use pictures to support children who do not yet have the reading skills required.

Ask the children questions so that they can identify the links between the plants and the places they were found. For example, *Where was the buttercup found? What plants did you find? Where did you find them? What colours were the petals?* Draw a line or arrow to link the daisy and field on the board and write *was found in* along the line. Continue with the other plants and places on the list, using the children's suggestions as prompts.

Work with the average attainers next to develop a concept map for the animals and where they were found. List or draw pictures on the board of the animals that were found. Ask the children, *What animals did you find? Were they on top or under the ground/bushes/grass? Were they on the ground or in water? How many legs, wings and feet did they have? Did any of them have a shell?* Ask the children to suggest one way in which they could be linked. For example, some have six legs. Join these with an arrow which says *all have six legs*. Similarly the birds, butterflies and ladybirds could all be joined with an arrow because they all have wings and can fly. Continue until you have several arrows linking animals for a range of reasons, including their features and habitats.

Finally, work with the higher attainers to develop a concept map noting reasons why the different animals were suited to their particular environments. For example, frogs, toads and centipedes can be linked because they like damp conditions; rabbits, moles and badgers because they live underground where it is safer.

Give the children similar lists to work with independently in groups. Let average attainers work independently while you work with lower attaining children to link first the plants with colours, then plants with their features and then the animals. Let those who are able make their own lists of animals and where they were found before identifying their own links.

WASHDAY

SUBJECT: HISTORY. QCA UNIT: 2 WHAT WERE HOMES LIKE A LONG TIME AGO?

LEARNING OBJECTIVE
To learn about aspects of home life in the past.

THINKING OBJECTIVE
To interpret information and make inferences.

THINKING SKILLS

The children will view old household items relating to washday in the past and interpret what they were used for. By identifying differences between washday in the past and the present, the children will be able to make inferences about the implications the items had on how people led their lives in the past.

WHAT YOU NEED

A collection of items associated with washday in Victorian times, including a bar of soap, washing soda, a grater, mangle, washboard, flat iron; a bowl of warm water, washing powder, a modern iron.

WHAT TO DO

Talk to the children about how their parents/carers wash their clothes. Ask questions, such as *Do they use a washing machine? Do they go to a launderette? What type of detergent do they use? How do they get the clothes dry? What do they use to get the creases out of the clothes when they are dry? Do you help?*

Show the class a bar of soap and ask how they think the soap could be used to wash clothes. Listen to their suggestions and then put a small square of the soap into a bowl of warm water and wait to see how long it takes to dissolve. Ask the children, *Does it take longer to dissolve than washing powder?* You could demonstrate how long washing powder takes to dissolve, too. Explain to the children that before washing powder was developed, people used to use soap to wash their clothes. Show the class how Victorians would grate the soap to make it dissolve quicker and more evenly in the water. Then show them the soda and explain that this was used to make the water softer which allowed the soap to dissolve easier.

Show the children the flat iron, or a picture of one. Ask questions to prompt the children to think about the item, such as *What do you think it was used for? How would it work?* Give any necessary clues to help them infer how the flat iron was used in the past. Then go on to ask, *What do we use today instead?* and show a modern iron if appropriate. Finish by asking, *Which of the two is an electrical item?*

Ask the children for any observations about what it would have been like to wash and iron clothes in Victorian times. Can any of them infer that it would have been hard work and time consuming? Explain how people in Victorian times used to do the washing on one day each week. Ask if anyone can think why they did this? Talk about the implications of the time it took to wash and dry all the clothes, sheets and towels using the methods they have looked at today. Point out that today we just load a washing machine and let it do most of the work for us.

AROUND THE WORLD

SUBJECT: GEOGRAPHY. QCA UNIT: 5 WHERE IN THE WORLD IS BARNABY BEAR?

LEARNING OBJECTIVE

To find out about different places in the world other than the immediate locality.

THINKING OBJECTIVE

To form opinions and make judgements.

THINKING SKILLS

The children will make judgements about what makes a place good or interesting to visit. They will learn how to form their own opinions, by looking at information on a world destination and listening to several points of view.

WHAT YOU NEED

Photographs, postcards and holiday brochures of a number of foreign holiday destinations; maps; computers or paper, writing materials and glue; board or flip chart.

WHAT TO DO

Ask the children about some of the places they have visited and list these on the board. Choose one place from the list and ask the children to find it on a map. Then ask them questions about the place, such as *Do you think other people would like to visit it? Why? Are there places of interest to see? What kind of activities could you take part in? What would the weather be like?*

Tell the children that you want them to decide whether a number of places would be good to visit. In small groups, ask them to look at a limited selection of photographs, postcards and brochures to find out as much about particular destinations as possible. Give the groups specific headings to find information about, for example the weather, interesting sites to visit, amusements, activities, beach facilities and places to shop and eat. Tell them they should discuss the information they have and listen to what other people in the group think.

Gather the class back together after ten minutes and talk about what the children have found out about their destinations. Encourage the class to ask each group questions, such as *Is it a sunny place? Are there lots of activities that people can take* part in? Would it appeal to someone who likes looking at buildings, or going to art galleries? What about people who like to shop? Ask the class whether they would like to go to each destination after it has been described.

On the board, model writing a short report about a destination, using the headings you gave to the groups earlier. Then ask the children to go back into their groups and write a short report about their destination. They could use a word-processing package to produce the report, perhaps including scans of postcards or pictures used during their earlier work. Otherwise the children could stick pictures next to their report if hand writing it. The children's work can be collated into a travel brochure to be looked at in the class or school library.

ROLLING VEHICLES

SUBJECT: DESIGN AND TECHNOLOGY. QCA UNIT: 2A VEHICLES.

LEARNING OBJECTIVE
To understand how vehicles move, and how to make a vehicle move faster or further.

THINKING OBJECTIVE
To deduce and give reasons.

THINKING SKILLS
By looking at how a toy vehicle moves and seeing the result of it travelling down a ramp set at different heights, the children will begin to make links between cause and effect and will begin to give reasons for why something is happening. By testing out their predictions they will start to revise their deducing skills.

WHAT YOU NEED
A ramp; a toy vehicle; a large space; distance-measuring equipment or markers.

WHAT TO DO
Pass the toy vehicle around and let the children spin the wheels and notice how they are attached to axles. Talk about how movement of the vehicle is created through the wheels and axles, and make sure they understand this. Then set up the ramp and tell the children that you are going to demonstrate how the vehicle can move. Ask them to make some guesses as to how far they think the vehicle will travel down the ramp when you let go of

it. They should give reasons for their answers. Then test out the children's predictions.

Ask the children how they could make the vehicle go further (or faster). If they don't suggest it, ask what they think will happen if you make the ramp steeper. Raise it and ask, *How far do you think the vehicle will travel now? Will it travel further now the ramp is steeper? And faster?* Test out the children's predictions again.

Then ask, *What will happen if we make the ramp too steep?* Make the ramp so high that the vehicle goes too fast and hits the floor so hard (and at such a sharp angle) that it 'crashes'. Ask the children to describe what happened and why. Did any of them deduce that this might happen?

Lower the ramp and experiment to find out which is the best height of the ramp for the vehicle to travel the furthest distance without crashing.

You could let the children try out the effectiveness of their own model vehicles by carefully testing them on the ramp.

ROBOT ROUTES

SUBJECT: ICT. QCA UNIT: 2D ROUTES – CONTROLLING A FLOOR TURTLE.

LEARNING OBJECTIVE
To learn to give precise instructions to move a programmable robot along a pathway.

THINKING OBJECTIVE
To make decisions.

THINKING SKILLS
The children will need to make decisions about how far they think a Roamer needs to travel, which way it should turn and the order in which to write the instructions to make it travel. The children will need to predict the distance the robot will travel and decide the number of units to programme in. This may be through trial and error to begin with, but after a while they will be able to estimate a suitable number. They will try out their routes and decide whether they have written the instructions correctly or whether they need revising.

WHAT YOU NEED
A floor turtle, a pathway for it to travel along; large sheets of paper; writing materials; board or flip chart.

WHAT TO DO
As a class activity, show the children how to programme the floor turtle. In small groups give them

the opportunity to explore how far forward it travels and turns per unit number entered, either in this lesson or in an earlier lesson.

Tell the children you want them to write instructions to make the Roamer travel across the length of the area in which you are working, maybe the classroom or the school hall. Give the children a few minutes to deduce and write down what number should be used to make it travel across the area. Gather the children together and discuss some of their predictions. Check to see if anyone was right by programming the Roamer and letting it move across the area. Ask the children, *On what did you base your predictions? Did you guess or did you base your suggestion on previous knowledge?*

Write instructions on the board for a simple pathway for the Roamer. Ask the children to try out the route by pretending to be a robot and walking through the instructions. Are the instructions written correctly or do they need revising? Ask the children in groups to think of another distance the Roamer could travel based on their knowledge, for example deducing how may units to programme in to make the Roamer travel the length of the library and back. Tell the children to write instructions to program into the Roamer, to input these and try them out to see if they were right. Ask, *Has the robot gone where you wanted? How must you change the instructions to make it go where you want? Do you need to tell it to travel further or less distance? Have you made it turn the wrong way?*

CONSTRUCTION LINKS

SUBJECT: ART AND DESIGN. QCA UNIT: 2C CAN BUILDINGS SPEAK?

LEARNING OBJECTIVE
To identify links between line, shape and pattern in observation of buildings.

THINKING OBJECTIVE
To explain and give reasons.

THINKING SKILLS
The children will be looking closely at a collection of lines, shapes and patterns to see how they are interlinked. This will support their own creative thinking when asked to represent their design ideas in pencil, paint and other artistic media. The important thing here is their ability to explain the links they can see and to give reasons for the links they are making. This is a simplified concept mapping activity, which helps the children to link their ideas and understand how shapes and patterns are formed.

WHAT YOU NEED
A collection of sketches, pictures and photographs which show different lines, shapes and patterns on buildings; board or flip chart; paper and writing materials.

WHAT TO DO
Look at one of the photographs together as a whole class and make a list down the left-hand side of the board of the different lines that the children can find. (Roof tiles and window frames have lines which travel in different directions, and often patterned tiles and ornaments can be found on buildings such as mosques, churches and Victorian houses.) Give each line a caption, such as *dotted or broken line, curved, diagonal, vertical* and *horizontal*.

Ask the children to identify and describe to you all the shapes they can see in the building. The children should be encouraged to see rectangles, squares, circles and triangles, as well as more unusual shapes like trapeziums, rhombuses and ovals. Record these as a list down the middle of the board.

Then ask the children to look closely at the list of lines and shapes and try to link the two together. Ask the class, *What shapes do some of these lines build?* and draw an arrow between any lines and shapes that correspond in your lists. Ask the children to give the reason for joining these, for example *the shape contains diagonal lines*.

Next, ask the children to find all the patterns in the photograph and to describe these. List them on the right-hand side of the board. Ask, *Do any shapes fit together to cover an area? Are there any diamond patterns? Is there a repeating pattern of lines and circles? Are any patterns symmetrical*? Get the class to match the patterns with either the lines or the shapes. Each pattern and shape can match with one or more line. For example, join a rhombus to a diamond pattern, a curved line to any stained glass patterns. The important thing is for the children to give reasons why they have joined their selection together.

Finish by giving groups of up to four children a photograph, sketch or picture to repeat the activity independently. Some children may need help with writing the lists. The discussion is more important, however, so move between groups listening to what they are saying and asking questions to promote discussion where necessary.

Rainbow Fish

Subject: Music. QCA unit: 7 Rain, rain go away.

Learning objective
To learn that an instrument can make various sounds and can be used descriptively.

Thinking objective
To make decisions and explain why they made them.

Thinking skills
The children will use their knowledge of how instruments are played to choose a particular one to depict the character of Rainbow Fish. They will link the sounds they have made with the movements of the fish and explain why they have chosen the sounds that they have.

What you need
The Rainbow Fish by Marcus Pfister (North–South Books); a range of musical instruments including bells, rain sticks, tambourines, drums, xylophones and glockenspiels.

What to do
Sit the children in a circle around your collection of musical instruments and remind them of, or read them, the story *The Rainbow Fish*. Ask the children if there are any parts of the story to which they would like to add sound effects. Use the children's ideas first. If they do not come up with any, suggest they try to portray the way Rainbow Fish looks, with its shimmering, shiny scales, or the feelings of the other fish.

Look together at the instruments and ask the children to suggest which would make a good sound for Rainbow Fish, asking them to give reasons for their suggestions.

Organise the children into small groups and let them develop sounds to depict Rainbow Fish. After five noisy minutes, gather the children back into a circle and ask each group to play their sounds to the rest of the class. Ask them to talk about why they have chosen the instruments that they have and why they decided to play them the way that they have. Use questions to prompt the children to give you reasons for their decisions, such as *Which instrument have you chosen to depict Rainbow Fish? Why did you choose that instrument? Is it because of the way that the instrument is played? Is it because of the material from which it is made?* Have any groups used different instruments to depict the same sound?

Start to read the story, letting the children add their sound effects. Stop them where relevant and talk about the dynamics and whether the sounds should be played loudly or quietly. Should the sounds be long or a series of short notes?

What's in the box?

Subject: RE. QCA unit: 1C Celebrations: why do Christians give gifts at Christmas?

Learning objective
To understand more about the meaning of the word *precious* and what it means to them.

Thinking objective
To form opinions.

Thinking skills
The activity will challenge the children's idea of what *precious* means. They will think carefully about their own opinions concerning what is important to them and why, after being confronted with material goods and personalised objects.

What you need
A large box containing a toy; a smaller box with a photograph of a special person or event in it; paper and writing materials; board or flip chart.

What to do
Ask the children to form a circle on the floor, and place the large and small boxes in the centre. Ask the children if they know what the word *precious* means. Get a child to explain to the class, or explain yourself. Then ask the children which box they think your most precious item is in. Ask them to give reasons for their choice.

Talk about the larger box and gather some guesses as to what may be inside. Ask, *What do you think is in this box? Do you think it is something big?* Open the box and show the children the toy. Do they think it is precious? Note the children's comments. Do the same thing with the smaller box. Take out the photograph and ask if anyone thinks it is precious. Which do the children think is most precious – the toy or the photograph? Talk about things which can be replaced easily and those things which would be more difficult to replace if broken or lost. (The point is not for them to decide whether the toy is precious, but to realise that it may be precious to you.)

Talk to the children about a favourite gift they have received at some time. What was it and why was it special? Ask them to think about someone special in their lives (this may be a parent, grandparent or a baby brother or sister). If they had the opportunity, what gift would they buy for this special person and why? Would it be something the person had always wanted, perhaps because they follow a particular interest or it would be particularly special to them?

Make a list on the board of all the things the children think are precious. Link this to a reason by drawing an arrow with *This is precious because...* on it. For example, *This (ring) is precious because it is valuable; This (teddy bear) is precious because the person to whom it belongs has had it since he was a baby.*

Finish by asking the children to write several sentences about what *precious* means to them. Write some examples for them if they find this difficult, such as *Something is precious if it means something special to the person who owns it or wants it; something which reminds someone of happy times is precious; something is precious if it is worth a lot of money.* Give the children lots of time to form their own opinions about what precious means. Reinforce this by asking the children to bring in a precious object of their own, or photographs of precious objects. Include some of your own.

GYM TRAILS

SUBJECT: PE. QCA UNITS: GYMNASTIC ACTIVITIES UNITS 1 AND 2.

LEARNING OBJECTIVES

To link movement phrases; to improve their work through investigation.

THINKING OBJECTIVE

To make deductions.

THINKING SKILLS

By practising different ways to travel safely around an obstacle course the children will learn to deduce which are the safest, quickest and smoothest ways to move between different pieces of apparatus. They will notice how to most successfully link movements to complete the courses.

WHAT YOU NEED

Four matching sets of low-level apparatus to form four identical obstacle courses (include hoops, mats, benches).

WHAT TO DO

Start with a suitable warm-up activity in which the children can move in different ways and at different levels, such as on their feet, on their hands and feet, and so on, developing stretches as the warm up continues.

Set up four identical obstacle courses, which should not be too challenging to begin with, and split the class into four groups. Allow the children to find different ways of getting across their course. When each group has completed the course, ask the children which parts they found easy and which parts they found more difficult. What made some parts more difficult? How could they make it easier to cross these parts? If necessary move some apparatus closer together, but encourage the children to think of smoother, quicker ways of travelling and moving, or better ways to link their movements between pieces of apparatus.

Tell the groups to have another go at their course, and challenge the children to try moving in different ways over each piece of apparatus, based on the previous discussion. Station yourself so that you have an overview of the activity and can teach the children suitable techniques.

Once you have assessed the children's abilities, make two of the courses more difficult, for instance, by raising one end of a ladder, making the gap between the end of a bench and a mat slightly bigger, turning one bench over to make a balance thinner or moving hoops slightly further away from each other so that the children have to stretch their legs further. Make sure that you are not encouraging the children to do anything dangerous, and reinforce this point to them. Move children as appropriate to the more challenging courses and reorganise the children to work again on designated courses (you may need more or less sets of more difficult courses depending on the children's abilities).

Encourage the groups to continue moving along the obstacle courses, trying to improve their techniques and movements each time.

EXTENDING REASONING SKILLS

Subject and QCA unit, NLS or NNS objective	Activity title	Thinking objective	Activity	Page
English NLS objective: To identify reasons for events in stories, linking this to plot	Kipper's Birthday	To infer and deduce	Giving reasons for incidents in a story using pictures and text	40
Maths NNS objective:To recognise coins of different values	Exchange it	To make decisions	Exchanging coins to the same value	41
Science QCA unit: 1F Sound and hearing	A noisy world	To give reasons	Understanding that sound is louder when closer, and fainter when further away	42
History QCA unit: 5 How do we know about the Great fire of London?	World Cup 1966	To interpret evidence and form opinions	Looking at a range of evidence about the World Cup final of 1966 and forming opinions about fact and fiction	43
Geography QCA unit: 1 Around our school – the local area	Where am I?	To make deductions	Looking at different photographs taken in the school grounds and identifying where they were taken from	44
Design and technology QCA unit: 1B Playgrounds	Swings	To make judgements	Making a model of a swing from straws and pipe cleaners	46
ICT QCA unit: 1A An introduction to modelling	A pirate's tale	To make decisions and choices	Creating a setting for a pirate story	47
Art and design QCA unit: 2C Can buildings speak?	Buildingscape	To give reasons for choices	Look at paintings as inspiration for creating their own pictures focusing on lines, colours and shapes	48
Music QCA unit: 4 Feel the pulse	Feel the rhythm	To deduce and explain	Deciding whether parts of a tune comprise the rhythm or the pulse	50
RE QCA unit: 1A What does it mean to belong?	What should he do?	To form opinions	Considering a moral dilemma and thinking about respecting others	51
PE QCA unit: Gymnastic activities unit 2	The great beanbag challenge	To use inference and deductions skills	Passing a beanbag along an obstacle course in teams so that it is not dropped	52

KIPPER'S BIRTHDAY

SUBJECT: ENGLISH. NLS OBJECTIVE: TO IDENTIFY AND DISCUSS REASONS FOR EVENTS IN STORIES, LINKING THIS TO THE PLOT.

LEARNING OBJECTIVE
To predict and discuss reasons for incidents in stories using pictures and text.

THINKING OBJECTIVE
To infer and deduce.

THINKING SKILLS
Teaching the children to use the skills of inference and deduction can be taught early in their reading development with the use of appropriate texts that interest and motivate them to think. Any book will lend itself to the development of such reasoning skills and *Kipper's Birthday* is the example used here.

40

WHAT YOU NEED
Kipper's Birthday by Mick Inkpen (Hodder Children's Books); flashcards with days of the week on.

WHAT TO DO
Read *Kipper's Birthday* to the class, up to the point where Kipper starts to eat his cake. Ask the children if the friends are late. (Note any children at this point who use their inference skills to say that the friends won't come. If any can, make sure they explain why – because Kipper has said *see you tomorrow* on the invitations, and he delivered them a day late.)

Read on to the next page, where Kipper's friends do not come to his party. Talk with the children about Kipper's disappointment. Then ask questions to get the children thinking about why Kipper's friends didn't turn up, such as *Why do you think that Kipper's friends did not come to his party? Did they not receive the invitations? Did they forget or did they decide not to come?* Give the children time to express their opinions and ask them to give reasons for these if they can.

Read the rest of the story, then ask the class, *Why did the friends come today? Why were they a day late?* (Note if anyone can infer why at this point, and again ask for reasons.) To get the children thinking, discuss first what Kipper had written on the invitations and see if the children can deduce why the friends were a day late from this. Get out your days-of-the-week flashcards and make sure the children understand Tiger's explanation when he tried to tell Kipper when today, yesterday and tomorrow were. Play a game pretending that today is Wednesday (or choose the

actual day you are on). Ask the children to work out when Kipper's birthday would have been (Tuesday). Ask them, *Which day should Kipper have delivered his invitations if he wanted his friends to come on Tuesday?* (Monday.) *Which day is tomorrow if he delivered them on Tuesday?* (Wednesday.) Point out, if you need to, that Kipper delivered them a day late, so the friends came a day late.

Move back to the point in the story where the friends arrive. Look at the picture of them each carrying a present and talk about the wrapping paper and shape of the presents. Can the children deduce what the presents might be from the shape and size of them? Tell the children which presents Kipper received for his birthday to help them if necessary, explaining that one friend brought candles, another a napkin and another a cake. Can the children deduce from the pictures who brought what? They should give reasons for their answers.

DIFFERENTIATION
Ask lower attaining children to focus mainly on the pictures, asking them to infer what is happening in the story by the look on character's faces, or anything happening in the background. Can they predict what will happen on the next page by inferring information from a picture?

Higher attaining children can look through other books with another adult to find examples where pictures and text imply what is happening or may happen next.

WHERE NEXT
During story time reinforce the skills drawn upon in the activity by reading other stories from which children can infer meaning. Make this a focus until you are happy that most children are recognising the clues in the pictures and text. Remind the children when they do not notice clues by questioning and prompting their memories.

Organise guided reading sessions to address skills of deduction and inference regularly during the year. Look out for stories, rhymes and poems which address these skills.

ASSESSMENT
When hearing the children read their reading books, or during the Literacy Hour, make a note of those who are beginning to use the pictures to help them

read unfamiliar words, or those who comment unprompted on what is happening in the pictures or the story.

Learning outcomes

The children will develop reading strategies using inference to help predict and comprehend the meaning in stories, often noting and appreciating subtle humour too.

Further English challenges

Why do Hue Boy's clothes look small?

Read the story *Hue Boy* by Rita Phillips Mitchell (Puffin Books) with the class and ask the children questions where they will be able to find the answer in the pictures. Hue Boy is shown in one picture growing out of his clothes. Asking questions such as *Why do you think that Hue Boy's clothes look small?* or *Have they shrunk?* will prompt the children to think about other possibilities and deduce other reasons.

Which character comes next?

Read the first page of *A Wolf at the Door!* by Nick Ward (Scholastic) to the children and talk about what they can see in the picture. By looking carefully at the picture can the children suggest what might happen next? Ask, *Can you suggest if a new character will appear on the next page? How do you know? What clue is there in the picture?* Continue to the end of the story to see if all the characters have appeared in the order deduced by the children. Challenge the children to find other stories with pictures which give clues to the next part of the story.

Exchange it

Subject: Maths. NNS objective: To recognise coins of different values.

Learning objectives

To learn that different coins have different values; to exchange coins to the same value.

Thinking objective

To make decisions.

Thinking skills

The children will be asked to think about the value of coins and how values can be made up of different combinations of smaller coins. Being asked to exchange coins to make the same value will draw upon the children's decision-making skills. This will not only help them develop an understanding of the value of coins, but will increase their confidence in the decision-making process.

What you need

A large die; a large number of coins of the values 1p, 2p, 5p, 10p and 20p (if you have a magnetic board and suitable coins this would be ideal).

What to do

Explain the basic premise of the game to the children: each dot on a die is worth 1p. Ask the children how many pennies they have if a 5 is thrown. How many do they have if a 2 is thrown? Continue with this line of questioning until most of the children understand.

Give each child a selection of coins, then throw a die. Ask the children to get out the right number of pennies to match the number. Then ask them to exchange their pennies for another coin of the same value. For example, if 5 is thrown can they exchange their five pennies for a 5p coin? If 2 is thrown can they exchange their pennies for a 2p coin? Challenge them to think of which coins they can choose if a 3 or a 6 is thrown.

Some children may need to stop here and play this part of the game a few more times with a classroom assistant until they understand the idea of exchanging. Continue the game with those who do understand.

Explain that you are going to throw the die as before and that each dot still represents a penny. The children can collect one penny from their coins for each dot when a number is thrown and then exchange them for 2p coins as soon as they can. When they have enough they can exchange their 2p coins for a 10p coin and so on, until they have made 20p. As the children exchange, model the language and then invite individuals to explain how they are making their decisions, using the correct language. For example, *I have two pennies and I can exchange my two pennies for one 2p coin*; or *This 2p coin is worth the same amount as two pennies.* Play the game until everyone has a 20p coin.

Differentiation

Give higher attaining children 50p and ask them to take away the appropriate number of pennies each time.

Only use 1p, 2p or 5p and 10p coins with lower attaining children and ask an adult to play with them in a group until you are sure the children understand the process.

WHERE NEXT

Adapt the game to develop the children's understanding of place value, using tens and units, and hundreds, tens and units. The exchanging game just practised can be used to develop this understanding of place value by asking the children to exchange ten units for one ten, and ten tens for one hundred. The children must also decide when to exchange ten units for ten, and ten tens for a hundred.

ASSESSMENT

Note which children are able to decide for themselves how many and which coins can be exchanged for larger coins, and can deduce that there is the value of 2 pennies in each 2p coin, five pennies in a 5p coin and so on.

Note any children who are able to make all combinations of coins up to 6p totals, and decide on the range of different coins to use for each total. How many children can go beyond this and make combinations of higher totals?

LEARNING OUTCOMES

The children will develop confidence in making decisions by learning to think through the process of exchanging before testing their decision and actually seeing its outcome by physically exchanging the coins.

FURTHER MATHS CHALLENGES

Money purses

Ask the children to draw outline pictures of purses which contain the least number of coin combinations to make a total of 7p, 25p, 18p, and other totals. They should decide for themselves which coins to include and give reasons why they think they have used the least number of coins.

When the children have decided on their coins, ask them if they can exchange several coins for one, for example two 10p pieces for a 20p piece, and so on. If they can, explain that they have found a way to make the same total with fewer coins. Continue until the children have exchanged to the lowest number of coins possible. Note which children approach the task in a logical way by deciding to use the largest coin below the total each time? For example, when making 7p do they start with a 5p coin? For 25p a 20p coin? For 18p a 10p coin?

Stamps for sale

Give the children puzzles to solve, such as: Alex only has 2p and 5p coins and he wants to buy a stamp for 8p. Will he be able to pay the exact money? Which value stamps will he not be able to pay for with the exact money?

A NOISY WORLD

SUBJECT: SCIENCE. QCA UNIT: 1F SOUND AND HEARING.

LEARNING OBJECTIVE

To learn that the closer the sound source, the louder the sound appears; the further away the sound source, the fainter the sound.

THINKING OBJECTIVE

To give reasons.

THINKING SKILLS

The children are required to decide whether they think sounds get quieter the further away they are from the source. They will begin to link cause and effect in scientific concepts by giving reasons for what is happening to the sounds as they move further away from the source, or the source moves further away from them.

WHAT YOU NEED

A tuning fork; a tape or CD player and recording of familiar songs.

WHAT TO DO

Talk with the class about how we hear sounds when they reach the ears, and how sounds travel through the air. Ask the children what happens to a sound when we move further away from its source, or the source moves further away from us. Ask the children what happens to sound if we are very close to it. Remind them about the dangers of listening to very loud noise, explaining that it can damage the ears and hearing. Explain that the sounds they will be listening to today are not going to be loud.

Sound the tuning fork and ask the children to describe the sound it makes. Can they hear it easily? Can they still hear it easily from the other side of the room? What about if they were outside? Would the sound still travel through the air so that they could hear it? Which is the furthest distance from which the children think they will still be able to hear the tuning fork? Try these scenarios out if appropriate to reinforce the concept that the further away from a sound source the fainter the sound becomes. Don't try to explain why at this stage, as it is scientifically difficult and the children may become confused with the ideas involved.

Take the class into the hall and ask an adult or an older child to stand at the other side of the hall and play one of the familiar songs at a very low volume so that the class can hardly hear it. Ask the children if they can name the tune. Repeat the process with the tape player moved closer to the children until they can hear the tune so clearly that they can recognise its name. Repeat the game with two other songs. Ask the children to reason why they can recognise the tunes when the tape player is closer. They may say straight away that this is because as the sound source moves closer to us, the louder the sound appears. Some may suggest that it is because the sound source is louder. Explain the difference if necessary to reinforce the concept.

Ask the children to close their eyes, then play the tunes one at a time again, moving away or towards the children as the music plays. Ask them to indicate by hand signals whether the sounds are coming towards them or going away. How do they know?

DIFFERENTIATION

Ask higher attainers to compose a piece of music which gets louder and quieter to represent the sound of a marching band moving closer or further away. Note whether they give the piece structure, where the sounds start quietly and get louder before getting quieter again. Record this on a tape for the other children to repeat the task. Make sure that children with hearing difficulties can join in, either by placing them nearer to the sound source so that they can hear it at the same time as the rest of the class, or by repeating the activity individually or in small groups.

WHERE NEXT

Talk about people who need to wear ear defenders for their work and list the jobs the children suggest. Discuss why these people need to wear ear defenders. Ask, *What are they defending their ears from? Why is the sound so loud? Why is too loud a noise dangerous for our ears?*

ASSESSMENT

Note those children who are able to give reasons for their decisions about when the sound source is closest to them and when it begins to move away. Who can relate it to the scientific concept that the further away the sound source, the fainter the sound appears?

LEARNING OUTCOMES

The children will learn to give reasons for their decisions. They will understand that we hear sound when it reaches our ears, and that the further away from the sound source we are, the fainter the sound appears. Also, the nearer we are to the sound source the louder the sound.

FURTHER SCIENCE CHALLENGES

Noisy instruments

Ask the children to set up a test to find out which musical instrument can be heard from the furthest distance away. Talk about making the test fair, and how they will measure and present the outcomes. Ask the children to use the results to explain their conclusions.

WORLD CUP 1966

SUBJECT: HISTORY. QCA UNIT: 5 HOW DO WE KNOW ABOUT THE GREAT FIRE OF LONDON?

LEARNING OBJECTIVES

To find out about a famous event from pictures and newspaper reports; to identify differences between fact and fiction.

THINKING OBJECTIVE

To interpret evidence and form opinions.

THINKING SKILLS

By beginning to consider the value of different pieces of evidence the children will start to interpret what each bit tells them about a particular event. From this they can form opinions as to whether the version of the event they have been told is accurate or whether the evidence could be interpreted in a different way. This is an important skill for children to learn when finding out about a famous event in history – establishing whether the information is accurate so we can say with more surety that events happened as they did.

WHAT YOU NEED

Video extracts of the 1966 World Cup final; newspaper or magazine articles, with pictures if possible, reporting what happened on the day; paper and writing materials.

WHAT TO DO

Give each child a copy of a simple newspaper or magazine article, or part of one, stating what happened on the day that England won the World Cup. (You could make a factual account yourself to match the reading level of the children in your class.) Read the article through together, then ask the children to make a list of all the facts about the match. To help them understand what a fact is, give the children a series of closed questions based on the article first. For example, *How many goals did England score in the final? Who scored the first goal? Which teams played in the final?* Explain that the answers they give you are all facts. Then ask them to make their list.

Next, move on to open questions which require the children to distinguish fact from fiction. Ask a series of questions about the article to see if they can do this, such as *Who can tell me how the German team felt at the end of the match? How did the England team feel when Germany scored in the final minutes of normal time? Does the evidence tell us? Who scored the most goals in the final?* Then ask who can tell you which of the answers to your questions are fact and which could be fiction.

Finally, look at any photographs or some video footage of the final and ask the children to say whether it agrees with what they have found out as fact so far. Ask, *Does video evidence help to separate fact from fiction about the event? Does the film show us exactly what happened? How do we know this is what happened? Is it someone's opinion or does what they see tell them the game was played in this way?*

Repeat this with another article about the final and tell the children they should add anything additional to their list of facts.

DIFFERENTIATION

Read the articles with lower attaining children and ask closed questions one to one, which will help them to remember some of the facts. Look at any photographs and talk about what they show, linking the action in the photographs to the articles. Ask higher attaining children to highlight the facts and opinions in different colours on their article.

WHERE NEXT

Relate the learning to other famous events, including the Great Fire of London. Discuss the range and type of evidence that was available for them to interpret when they were looking at the World Cup final. Which types of evidence would not be available when looking at the Great Fire of London?

ASSESSMENT

Note the children who can form opinions about the reliability of factual evidence, and the strengths and weaknesses involved with interpreting eyewitness accounts from spectators. Which children know that events can be presented in different ways depending on how evidence is interpreted?

LEARNING OUTCOMES

The children will learn to recognise that historical events happened in the past and that we know about them because of the range of evidence available. The children will learn that this evidence may tell us different things and that it needs to be interpreted, as some evidence is based on fact and some on opinion.

FURTHER HISTORY CHALLENGES

Evidently

Ask the children to look at a range of evidence for different historical events and to form opinions about the accuracy of this evidence. Ask them to decide whether the evidence gives a true picture of what happened or whether there could be a different interpretation. Events to use could include Captain Cook's discovery of Australia, whether Christopher Columbus was the first European to discover America, the first successful climb to the summit of Mount Everest, and the race to the South Pole. Ask them to list the evidence available for each event. Is there any piece of evidence that is constant, where a solid interpretation can be formed, such as logs or diaries, photographs and paintings? Are there any kinds of evidence we have today that were not available years ago?

Hear the news

Give the children a list of facts about a famous event and ask them to put the facts together into a newspaper article. Gauge the number of facts according to the range of children's abilities. Next, ask them to add a quote from a spectator or eyewitness, which does not necessarily relate to the facts. This is a good way for the children to highlight the difference between factual information and fiction, and to see how other people would need to interpret their article.

WHERE AM I?

SUBJECT: GEOGRAPHY. QCA UNIT: 1 AROUND OUR SCHOOL – THE LOCAL AREA.

LEARNING OBJECTIVE

To recognise and describe where features are in the local environment.

THINKING OBJECTIVE

To make deductions.

THINKING SKILLS

The children will use their knowledge of the school locality to deduce the spot from where photographs have been taken. Activities which ask children where features found on photographs are located are commonplace, but this activity asks the children to extend their skills by looking at things from a different point of view. They will need to use their knowledge of the school area and their mapping skills to deduce where photographs were taken from, using the clues in the photographs to explain why they think this.

WHAT YOU NEED

Photographs taken of different features in and from the school grounds (depending on your location include natural features, such as hills, rivers, fields and trees, and man-made features – include some of the school grounds, such as hedges, fences, playground, houses around the perimeter, telephone poles, and so on); chalk; a large sheet of paper; coloured pencils.

WHAT TO DO

Before embarking on this activity, carry out a risk assessment of your local area and follow your school and LEA policies for taking children out of the classroom.

Ask the children to look at the photographs taken around the school and to talk about the features in them. Get the children to agree on what the photographs show, then write what they are on the back. Can they identify whereabouts these are in the locality? Explain to the children that they are going to find the exact spot where you took the photographs.

Go outside together as a class with two of your photographs. Find the features shown in the photographs and go to the place where the children think the picture was taken from. Ask, *Why do you think the photograph was taken from here? What clues help you decide? Which view of the feature can you see from here? Which view can you see from the photograph? Are they the same view?* Talk about the reasons why the children think that the photograph was taken from the chosen spot. Hold up the photograph and make sure that the view is the same. Mark the spot where the children think the photograph was taken with a large chalk X.

Give pairs of children photographs and ask them to find the spot where the photograph was taken and mark the spot with an X in the same way. Continue until all the spots have been marked. Then ask the children to swap photographs with another pair and challenge each pair to find the correct marked spot for their new photograph.

Back in the classroom, place the photographs onto a large piece of paper. Get the children to draw a frame around each one with a different colour. Then ask the children to identify on a large map of the school grounds where each photograph was taken from. Get them to mark this spot on the map with an X in a matching colour. Make sure they are all correct and pose questions to check why they deduced the spot they did.

DIFFERENTIATION

Ask an additional adult to stay with lower attaining children whilst out in the school grounds, to make sure that they are clear about where they are in relation to the photographs. Check that they can see the feature shown in the photograph before marking the spot. Do one example only for higher attaining children. Let those who understand straight away continue with the activity independently. Once you are confident that they are secure with the activity, challenge the children to find interesting 'shots' for others to find and to record these using a digital camera.

WHERE NEXT

Repeat the activity on a walk around the local area.

ASSESSMENT

This activity is based on children using their deduction skills. However, in order to do this they will also need to use their mapping and fieldwork skills, so you need to assess their ability in both areas.

LEARNING OUTCOMES

Many children will be able to locate where things are on a map and some will begin to use clues to help them to locate positions using their deduction skills. The children will use geographical language to describe the features they use to deduce where each photograph was taken from.

FURTHER GEOGRAPHY CHALLENGES
Where was the photographer standing?
Give the children a large map of your locality or a contrasting place (this could be a seaside location, a picture map of the Isle of Struay or Coll, or a city). Give them a set of photographs or postcards and ask them to deduce where each image was taken from on the map.

A guessing game

Take photographs of interesting features of buildings, street furniture or signs in the locality from unusual angles. Ask the children to deduce from which angle the camera was held.

Take another set of photographs of simple features, for example drain covers, paving slabs laid in various patterns, a pedestrian crossing, postboxes, signs and bushes, but from odd angles. Challenge the children to deduce what these features are.

SWINGS

SUBJECT: DESIGN AND TECHNOLOGY. QCA UNIT: 1B PLAYGROUNDS.

LEARNING OBJECTIVE

To learn how to join and combine materials to make a stable frame.

THINKING OBJECTIVE

To make judgements.

THINKING SKILLS

The children will explore different materials and deduce how they can be used to make a frame for a model swing. They will think about how they can best combine the materials and join them to make a rigid frame before making judgements about how to make the frame more stable, and strong enough to hold a small Lego person.

WHAT YOU NEED

A picture of a swing; plastic straws, pipe cleaners, wool, string, card, sticky tape, scissors; a variety of Lego people.

WHAT TO DO

Ask the children about the times they have played on a swing. Talk about how the swing moves. Look at a picture and ask the children to label the components of the swing. Together make comments about how these components are joined together.

Show the children the materials and tell them that they are going to make their own model of a swing from the materials. Explain that first they will need to make judgements about how to attach the top bar to the two side structures. Give each child a set of materials and allow them about ten minutes to join the materials together to make a frame. Some may bend the straws or decide to join them with sticky

tape. This is fine, so long as the models stand up unaided.

If they have not already done so, talk to the children about how they can use the pipe cleaners to join the straws. Show them how they could do this (bend them and feed them inside the straws to allow the straws to stand upright) and ask, *Does this still allow the straws to stand upright unaided? Is the structure stable?* Some children may judge that another way is more effective, but point out how flexible the pipe cleaners have made the straws, that now the straws can stand up into different shapes.

Finish by asking the children to make a seat and join it to the frame. Ask, *What can you make a seat from? How can you join the seat to the frame to make it swing?* They could use cardboard for the seat with string to attach it to the framework. When the children have completed their swing ask, *Is the framework still stable? Is it strong enough to hold a Lego person?* Ask the children to try this out.

DIFFERENTIATION

Work closely with lower attaining children and question them to lead them towards thinking about how best to join the materials together. Challenge higher attaining children to find a way to make a T-join independently to join the side frame to the top bar.

WHERE NEXT

Ask the children to use the same materials to make other models of playground equipment. Or use commercial kits, such as Quadro, to make a large class model of a swing.

ASSESSMENT

Note the children who can judge which materials to use and how to join the parts of their swing together. Note those who can deduce how to make a T-join independently.

LEARNING OUTCOMES

Most children will learn to judge effective ways to join materials together to make a stable frame. Some will deduce how to bend pipe cleaners to join the straws into a variety of shapes. Some will deduce how to make a T-join to join vertical and horizontal structures.

FURTHER DESIGN AND TECHNOLOGY CHALLENGES

Picnic tables

Ask the children to use the straws and pipe cleaners to make a frame for a picnic table. Challenge them to make the frame strong enough to hold a top made from card that will support several wooden cubes. How can they stop the table from collapsing under the weight?

Climbing frames

Challenge the children to make a model of a climbing frame from straws, pipe cleaners and sellotape. How can they join the horizontal and vertical bars? If they do not think of this themselves, show them how to twist two pieces of pipe cleaner together to make a T-join to join them. Can they make ladders in the same way? Challenge some children to make a model of a slide and to find a way to attach to it to the climbing frame using pipe cleaners or sellotape.

A PIRATE'S TALE

SUBJECT: ICT. QCA UNIT: 1A AN INTRODUCTION TO MODELLING.

LEARNING OBJECTIVES

To use a computer to create scenarios; to understand that computers can make representions of fantasy situations.

THINKING OBJECTIVE

To make decisions and choices.

THINKING SKILLS

By creating a visual scene on a computer set within very clear parameters, the children will need to make decisions about what will appear in their scene. The children will decide which components best set off their story. Deciding what to include, and more importantly what to leave out, to depict precisely the setting in a story is a difficult skill for children of this age. The decision-making skills they learn can be related to different scenarios for structuring future story writing. Once they have learned the skills of using the menu, inserting pictures into a background, changing size and colours and so on, they can use the computer to create settings for different stories in future work. This will help spark their imagination and develop their ideas.

WHAT YOU NEED

Computers (enough for the children to work in pairs), an object-based graphics package, clip art pictures; board or flip chart.

WHAT TO DO

Before the start of the lesson, tell the children that you want them to imagine what a setting for a story about a pirate might look like. Give them a few minutes to think about this and then discuss it as a class. What do the children think should be included in their settings? Make a list on the board of all the things the children suggest. Then explain that you want them to create their own settings using a computer.

Revise any ICT learning you feel is appropriate, such as the tools required to create a setting, how to use the palette to change the background or how to use fill and colour and create shadows. Demonstrate by importing a picture from a selection of clip art or from the menu in the software you are using. Place it in a chosen spot, resize and add a shadow to it to create a 3-D effect.

Let the children work in pairs to create their settings so that they can bounce ideas off each other before making decisions. Let them explore the program and try out different scenes before they decide on one they like. Monitor them closely to make sure that they are taking it in turns to carry out the computer tasks. Talk to them about why they have chosen the pictures they have and ask questions, such as *What mood does the setting create? Why do you want this particular mood for the story? What is going to happen in the story that might need to be included in the picture?* (Perhaps finding a treasure chest under the roots of a large tree.) *What can you add to make it more realistic?*

As you go round the classroom, show the children how to enhance their settings, such as how to add a darker shade of colour or a shadow effect to add drama, or how to make a picture brighter. Ask them to add characters, speech bubbles and captions to the story setting. Ask how they will decide to convey their characters' feelings and thoughts.

At the end of the lesson, save the work to disk

so that the children have a chance to revisit their work during the week, perhaps during literacy group working time.

During a whole class plenary, talk about the settings that have been created. Note how the settings are all different and point out how people have made different decisions and choices. Can anyone suggest why this is? Talk about how the settings have been created to support the outline story in the mind of individual authors. Reinforce the importance of individual decisions and choices.

DIFFERENTIATION

It is always useful to have an additional adult to support the children's computer practice. However, as this is an activity that focuses on the children making decisions, pair a more able child with a lower attaining one to support them with the technical computer skills.

WHERE NEXT

Give each pair of children a small part of a story to create a setting for on the computer. Put these together to form a class story.

Get the children to apply their skills to other contexts, depending on your current topic, such as 'A Journey into Space' or 'A Walk in the Jungle'.

ASSESSMENT

Note the children who take a lead in the discussions and make sure that they are paired together for any follow up activities. This will allow them to work independently to discuss ideas and decide on a paired setting for another story.

LEARNING OUTCOMES

The children will be able to describe their setting, giving reasons for their decisions. They will find out that different people make different choices for different reasons.

FURTHER ICT CHALLENGES

Find the treasure

Draw a large treasure map which includes all the features in the children's pirate story settings. Ask the class to plot where treasure can be found and to write an adventure story for the characters to embark upon. Encourage the children to give the characters decisions to make in the story, such as *Pirate Pat comes to a fork in the road. Should she go to the right or to the left? The pirates reach the river. Do they swim across or walk along to the bridge?* Write the possibilities for both choices on different pages so

that there can be a different decision each time the story is read.

Pirate Pat

Get the children to use a suitable painting or graphics package to create the character Pirate Pat. Tell them they need to decide whether the character is male or female, tall or short, fat or thin. They should also choose what features she will have. Prompt them to think about her colour and shape and the expression likely to be seen on her face. They could also choose to add suitable accessories, such as an eye patch and parrot.

BUILDINGSCAPE

SUBJECT: ART AND DESIGN. QCA UNIT: 2C CAN BUILDINGS SPEAK?

LEARNING OBJECTIVES

To ask and answer questions about the starting points of their work; to try out tools and techniques to print and make collage pictures.

THINKING OBJECTIVE

To give reasons for choices.

THINKING SKILLS

The children will think carefully about how to achieve a particular effect in printing their own buildings and skyscapes. Some will consider colour when depicting the scape at night, and others about contrasting colours for seasonal pictures. They will need to be able to give reasons why a particular pattern, colour or shape has been used in their finished artwork.

WHAT YOU NEED

Pictures and photographs of local buildings showing patterns and distinctive shapes; a painting by Lowry;

blocks of wood, polystyrene and sponges of different cuboid shapes and sizes; sheets of card of different thicknesses; paint in a range of colours; large sheets of paper; painting equipment.

WHAT TO DO
Show the children pictures and photographs of buildings in your local area. Talk about the patterns, colour and shape on each one. Focus, for instance, on the tile pattern on the roofs, the shapes of windows and their panes of glass, on doorways and columns. Perhaps there are Georgian features or Tudor designs in your area.

Then show the children the painting by Lowry and talk about the colours, shapes and patterns. Talk about the figures and the buildings. Ask questions to encourage discussion, such as *Did he paint shapes? Which colours did he use mostly and why do you think he chose those colours? What kind of lines did he paint?*

Show the children, as a whole class or in groups, how to create the different shapes and lines of the parts of the buildings they have been looking at. Explore how to use the different sizes of blocks, the flat face and edges of the card to make thick and thin walls to create distance and size. Help them to investigate how to make shades of the same colour.

Then organise the children into small groups if you haven't done so already and tell them that you want them to create their own building landscape. Explain that you want them to plan their picture before they begin and that, to start with, you want them to make skyscapes by creating the outline of the buildings (roofs and walls). Explain that when this outline is dry they can add details of windows, doorways and pattern on roof tiles. Tell them that you want them to include some of the lines, shapes and patterns that they found in buildings in the earlier part of the lesson.

Suggest the groups vary their pictures by setting one at daytime, one at night time and others at different times of the year. Give out the materials they will need to print their pictures. As they plan their picture, talk with each group about the colours they intend to use, and the techniques they want to use to make the buildings. Ask, *Will the night picture need darker shades of paint? Will buildings in the distance need to be smaller? Why?*

Focus the groups' attention on the lines and patterns they have included in their paintings by posing questions, such as *Why did you use this shape, line, and colour? Why did you use a smaller block for this bit? How did you make this pointed roof? How did you draw the lines here?* Make sure the children can give you reasons for including the shapes and patterns they have.

Evaluate the pictures and allow the children to make any final improvements. Display the finished pictures.

DIFFERENTIATION
Give the children with motor difficulties larger blocks with which to work and get them to develop the same ideas on a much larger scale. Give children with visual difficulties textured papers and glitter paint to work with. Ask them why they have used a particular textured finish for certain buildings. Is it because they want them to stand out? Why is this? They can work with a partner to produce a textured picture if appropriate.

Skilled artists should work on the nightscape picture and learn how to make darker shades of colours by mixing colours. They should think about the effects of lighted lamps on tones of the buildings.

WHERE NEXT
Collect pictures of buildingscapes in colour and black and white, and display these with the children's paintings.

Take the class outside and ask the children to draw parts of buildings, concentrating on the shapes, lines and colours they can see.

ASSESSMENT
Note the children who are confident in giving reasons why they have used their choice of shape, colour and line. Remember, it is their picture and as long as they give plausible reasons for their choices, the finished picture is their personal composition. Note which children are able to make comparisons between the elements they have used and those used by Lowry in his paintings.

LEARNING OUTCOMES
The children will learn to give reasons for their choices of shape, colour and line to create a particular view or effect in their artwork. They will talk about the work of another artist and consider how he created his pictures through the use of shape, colour and line. Some children will learn how to change the tone of a colour to create a different effect, change the sizes of the shapes to add perspective and use contrasting colours to make a particular feature stand out. The children will start to give reasons for the choices they have made within a given context.

FURTHER ART AND DESIGN CHALLENGES

Towering peaks

Ask the children to design sculptures with wood, bricks and ceramic tiles. Challenge them to find a way of making a tower by stacking 20 tiles or bricks in different ways. Can they make a spiral tower? How can they make the wood stand up and not fall over? Can they balance anything on top to make a roof? Why have they put certain colours together or have they used them randomly?

Photograph the children's sculptures and put them together to make a picture of towers. Ask the children to draw their sculptures, picking out the shapes, lines and colours they have used.

Buildings to touch

Give the children sponges in pastel colours, fabric, small boxes, laces, ribbon and other collage materials for them to make 3-D buildings (castles are fun to make). Can they find a way to present the materials to show the distinctive shapes, colours and lines of their buildings? What effects have the children created? How did they do this?

FEEL THE RHYTHM

SUBJECT: MUSIC. QCA UNIT: 4 FEEL THE PULSE.

LEARNING OBJECTIVE

To understand what is meant by pulse and what is meant by rhythm, and to recognise these elements in a song.

THINKING OBJECTIVE

To deduce and explain.

THINKING SKILLS

By taking part in singing and clapping along to a song, the children will learn the difference between a pulse and a rhythm. They will need to deduce which is which and be able to explain why. Both pulse and rhythm are important elements that the children will need to know about when composing their own pieces of music. They may want to create music with a steady beat, which is made more interesting by repeated or syncopated rhythms.

WHAT YOU NEED

'Yellow Submarine' by The Beatles; a tape, record or CD player to play the song on.

WHAT TO DO

Play 'Yellow Submarine' to the children. Let them listen to it to start with, and then teach them the chorus and get them to join in, singing along with the recording.

When the children are comfortable with the song, listen to it again and this time ask the children to clap along with the steady beat. Ask the children to note when the chorus has a more emphasised beat and explain that this is the first beat in each bar. Note every time the beat is emphasised and count *one* for these with the children until they can hear the emphasised beat. Explain that there are four beats in the bar because you count to four each time before the emphasised note appears again. Explain that this is called the beat or pulse of the song and that it stays regular.

Then get the children to listen to and identify the rhythm of the words in the chorus. Ask them to focus on specific words or small word phrases and to become familiar with the rhythm of these to start with, such as *sub-ma-rine* or *we all live in a yellow submarine*. Clap these phrases, too, so that the children can guess which part of the chorus it is. Explain that what they are doing is focusing on the rhythm of the chorus. Point out how this is different from the pulse.

Divide the class into two and ask one half to clap the pulse and the other half to clap the rhythm of the chorus. You may need an additional adult or more confident child to support you with this.

Swap over the children's roles so that they all have the opportunity to clap the pulse and the rhythm in turn. Ask the children in each group to tell you what they are clapping – the pulse or the rhythm – and to explain why they think this.

Clap the pulse in the words *yellow submarine* (four claps). Then clap the rhythm of the words (five claps). Can the children tell you which is the pulse and which is the rhythm? Ask the two groups to clap out the words, one clapping the pulse while the other claps the rhythm.

Finish by playing the song again and asking the children to clap the rhythmic phrase *yellow submarine* throughout the chorus. Ask the children, *Are you now clapping the pulse of the chorus or part of the rhythm? Why do you think this?*

DIFFERENTIATION

With lower attaining children concentrate on either the pulse or the rhythm. Get them to explain the particular element to you. Introduce the other element the following week if appropriate. More able musicians can devise their own rhythm for the song or another one they know and play this as a small group. To do this the children will need to decide which rhythm is interesting and deduce how to reproduce this on their chosen instruments.

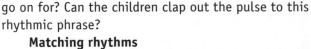

WHERE NEXT

Choose other songs and ask the children to deduce which is the pulse, explaining why they think this, and to copy the rhythm of any phrase from the song.

ASSESSMENT

Note the children who can deduce rhythms and play them independently. Make a note of who can pick out the pulse of songs. Also note who is able to explain competently the difference between pulse and rhythm.

LEARNING OUTCOMES

The children will be able to separate the pulse and rhythm of words in a song, explaining which is which. They will practise performing a rhythmic pattern to a steady pulse.

FURTHER MUSIC CHALLENGES

The rhythm of the beat

Play 'Mars' from *The Planets Suite* by Holst to the children and help them to identify the strong rhythmic phrase at the beginning of the piece. Get the children to listen carefully to the first few minutes of the movement and ask them to say when this rhythmic phrase stops. How long does it go on for? Can the children clap out the pulse to this rhythmic phrase?

Matching rhythms

Make flashcards of rhythms and pulses with crotchets, quavers and crotchet rests. Ask older children in the school to make a tape of these rhythms and pulses, played on a range of familiar percussion instruments. Play a game asking the children in the class to identify which of the recordings match the rhythms and pulses shown on the cards. Ask them to give explanations for their choices.

WHAT SHOULD HE DO?

SUBJECT: RE. QCA UNIT: 1A WHAT DOES IT MEAN TO BELONG?

LEARNING OBJECTIVES

To think about what 'belonging' means; to develop respect and value for others.

THINKING OBJECTIVE

To form opinions.

THINKING SKILLS

The children will be presented with a moral dilemma where they will be asked to give their opinions regarding what they think is right and what is wrong. They will learn to listen carefully to each other's points of view and put forward their own opinions, which may change after listening to others. They will be challenged to think about the moral issues concerning following rules regardless of another's behaviour.

WHAT TO DO

Reinforce the children's understanding that everyone belongs to the school. Talk about the school rules and how the children should behave towards one another.

Tell the children you are going to give them a moral dilemma to think about and give their opinions on. Make up a story about someone (Toby) who was excluded from a game at playtime by a particular boy or girl (Meena). Give the characters names if you wish, making sure that you do not use the name of someone in the class. Tell the children that eventually Toby found someone to play with because another kind child invited him to play. The next day, Meena had no one to play with. Should Toby invite her to join his game? Should he be her friend? What would the children do?

Talk about the moral dilemmas involved in the story. Ask, *How do you think Meena would feel if she had been allowed to join in the game? Would she feel guilty about the day before? How would she feel if she was not allowed to join in? Would she learn how to be friendly?* Listen to all the children's thoughts and opinions. What do they think would be the nicest thing for Toby to do?

If appropriate, encourage the children to talk about any similar experiences they may have had. How did they cope with rejection? Conversely, were there any times when they wouldn't let someone join in with their games? Why? Ask other children to give their opinions (constructively) on the situations described. Have any children changed their opinion after listening to their classmates?

DIFFERENTIATION
Adapt the moral dilemma to suit the make-up of your class, by changing the names, gender or type of situation that is involved.

WHERE NEXT
Relate the story of the Good Samaritan to the children and talk about the similarities. Ask, *Why did the first group of people ignore the injured man? Why was what the Samaritan did so special?* Tell stories from different religions which reinforce the meaning of 'belonging'.

Ask the children to consider what they could do if they found they had no one to play with. Help them set up a system which allows children to find a friend to play with, such as a 'Friendship bus stop' or 'Friendship seat'.

ASSESSMENT
Listen carefully to the children's responses. Question those who think that Meena should not be included in the game. Young children often see things in black and white and express tit-for-tat views. This gives you an opportunity to extend the children's thinking beyond this.

LEARNING OUTCOMES
The children will learn that everyone belongs somewhere. This may be a school or a religion. They will debate and give opinions on what it means to them to belong and the special things that must be done to make everyone feel that they belong.

FURTHER RE CHALLENGES
Belonging
As a class, plan playground activities and write rules to make sure that everyone has the opportunity to join in at some time. These may involve taking it in turns to play, or organising more of the children's favourite games when space dictates that only a certain number can be involved in certain activities at any one time. Make sure that the children think about those who do not necessarily want to be active. Think about the weather issues, too. For example, those children who prefer to stand and chat, draw pictures or look at a book – how will they do these things outside in the playground when the weather is windy and cold? What steps could be taken to make sure that they enjoy these activities even on a cold day?

Playtime buddies
Ask the class to design a monitor's badge for those children who are responsible for inviting people to join in with their games. This means that those who want someone to play with or who are new to the school will know who to approach to get a friendly response. The children could also write a job description for the people chosen to take on this role.

THE GREAT BEANBAG CHALLENGE

SUBJECT: PE. QCA UNIT: GYMNASTIC ACTIVITIES UNIT 2.

LEARNING OBJECTIVE
To move confidently across and over apparatus with thought to their own and other's safety.

THINKING OBJECTIVE
To use inference and deduction skills.

THINKING SKILLS
The children will learn to work together as a team to identify a strategy for carrying a beanbag over a range of apparatus without dropping it. They will start to use inference and deduction skills to work

out a way to get the beanbag across a space within the confines of the rules of a game.

WHAT YOU NEED
Three beanbags; a range of low-level gym equipment, such as mats, benches, climbing tables and hoops.

WHAT TO DO
Set up three identical simple obstacle courses with a mixture of benches and climbing tables and good lengths of space. Put the children into three teams and explain that they have to work out a way to get both their beanbag and their team from one side of the course to the other without dropping the beanbag. Explain the two rules to them:

- ◉ No one must carry the beanbag if they are climbing on or over equipment.
- ◉ Only one person can be moving at any one time.

Give each child a beanbag to practise with and let them explore the problem to begin with. Watch to see how they work out the strategy of getting their beanbag across the tables and benches without carrying it across. Are they using their inference skills to anticipate problems? Have they naturally started to work in pairs or small groups to help each other?

After a while stop the activity and talk about what the children are doing. How many have deduced that if they work in groups of three they can transport the beanbag very easily across the benches and tables? Ask questions to develop the children's inference and deduction skills: *Who can think of a way to get the beanbag over the table when you can't carry it over personally? Do you need someone to help? How can this person help? Can they come with you, or will they have to go first and wait for you or follow you once you get to the table? Does that person need to go back for their beanbag or can someone else bring it for them?*

Tell the class you want to see which team can get their beanbags back to the start, over the apparatus the other way. If appropriate, organise this into a game to see how long it takes to complete the problem. You will need to know your class to see if you need to establish more rules, such as no running, and so on. Ask, *How are you going to get your team back to the beginning? Are you going to take it in turns to go back, or go in groups of three?*

Observe each team as they transport their beanbags. Discuss with the children which team was the most successful and why.

DIFFERENTIATION
Stand where you can see all of the area in which the children are working. Make sure you have the children who have difficulty following rules closest to you.

WHERE NEXT
Make the courses more challenging.

ASSESSMENT
Watch the children as they try to work out how to get their team and their beanbag from one place to another. How do they approach the challenge? Do they use inference and deduction to talk about and plan how they are going to do it first, or do they solve the problem through trial and error?

LEARNING OUTCOMES
The children will learn to work together as a team to solve a problem. They will develop their inference skills and deduce some tactical ideas by working out how to get the beanbag and the team across the course.

FURTHER PE CHALLENGES
Crossing the rickety–rackety bridge
Give the children this challenge:

> The Three Billy Goats think they have found a way to get across to the other side of the river to eat the grass without waking up the Troll. They have managed to find three squares of carpet which they know will make their footsteps quieter.
>
> The Little Billy Goat Gruff decides to go first. He puts one square down onto the bridge and hops onto it. Then he puts down another square and hops onto that. He puts down the third square and hops on top, but he still hasn't reached the other side of the bridge.
>
> If he takes the squares with him, his two brothers won't be able to cross the bridge. He could go on and eat the grass on his own, but he must get back to his brothers before the Troll wakes up and sees that he has managed to get across the bridge without waking him. Also, his brothers may get hungry and it wouldn't be fair to leave them behind.
>
> How can the Three Billy Goats all get across the bridge without waking up the Troll?

ENQUIRY SKILLS

INTRODUCTION

The enquiry process is a means through which children can be fully involved in their own learning. This process gives them the opportunity to identify why they are learning something, as well as how and what. The ability to ask questions is fundamental to the development of children's independent enquiry skills. Once children are able to ask questions, the next step is to identify when they have asked the right questions to suit the needs of their research requirements. These questions can only be identified if the children can note what the problem is and what they need to find out in order to solve it. Only then can they begin to plan research into a topic or area.

Too often the children are presented with a ready-made set of questions and, therefore, play no part in developing the skill of asking questions themselves. The process undertaken with scientific enquiry can be applied to other subjects and is a good starting point through which to develop the children's enquiry skills. Often, with young children, teachers start with a question in science and yet rarely do so for other subjects. By identifying questions for each unit of work in all subjects, you will be setting up the enquiry process, allowing the children to find things out for themselves and to develop enquiry skills. This will allow the children to achieve the average National Curriculum Level 2 descriptors by the end of Year 2. However, this will not move the children on to achieve the higher Level 3 as this requires them to start planning their own research. This research involves them asking their own questions to start off an independent enquiry. While teachers generally model the asking of questions clearly in science to help identify a problem, enquiry or investigation (which gives the children the opportunity to plan their investigation and carry out a test), they tend not to revisit the investigation to improve ideas or refine the hypothesis, which may lead to a redefinition of the problem to make it more precise. This is the point at which children may begin to ask their own questions to lead them into investigations and to conduct research, which takes their achievement beyond the average. Thinking becomes visible from this point forward.

The enquiry process is generally addressed as a whole, and the links between the range of skills are established easily. The activities in this chapter are planned to focus on particular aspects of the enquiry process, but at the same time recognise that these are probably set within a whole research project. It will, therefore, be difficult to see the skills on their own in all activities and the overlap between them.

The enquiry processes and skills are:
⊙ asking questions
⊙ defining a problem
⊙ planning research
⊙ predicting outcomes
⊙ anticipating consequences
⊙ testing conclusions
⊙ improving ideas.

INTRODUCING ENQUIRY SKILLS

Subject and QCA unit, NLS or NNS objective	Activity title	Thinking objective	Activity	Page
English NLS objective: To pose questions and record them in writing	Amazing facts	To ask questions	Finding answers in text and locating different parts of text	56
Maths NNS objective: To estimate, measure and compare capacities	How much does it hold?	To predict and test conclusions	Practically measuring liquid	56
Science QCA unit: 1C Sorting and using materials	I'm thinking of something	To ask scientific questions	Playing a game to determine the properties of different objects	57
History QCA unit: 2 What were homes like a long time ago?	Knobs and handles	To plan research	Looking at a collection of knobs and handles and comparing them across historical periods	57
Geography QCA unit: 3 An island home	Katie Morag at home	To ask geographical questions	Identifying human and physical features of a real and a fictional island	58
Design and technology QCA unit: 1A Moving pictures	Moving pieces	To anticipate consequences	Using their knowledge and understanding of how things move when making a model	59
ICT QCA unit: 1F Understanding instructions and making things happen	Starting or finishing	To anticipate consequences and predict outcomes	Interpreting a set of instructions and following routes	59
Art and design QCA unit: 1C What is sculpture?	Statues	To ask questions	Learning about the aesthetic qualities of sculpture	60
Music QCA unit: 4 Feel the pulse	Feel the beat	To test conclusions	Identifying different parts of composition in several pieces of music	61
RE QCA unit: 1D Beliefs and practice	Divali	To plan research	Learning about the festival of Divali and understanding where information can be found	61
PE QCA unit: Games activities unit 2	Dressing up	To define a problem and anticipate consequences	Trying out different orders to put on clothes in a dressing-up race	62

AMAZING FACTS

SUBJECT: ENGLISH. NLS OBJECTIVE: TO POSE QUESTIONS AND RECORD THEM IN WRITING, PRIOR TO READING NON-FICTION TO FIND THE ANSWERS.

LEARNING OBJECTIVE

To find answers to questions in text and locate different parts of text that give particular information.

THINKING OBJECTIVE

To ask questions.

THINKING SKILLS

The children will begin to ask questions about things that interest them, or about things which they wish to look at in more depth, from reading a piece of information. They will use the text to locate the answers to the questions they have asked. During this activity, the answers may lend themselves to further questions, thus developing their questioning skills further.

WHAT YOU NEED

A fact sheet, extract from an information book or an information poster containing facts and figures about a favourite class topic; board or flip chart; paper and writing materials.

WHAT TO DO

Read through a fact sheet, book or poster with the children. This could be a set of safety rules for Bonfire Night, books about animals or dinosaurs, or a fact sheet about how to plant seeds; as long as it gives information in pictorial and text forms.

After an initial reading ask the children for any questions they would like to ask about the piece. For example, what does the brontosaurus eat? Which is the biggest dinosaur in the poster/book? Which dinosaur lived the longest time ago? Record these questions on the board. Try to make sure there are included questions about a fact, a figure and something that is relevant to the content of the piece and is truly amazing. For example, questions about the tyrannosaurus might include: *What does the tyrannosaurus eat? How tall is it? Why is it called tyrannosaurus?*

Ask the children to work in groups to find answers to the list of questions on the board. Give each group a copy of the information text and ask them to find the information within it. Explain that they should look closely at what sort of information is given in different parts of the text and the different ways it is presented. Work with the groups, pointing them

towards clues such as format, headings and captions. Ask, *How are the facts presented? Are bullet points used or are points numbered? Does this help you find information?* Make sure the children look at any pictures or charts, and discuss with them how these support the facts in the text. Do these features help them to locate any answers to the questions?

At the end of the lesson share the children's answers and consider all the amazing facts that the children have found.

HOW MUCH DOES IT HOLD?

SUBJECT: MATHS. NNS OBJECTIVE: TO ESTIMATE, MEASURE AND COMPARE CAPACITIES.

LEARNING OBJECTIVE

To know that liquid volume can be measured in litres.

THINKING OBJECTIVE

To predict and test conclusions.

THINKING SKILLS

The children will predict and test out whether different shaped containers hold the same volume of water even though they may be taller, fatter, shorter or thinner than each other and might look as if they hold more or less. They will learn to test their predictions by carrying out the test systematically.

WHAT YOU NEED

A water tray for each group with enough water to fill at least five containers; five containers of different shapes and sizes that hold the same amount of water, labelled from 1 to 5 for each group; 1l, 500ml and 250ml measuring jugs; a collection of familiar containers which hold different volumes, such as drinks bottles, cartons, cans, sauce bottles and liquid soap bottles (include some that hold exactly 2l, 1l, 500ml and 250ml and make sure they have not contained anything harmful); paper and writing materials; board or flip chart.

WHAT TO DO

Show the children the range of familiar containers and talk about how much each one holds. Get them to look at the labels to find this information, and record the volume of each in a list on the board. If relevant ask the children to find containers with different volumes as a homework activity to reinforce the learning in this area.

If the children are ready, explain that 500ml is half a litre and 250ml is a quarter of a litre. Challenge the children to tell you how many millilitres in 1 litre. If they can't, tell them that 1 litre is 1000ml.

Show the children the five containers that hold the same amount of liquid, but don't tell them this. Split the class into groups of six, organised into pairs, around a set of containers on their table. Ask them to either draw or write the numbers of the containers in order, from which they think will hold the most to the least amount of liquid. When they have done this, ask the children how they could test their predictions.

Ask the children to check their predictions. Give each group a water tray, a set of measuring jugs, a set of the five containers and recording materials. If they get stuck, suggest that a good way to work would be to fill one container with water and pour the amount into another to see if it holds more or less than the first one.

Ask those children who are ready to predict which of their containers hold most, more, less and least, before using the measuring jugs to sort them into sets. The sets could be according to whether they hold more or less than 1 litre, more or less than 500ml, more or less than 250ml (depending on the children's abilities). When they have carried out their measuring ask the groups, *Were your predictions right? Are you surprised to find that they all hold the same amount of liquid?* When all the groups have finished their testing, call the class together and ask if their test results were different from their predictions.

I'M THINKING OF SOMETHING

SUBJECT: SCIENCE. QCA UNIT: 1C SORTING AND USING MATERIALS.

LEARNING OBJECTIVE
To learn that materials have different properties, which are suited to their uses.

THINKING OBJECTIVE
To ask scientific questions.

THINKING SKILLS
The children will ask direct questions in order to gain information, and there is an added incentive for them to use scientific vocabulary in their questions which supports their science learning. There is also a focus on the way that the properties of each material are suited to its use, as well as merely identifying the name and properties of each material.

WHAT YOU NEED
A collection of objects made from a variety of materials with a range of different properties; a board or flip chart with everyone's name written in a list to add scores to.

WHAT TO DO
Tell the children you want them to play a game. Tell them that they have to ask you questions to try to work out which object you have under the table. Explain that the objects you have in the collection are all made from different materials and that is their main difference. Tell the children that every sensible question will earn them 1 point and if they use scientific vocabulary they will get an extra point. Model some questions first so they get the idea of the game, for example *Is the object made from a material which is bendy? Is the object made from a material which is soft? Can you see through the object? Is it transparent? Is the material magnetic?* Explain that you are only allowed to answer each question with *Yes* or *No*. Tell them that they are not allowed to make wild guesses about the object and each time they do you will take a point off their score, and that the person who guesses the object correctly will get 2 points. Ask a higher attaining child to record the scores on the board, adding the points earned next to the children's names on the list.

Start the game, sitting close to the scorer to point out the names in order to speed things up. It may take a while before the children get the hang of the game. If they get stuck, encourage them by talking about the object you have chosen and thinking of some questions the children could ask about that item.

As the children improve with the game start the scores again from 0. Encourage the children to use questions that develop their understanding of the suitability of the materials to the object's purpose. For example, *Is the material waterproof? Does it fold like fabric? Is it an umbrella?* You could model these sorts of questions by giving a higher attaining child the job of thinking of an object while you act as guesser with the other children. This way you can ask more questions which focus on specific scientific information.

KNOBS AND HANDLES

SUBJECT: HISTORY. QCA UNIT: 2 WHAT WERE HOMES LIKE A LONG TIME AGO?

LEARNING OBJECTIVE
To compare a household object from two different historical periods.

THINKING OBJECTIVE
To plan research.

THINKING SKILLS
The children will explore why knobs and handles are designed; their shape, their context and colour depending on their age and period style. The knobs and handles from Victorian or Edwardian times are very different from those which were designed at different times during the 20th and 21st centuries. The materials used are different, and themed knobs are frequently found today.

WHAT YOU NEED
A collection of modern knobs and handles of different shapes, sizes, pattern and purpose; pictures of furniture with knobs and handles clearly visible from a different historical period, such as Victorian or Edwardian periods, or from the 60s and 70s; sample drawer fronts; board or flip chart.

WHAT TO DO
Look together at the collection of modern knobs and handles. Ask the children to sort them into sets with different criteria, for example according to purpose, material, colour, design (those that screw in, those that are attached by screws externally) or shape (flower designs, round, square).

Tell the children that you want them to find out about the handles and knobs that were used at different times in the past. Explain that you want them to find out how they were different and how they were the same as the modern ones they have been looking at. Ask, *How can you plan your research? How can you find out this information?*

Prepare a class planning sheet for the research. On the board, write any questions the children feel will be helpful in planning their research. These might include, *What are we trying to find out? What resources will we use? What questions do we need to ask? Where will we find the answers? What have we found out? Is the information useful in helping us decide what is the same and what is different?*

Then list with the children all the places where they might find information about knobs and handles from different periods. This will include looking at photographs showing old and modern furniture, books containing pictures and information. Look at the evidence sources in your collection and ask the children to identify which things will be useful.

Show the children the pictures of furniture from a different historical period and ask what they notice about the shape and size of the knobs and handles they can see. Ask, *How are they the same as the modern ones we've been looking at? How are they*

different? Are they fit for their purpose or are they more cosmetic? From what material are they made? Are there any plastic ones? Why not? How are they attached to the furniture?

When the children have completed their research of one knob or handle, go back to the questions on the board and revise what they planned to research and whether this was useful.

Set up drawer fronts in the classroom and let the children experiment with different combinations from the knobs you have brought in. Challenge them to choose knobs which look like those from the older period in the pictures.

KATIE MORAG AT HOME

SUBJECT: GEOGRAPHY. QCA UNIT: 3 AN ISLAND HOME.

LEARNING OBJECTIVES
To learn to identify the geographical features on a map; to find out about facilities of different locations using brochures and the Internet.

THINKING OBJECTIVE
To ask geographical questions.

THINKING SKILLS
The children will learn to ask their own questions as a starting point for research. They will begin to think about where to find information about the geographical features of a place and to locate this information in books and on the Internet. They will consider how and why certain features attract visitors to islands.

WHAT YOU NEED
A copy of any Katie Morag story book which shows the geographical features of the Isle of Struay; a map of any other island, such as the Isle of Man or the Isle of Wight; board or flip chart.

WHAT TO DO
Talk with the class about Katie Morag's island and look at a picture of the Isle of Struay together. Play a questioning game for which the answers can be found in the picture. Model the game by asking questions such as *What is the name of the physical feature that Katie has to walk around to get to Grannie's house?* (The bay.) Continue the game until you think the children understand how to ask questions themselves.

Then invite them to take it in turns to ask the class questions that will identify the human and physical features on the island. Then extend the game and play 'I-Spy', including clues that note how the features are used. For example, *I spy with my little eye a physical feature beginning with B*. Give a clue, such as *Where is the place where I can build a sandcastle?* Again, invite the children to be the leader and provide the clues.

Look carefully at the map of the other island together to see what features there are. Find the beach, church, playground, river, railway station and so on. Play 'I-Spy' again if you wish. Ask the children whether there are different features from those on Katie's island. Make a list of activities that can be done on an island, including going on a boat trip, building a sandcastle, visiting a castle or buying souvenirs. List these as questions on the board and ask the children to find each location on the maps of both islands where they could do these.

Prepare a list of questions with the children about whether to choose the islands as a holiday destination. For example, *Is there somewhere to go for a walk? Can you build a sandcastle? Are there rock pools to explore? Can you go on a boat trip?* Record these questions on the board and ask the children to work in groups to find the answers to some of them. Using the answers, can they decide whether or not each place would be a good one to visit? Additionally, the children could use the Internet to find out about the weather.

Moving pieces

SUBJECT: DESIGN AND TECHNOLOGY. QCA UNIT: 1A MOVING PICTURES.

Learning objective
To learn that levers and other mechanisms make things move.

Thinking objective
To anticipate consequences.

Thinking skills
Although no longer such a focal part of the design and technology curriculum, it is sometimes useful for the children to take things apart to find out how they work. Here, the children's enquiries into mechanisms can help them gain knowledge and understanding

that they can then use in their own designing and making tasks.

What you need
Books and cards with moving components; scissors, tongs and pliers; strips of Meccano (enough for two for each pair of children); small pictures; small paper hands (enough for a pair of hands for each pair); split pins, cardboard, drawing materials.

What to do
Look with the class at the books and cards with moving components. Discuss with the children the things that move in them and how they move. Focus on whether they move in and out, up and down, or together and away. Then look at particular moving components in turn and before pulling or sliding a mechanism ask the children to predict how it will move its component. Are they right each time?

Then look together at how scissors, tongs and pliers work and the movement involved. Ask, *How do they move?* (Together and apart.)

Join five strips of Meccano of equal length together and manipulate the structure to make different shapes. Ask the children to describe how the different shapes are created, anticipating what effect a change in direction of one of the strips will have. Talk about how this can change the position of objects placed at the end of the strips too. Stick some small pictures to each corner of the structure and make sure the children understand how they are moving with the strips of Meccano.

Working in pairs, give the children two Meccano strips and ask them to connect them together to make a scissor movement. Give out two paper hands per pair and tell them to stick a hand to the end of each strip and make the hands clap together. When they have mastered this, ask them what would happen if they joined the two pieces together at different points. (They should move further apart.)

The children could make greetings cards with a scissor movement inside, made from cardboard strips and split pins. Let the children design their own pictures to move together, but ideas could include a bee landing on a flower head, a chicken moving from behind an egg, a car going in and out of a garage.

Starting or finishing

SUBJECT: ICT. QCA UNIT: 1F UNDERSTANDING INSTRUCTIONS AND MAKING THINGS HAPPEN.

Learning objective
To interpret a set of instructions and to understand how important it is that they are precise.

THINKING OBJECTIVE
To anticipate consequences and predict outcomes.

THINKING SKILLS
The children will learn to anticipate consequences and predict outcomes when following a list of instructions. They will use this knowledge to rewrite more precise and correct instructions. Some will discover how to work backwards through a set of instructions to find a starting point.

WHAT YOU NEED
Different sets of instructions on how to get from one point to another following a pathway, for example from the classroom to the hall, from the playground to the library, with at least one deliberate mistake in each set (have as many different pathways as you can, written in very clear and precise language); for higher attaining children include some instructions that have the finishing point identified but the starting point removed.

WHAT TO DO
Read one set of instructions to the children. Explain that they are going to follow the instructions to get to the finishing point. Read the first instruction again, which should give the precise starting point. Ask the children to say where they think they will be when they have followed this instruction. Read the next instruction and ask the children to predict where they will be after they have followed this. Increase the number of instructions to three at this point, making sure that it involves a travel, a turn and some further travel. For example, *Go forward ten paces, turn left and go forward three paces.* Deliberately make the turn the wrong way so that the walker would walk into a wall or door. Have any of them noticed? Ask the children to consider what would have happened if they had not anticipated the consequences of this wrong instruction. Rewrite the instruction together so that the turn is now the correct way.

When you have finished the first pathway, revise why it is important to turn the correct way. Ask, *Why is it important to get the instructions precise for a robot? Will a robot be able to think that maybe the instructions are wrong, or will it simply stop when it reaches an obstacle?*

Repeat the exercise with a second set of instructions, but this time before starting, tell the children where the finishing point will be. Read the first three instructions which will clearly send you in the wrong direction, away from where you need to be travelling. See if any of the children can anticipate this outcome before you ask one of them to start to follow the instructions. If not, allow the volunteer to follow the route practically until the children can anticipate that they are going in the wrong direction. Again, talk about the importance of precise instructions.

Let the children work in pairs to follow different routes. Explain that there is a mistake in each of their directions and that they will not reach the intended destination if they do not anticipate where this is. As they follow the instructions, talk to them at various stages to see if they can anticipate where the instructions are asking them to turn or travel in the wrong direction.

Give higher attaining children the instructions which ask them to work backwards from the finishing point to find the starting point.

At the end of the lesson reinforce the objective that it is important to write precise instructions and directions so that the correct pathway is followed. Otherwise the person or robot may get lost and not finish at the intended finishing point.

STATUES

SUBJECT: ART AND DESIGN. QCA UNIT: 1C
WHAT IS SCULPTURE?

LEARNING OBJECTIVE
To establish why sculptures are made and where they are found, and identify materials they are made from.

THINKING OBJECTIVE
To ask questions.

THINKING SKILLS
The children will ask questions to find reasons why particular statues and sculptures have been made and placed where they have in the local environment. They will also be encouraged to ask open questions about any personal element they are interested in regarding a sculpture.

WHAT YOU NEED
Pictures of famous statues and sculptures found in towns and cities; travel brochures which show statues or sculptures in travel destinations (Hawaii and the South Sea Islands, Alaska and Canada usually provide good examples of stone and wooden statues and totem poles. Cruises to Italy are another source of information and you may find an ice sculpture on one of the pages.); plan a walk around the local area or a visit to a museum or art gallery to see sculptures; board or flip chart.

WHAT TO DO

Look at (a photograph of) one of the sculptures. Ask the children questions about it, such as *From what is the sculpture made? Will it last a long time or will it eventually disappear?* If you have an actual sculpture, let the children stroke it and feel the texture. Ask, *How does it feel? What does it makes you think of? Does it remind you of anything?* Ask the children why they think statues and sculptures are made. Is it because of the subject? Is it something to do with the local town or city? Why do they think the artist used this particular idea?

Look at another sculpture together. Invite the children to ask questions about it. Prompt them by asking, *What do you want to know about this sculpture?*

Show the children the travel brochures and the pictures of different statues and sculptures in them. On the board, make a list of questions the children would like to ask in order to find out about what the statues are made from and how and why they were made.

Take the children on a visit to a garden centre and/or go on a walk around the local area if there are good examples of sculptures and statues, or there is a topiary enthusiast about. Ask the children why they think the statue or sculpture is where it is. *What is the subject about? Why has this particular subject been chosen by the artist?* Encourage the children to think of their own questions regarding any sculptures to spark enquiry into its purpose.

FEEL THE BEAT

SUBJECT: MUSIC. QCA UNIT: 4 FEEL THE PULSE.

LEARNING OBJECTIVES

To learn to identify the tune, pulse and accompaniment in pieces of music; to repeat short rhythmic phrases confidently.

THINKING OBJECTIVE

To test conclusions.

THINKING SKILLS

The children will listen to a range of musical extracts and identify different elements in them, such as the tune, pulse, rhythm and accompaniments. They will repeat these along with the music and conclude whether or not they have identified these correctly.

WHAT YOU NEED

Extracts from different music where each element is clearly separate, for example 'Troika' from *Lieutenant*

Kije by Prokofiev (tune and accompaniment), *Bolero* by Ravel (rhythmic accompaniment), 'March of the Toreadors' from *Carmen* by Bizet (pulse), the Anvil Chorus from *Il Trovatore* by Verdi (accompaniment and tune); a tape recorder; percussion instruments.

WHAT TO DO

Play 'Troika' and ask the children to identify the tune. They can sing along with this, as it is easy enough to copy. Focus on the accompaniment and ask them to identify this part of the music: *Why did the composer choose these instruments and this rhythm?* Give a small group of children bells and ask them to play along with what they think is the accompaniment part of the music, while the rest of the class continue to sing what they have identified as the tune. Record the children's performance and play it back to them afterwards to evaluate whether they identified the tune and accompaniment correctly.

Repeat this with the other extracts of music, talking about which parts are the tune, pulse, rhythm and other accompaniments. Can the children name the instrument(s) being played too? Ask, *How have you made your decisions?* Identify the different elements of the pieces for the children, explaining why each part is the pulse, or the rhythm, for example stating that, *The rhythm is often repeated or follows a steady beat.* Assess whether the children's decisions were correct.

Finally, listen to a short extract from *Bolero* and get the children to pick out the rhythmic accompaniment, which repeats a rhythm throughout. Clap this together, and then get the children to transfer the rhythm to instruments. They can play along with the rhythm on different non-pitched percussion instruments. Ask questions so that the children can test their own conclusions this time, such as *How do you know this is the rhythm and not the tune? Which is the tune? Can anyone sing a short extract of the tune?*

DIVALI

SUBJECT: RE. QCA UNIT: 1D BELIEFS AND PRACTICE.

LEARNING OBJECTIVE

To learn the main belief represented by a festival.

THINKING OBJECTIVE

To plan research.

THINKING SKILLS

The children will identify what they want to find out about Divali rather than learning by only listening to a story or account. They will plan where and how they will find answers to their questions before relating these to the rest of the class. This will add more meaning to the festival of Divali and what it means to Hindus and Sikhs.

WHAT YOU NEED
Books with pictures and simple texts about Divali; photographs and/or posters of a Divali celebration; the story of Rama and Sita; board or flip chart.

WHAT TO DO
Explain to the children that Divali is a religious festival celebrated by Hindus and Sikhs. Tell them that you want them to find out what they can about it. Start by asking the children what they would like to know. Invite them to ask you questions, and record these on the board. When you have about ten questions, choose one and ask the children to say which resources they could use to find the answer to it. For example, if the question is *Are there any special objects used in the festival?* they might suggest finding a book, using the Internet or asking any Hindus or Sikhs in the school. Try one of the sources the children have suggested and talk about whether the source was helpful. Did it show a Divali lamp or cards, for example?

Divide the children into groups. Give each group a question from the board, and books and posters (and Internet access if possible) in which the children will find the answers to their question. Move around the groups, encouraging them to talk about what they are using and why. Make sure that lower attaining children have pictures help them find the answer to their question and keep returning to this group to prompt ideas.

After about five minutes, bring the children back together and share the answers to their questions.

Finish by read the story of Rama and Sita to the children, relating the content to the Hindu celebrations of Divali where relevant.

DRESSING UP

SUBJECT PE. QCA UNIT: GAMES ACTIVITIES UNIT 2.

LEARNING OBJECTIVE
To choose, use and vary simple tactics.

THINKING OBJECTIVE
To define a problem and anticipate consequences.

THINKING SKILLS
The children will work out the best order in which to put on a series of clothes in order to do this in

the fastest time to win a race. They will need to think about the problems they may encounter and anticipate the consequences of not organising the order properly.

WHAT YOU NEED
Enough clothes for five teams to play a dressing-up race (include gloves or mittens, a scarf, a hat and large jumper); a stopwatch.

WHAT TO DO
Show the children the clothes you have in your collection and talk about how each item is put on. Invite four children to model one item of clothing, demonstrating how to put it on.

Then ask the children to suggest a possible order that they could put the clothes on for a dressing-up race. Ask the children to suggest which item would be best to put on first. Why did they choose this? Give the children the opportunity to make alternative suggestions, giving reasons for these. If they do not come up with an alternative ask, *What would happen if you put the hat on first?* Encourage the children to think of possible problems with this and to anticipate consequences for the rest of the clothes they need to put on. For example, if they put the hat on first would it be easier or harder to put on the jumper?

Ask which should be the second item the children would put on, repeating the questions and giving the children the opportunity to define any problems they can foresee and anticipating any consequences of putting on certain garments second. Can the children predict the best order in which to put all the clothes on?

To test out the children's prediction, split the class into four groups and run the race. One child from each group should take part in each race. Explain to the children that you will time how long each child takes and the winner will be the one who can put all the clothes on fastest. After the first race, discuss with the children whether their ideas about the order the clothes should be put on were correct. Do they want to change this order? Allow them to discuss this in their groups before running the race again.

Repeat the race until you are happy that the children have found the best order. Bring the children together and discuss what order this is.

EXTENDING ENQUIRY SKILLS

Subject and QCA unit, NLS or NNS objective	Activity title	Thinking objective	Activity	Page
English NLS objective: To describe story settings and characters	Robot mania	To ask and answer questions	Identifying questions that they want to know about a story	64
Maths NNs objective: To read the time on analogue and digital clocks	What's the time?	To ask and answer questions in order to solve problems	Developing the language and understanding of time by identifying TV or radio programme start and finish times	65
Science QCA unit: 1E Pushes and pulls	Flap the kipper	To predict outcomes, test conclusions and improve ideas	Finding out which are the best materials to use in a 'Flip the kipper' game	66
History QCA unit: 4 Why do we remember Florence Nightingale?	Florence Nightingale in the hot-seat	To ask and answer historical questions	Devising interview questions to ask Florence Nightingale	68
Geography QCA unit: 22 A contrasting locality overseas – Tocuaro	Mexican heatwave	To ask geographical questions	Looking at changes in physical and human features in a place they have studied	69
Design and technology QCA unit: 1C Eat more fruit and vegetables	Vegetable variety	To research and improve ideas	Making a vegetable stir-fry	70
ICT QCA unit: 1E Questions and answers	Going on holiday	To plan research	Planning a database using information they have collected and using it to answer further questions	71
Art and design QCA unit: 2B Mother Nature, designer	Natural art	To plan research and improve ideas	Making papier mâché dishes and decorating them with designs inspired from the natural world	73
Music QCA unit: 5 Taking off	Swings and roundabouts	To test and improve ideas	Creating sequences of sound that represent apparatus in a playground	74
RE QCA unit: 2B Why did Jesus tell stories?	Telling stories	To ask questions for given answers	Playing an 'identify the question' game to given answers, in order to draw upon knowledge of the stories Jesus told	75
PE QCA unit: Games activities unit 1	Ball fun	To plan research, predict outcomes and test conclusions	Throwing a ball accurately in different ways	77

ROBOT MANIA

SUBJECT: ENGLISH. NLS OBJECTIVES: TO DESCRIBE STORY SETTINGS AND RELATE THEM TO THEIR OWN EXPERIENCE; TO IDENTIFY AND DESCRIBE CHARACTERS, EXPRESSING THEIR OWN VIEWS AND USING WORDS AND PHRASES FROM THE TEXT.

LEARNING OBJECTIVE
To identify and describe characters, events and settings in a story.

THINKING OBJECTIVE
To ask and answer questions.

THINKING SKILLS
The children will learn to ask questions which will help them to identify the characters, settings and events of a story, important skills to help them write stories of their own. It is also an important ability to help with the development of prediction, inference and deduction skills.

WHAT YOU NEED
Harry and the Robots by Ian Whybrow and Adrian Reynolds (Gullane Publishing); board or flip chart divided into three columns.

WHAT TO DO
Show the children the back cover of the book and read the blurb. Ask the children what they think the story might be about. Ask, *Is it about playing with robots, mending or making robots, a visit to a hospital or something else?* List the children's ideas on the board.

Read the first two pages of the story. Ask the children who the characters are so far and where the story is set at the beginning. Write the names of the characters in one column on the board and the setting in the middle. Write what has happened so far in the right-hand column. Use different coloured pens if you wish.

Read the next two pages of the story. Invite the children to ask questions about the characters and setting. Prompt them to focus on particular characters, for example *Who are the people standing in the background? Are they new to the story? Have they been mentioned yet? Can we be sure of who they are?* Add the new characters and settings to your list.

Read the next four pages. Ask, *Who is Sam? Have we seen this character before*? Add the name to the character column, along with Mum. Talk about what has happened to Nan and add this to the events column. Invite questions about the setting.

Read the next page and talk about how Sam is feeling. What questions can the children think to ask to find out how Sam and Harry are feeling? Examples might be, *Why doesn't Sam want Harry to use Nan's scissors? Why did Harry throw his Stegosaurus at Sam? Who did Harry make his new robot with? Why did Mum let him use Nan's scissors?* Ask the children what clues they used to help them think of their questions.

Encourage the children to continue reading the story in groups, inviting questions about how Harry is feeling, whether his robot can really talk or whether Harry has a vivid imagination. Continue to add relevant and significant events to the list, along with any additional characters and settings.

Ask an additional adult to work with one group of children, modelling and identifying a set of comprehension questions they want to ask about the ending of the story. These might include, *Did Nan get better? What made Nan get better? How many robots did Harry make? Why did Harry make the robots?*

Finish by looking at the columns you have made on the board. Ask the children, *How many characters are in the story? How many settings are there?* Read through the events and identify the beginning, middle and the end of the story. Talk about how the questions helped the children find out about what was happening in the story.

DIFFERENTIATION
A higher attaining group should identify the questions independently and this will help them to decide what they think may happen in the story. Lower attaining children should work with supervision to identify characters, settings and events.

WHERE NEXT
Ask the children to think of a set of questions which will help others to retell the story in the correct sequence. The children could also ask questions which, when asked, will help a younger child sequence the pictures of a different story in the correct order.

ASSESSMENT
Note the children who can identify questions to help them understand what the story is about. Note those who understand how the questions have helped them get to know the characters, settings and events.

LEARNING OUTCOMES
Most children will learn to ask questions and use these to get to understand the meaning of the story.

Many will begin to identify the meaning beyond the literal by questioning how the characters feel about things, using pictures as clues.

FURTHER ENGLISH CHALLENGES
Picture questions
Look at any picture from any story which shows at least two characters with particular expressions on their faces. Challenge the children to think of at least five questions which, when answered, will indicate how the characters are feeling.
What happens next?
Invite the children to find a picture in *A Wolf at the Door!* by Nick Ward (Scholastic). Challenge them to think of three questions which will help the reader predict what will happen next in the story.

WHAT'S THE TIME?

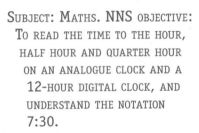

SUBJECT: MATHS. NNS OBJECTIVE: TO READ THE TIME TO THE HOUR, HALF HOUR AND QUARTER HOUR ON AN ANALOGUE CLOCK AND A 12-HOUR DIGITAL CLOCK, AND UNDERSTAND THE NOTATION 7:30.

LEARNING OBJECTIVE
To learn to tell the time in analogue and digital form and solve problems using the information.

THINKING OBJECTIVE
To ask and answer questions in order to solve problems.

THINKING SKILLS
The children will build on their skills of information collecting by identifying questions they need to ask in order to find answers to questions about time.

WHAT YOU NEED
A digital and analogue clock; timer or stopwatch; copies of programme listing times from a radio or television guide; board or flip chart; paper and writing materials.

WHAT TO DO
Play the game What's the Time Mr Wolf? with the class and afterwards look at how *o'clock* is recorded in analogue and digital format.

Discuss how many minutes there are in an hour, half an hour, a quarter of an hour and three quarters

of an hour. What do the children notice about the number of minutes in each of these and the way that the time is recorded digitally? Make sure that the children are able to understand how each of these amounts of time are recorded in analogue and digital formats. Consolidate this by asking the children to write two examples for quarter past and quarter to an hour on the board.

Give groups of children copies of the programme listings and tell them to work for ten minutes as time detectives to look for programmes that start at o'clock, half past the hour, quarter past or quarter to the hour. Identify with the children that they are asking the question, *What time does the programme start?* Explain that when the children have found a time one child in the group should record this as part of a list, and that they should take it in turns to record this information. Set a timer for ten minutes to give the children a time challenge. Afterwards, ask the groups to name one programme they have found for each time in turn.

Tell the groups that you would like them to think of ways of finding out when the same programmes on their list finish. Ask, *How will you know*? (Does anyone understand that one programme finishes when the next one begins?) Identify with the children what questions they need to ask to find out how long the programme lasts, such as *What time does the programme start? What time does the programme finish? How many minutes have passed between these two times? How can I find out?* Record their questions on the board. Give a lower attaining group programmes that start on the hour and record the start and finish times alongside the listed programmes.

DIFFERENTIATION
Lower attaining and younger children will need to work with o'clock and half past times only. Help them to identify the questions which will help them find the programmes that start at these times in the listings. Higher attaining children can record the times in both analogue and digital format to reinforce their understanding of both forms of recording the time. Move them onto identifying questions for working out how long particular programmes last in minutes.

WHERE NEXT
Organise the children's information as a graph. Use the graph to ask questions which will help the children to interpret what they have found out about the length of their favourite programme.

During the week ask the children questions like, *How long is it to playtime, assembly or to our favourite television programme?* Point out the time on the clock and move the hands around if necessary, so that the children can see the passage of time. Choose times which require an answer of half or quarter past or to the hour.

ASSESSMENT

Look at the lists the children have made to note who has correctly identified the start times and who has managed to use the information to find out how long some programmes last. Which children know which questions to ask to find out this information? Note those who are confident with quarter hours and who are ready to move onto smaller units.

LEARNING OUTCOMES

Most children should develop the vocabulary needed to ask questions about the passage of time. They will have learned to use their enquiry skills to find answers to these questions. This will enable some children to solve simple problems about the passage of time.

FURTHER MATHS CHALLENGES

Planning a party

Give the children a worksheet which outlines the activities at a party with the amount of time it takes for each activity to be completed. Ask them to think of questions which will help them to organise a timetable so that they have an interesting programme for the party. For example, *What time does the party start? What time does the party end? How long does each game last? What time do we want to eat?* Give the children timesheets to help them organise the times of activities, either by writing in each one or by placing blocks of time on the sheet. This will allow them to move things around if they wish. Get together at the end of the lesson and talk about the different party timetables created. The children can work individually or collaboratively in a group.

A fun day to remember

Organise an end of term fun afternoon in the same way as the 'Planning a party' activity above. Ask the children to identify the questions they need to ask themselves when organising this day. Collect the children's suggestions for activities for the day and work out together how much time each one is likely to take. Put together a programme for the afternoon and when suitable run this to find out whether the children have correctly estimated the amount of time for the activities.

FLAP THE KIPPER

SUBJECT: SCIENCE. QCA UNIT: 1E PUSHES AND PULLS.

LEARNING OBJECTIVE

To find out about what causes movement.

THINKING OBJECTIVE

To predict outcomes, test conclusions and improve ideas.

THINKING SKILLS

The children will consider different variables involved in testing different materials to see which causes movement. This will allow them to deduce when a test is unfair, a prerequisite to knowing how to make a test fair, and help them make improvements to their predictions. They will learn to organise investigations to make sure that they have tested all the different materials available and which causes the best movement. They will discover how important

it is to record their findings in a way that can be interpreted to help them test their conclusions. They will decide whether the information they have discovered allows them to answer their questions or whether they need additional information.

WHAT YOU NEED

A range of papers including tissue, crepe, newspaper and sugar paper for the kippers; thick card, plastic sheeting, rolled-up newspapers and foil for the flappers; stopwatches; board or flip chart; a set of areas to race the kippers in; paper and writing materials.

WHAT TO DO

Before the lesson, cut the flapper materials to the same size. These should be rectangles measuring between A4 and A3 size, as small hands will be able to manipulate these easily. Cut the fish shapes for the kippers. Kippers should be no more than 30cm long and 20cm wide (the same size as a page from the *Radio Times*!). Use no more than four different materials for kippers or flappers.

Demonstrate to the children how to make the kippers move with the flappers. Place a kipper on the floor and flap a flapper to try to make it move. Allow the children to play with the kippers and flappers and to develop their technique. Remind them not to touch the kipper with the flapper. During this time ask questions to direct their learning, such as *How fast should you flap? Should you bang the floor with the flapper? When you have managed to lift the kipper what do you need to do then – keep flapping or stop to watch it?*

Then play the game 'Flap the kipper' with the children. Either choose a small group of children to play or let everyone play individually, depending on how much space and how many kippers and flappers you have. Don't make the racecourse too long. Use sugar paper kippers and rolled-up newspaper as flappers to start with. Afterwards, talk about who won the game and the possible reasons for this. Write the children's suggestions on the board. Ask, *Was the sugar paper kipper easy to move? Was it easier to move if the flapper was used while the kipper was still in the air? What made the kipper move? Was it the flapper, or the air that was disturbed by the flapper?* Try to get the children to describe the movements of the kipper and what made it move.

Ask the children if they think a flapper made from a different material would work better. Look at each of the different flapper materials in turn and ask the children for their opinions on whether they would make good flappers. Invite the children to give you reasons for their thoughts, encouraging them to think scientifically by relating their reasons to the properties of the materials, such as thickness, rigidity and flexibility. List the different flappers in a table on the board, giving each one a mark out of ten for how effective the children think each one would be. Ask questions to help them, such as *Do you think this flapper will make the kipper move quite well, very*

well, just a little bit or really fast? Do you think this flapper will make the kipper move really slowly, quite slowly or not at all? What mark shall we give to this flapper? Why are you only giving this one three out of ten?

Briefly talk about how they could find out which is the best flapper. Ask the children if they could find out by using a simple stopwatch to time how long it takes each kipper to cover the course with each flapper. Allow each child to test each flapper out with the sugar paper kippers, afterwards asking them to give each one a mark out of ten, with the highest number being given to the one that moves the kipper the easiest and fastest. This will require the children to make comparisons through noting which kipper moves through the course fastest and thus which flapper was the most effective. With the higher attainers, talk about whether the test was fair and if not how to make it fair.

Record the results on the board. Ask the children whether what happened was what they had expected. Give each flapper a rank order and ask the children to use the results to write a brief conclusion.

Now tell the children that you want them to be champion kipper flappers. Explain that you have found out which is the best flapper (which one will depend on your results), but will the flapper move a tissue paper kipper better than a sugar paper kipper, for example?

Organise the children into groups, giving each group a different kind of flapper. Ask each group to use their flapper to test the materials from which the kippers are made to find out which is the best combination of kipper with their flapper. Ask each group to predict which material they think will make the best kipper. After testing, ask them which material made the best kipper to use with their flapper. Ask a spokesperson to say how they decided this. When each group have given their answers ask the children which is the best combination of kipper and flapper.

Ask the children if they have enough information to say which are the best kippers and flappers. If you have timed how long each kipper took to cover the course you may have already, but otherwise finish the lesson by holding a race of the best flappers and kippers from each group to find the supreme champion. Point out that the winner may be because of the way the kipper was flapped rather than because of the materials from which the kipper and flapper were made.

Later, or straight away, depending on the children's mood, talk about how to improve the investigation or identify what else you can do to find out if there is an even better combination of kipper and flapper.

DIFFERENTIATION

Lower attaining children will need to work in a group with average attainers so that they can finish their investigations. Afterwards talk to these children in a smaller group to find out whether they can say individually what they did and what they found out. Remember they may all have found out something different.

The higher attainers should be able to measure the length of time taken to complete the course to have a more accurate measure of which materials make the best flapper and kipper. Talk about how this makes the test fair. This group may also wish to consider why scientists usually repeat their investigations and how many times they think they ought to repeat theirs in order to test their predictions accurately. Allow them to do this if possible.

WHERE NEXT

Get the children to test out flappers and kippers made from other materials. They can measure the times taken to cover the course and write down all the variables which have made each one flapper or kipper better or worse than the one before. Look at the list of variables so that the children can see the importance of making everything the same or as near the same as they can. This will help them to understand the notion of fair testing.

Make a display with a table of results for all the groups. Use this to ask and answer questions about the investigation.

ASSESSMENT

Note the children who test out their ideas, make improvements in response to what they have found out and form conclusions about what makes the best flapper and kipper.

LEARNING OUTCOMES

Most children will learn how to make their predictions more precise and explain why. They will learn to draw conclusions based on testing out their ideas and will learn to use this knowledge to make improvements to their kippers and/or flappers.

FURTHER SCIENCE CHALLENGES

Balloon kippers

Replace the kippers with balloons and challenge the children to find a way of moving them from one end of the racecourse to the other without touching them. Can the children predict whether they will be more or less difficult to control than the paper kippers? Can they say why? Do they test out their ideas and make improvements during the game in response to what is happening?

Flying kippers

Challenge the children to make a kipper and flapper which will keep the kipper in the air for as long as possible. The children should use their prediction skills by choosing the materials which they think will be best before trying these out practically. As they test out their ideas, get them to make improvements to their chosen kipper and/or flapper before checking out their conclusions in a practical game. Decide whether the winner won because of the kipper, the flapper or the flapping technique.

FLORENCE NIGHTINGALE IN THE HOT-SEAT

SUBJECT: HISTORY. QCA UNIT: 4 WHY DO WE REMEMBER FLORENCE NIGHTINGALE?

LEARNING OBJECTIVE

To recognise why people did things, why events happened and what happened as a result.

THINKING OBJECTIVE

To ask and answer historical questions.

THINKING SKILLS

Asking historical questions is something the children must learn before they can carry out research and enquiry into various themes. The research will be more purposeful if the children are very clear about what they are trying to find out and why.

WHAT YOU NEED

Clothes of the Victorian period to dress up in; pictures or artefacts of the time; board or flip chart; question cards.

WHAT TO DO

The children should know some of the facts about Florence Nightingale before attempting this lesson. Before play or lunchtime briefly remind the children about her story. Talk about why she wanted to become a nurse and go to the Crimea. Show the children the pictures and artefacts and talk about what they were used for. Ask the children what they would ask Florence if they were able to talk to her. Questions could include:
⊙ What conditions did you work in?
⊙ What did you enjoy about the work that you did?

- What sort of things did you use?
- How long was your day?
- Where did you sleep?

Record their questions on the board. Afterwards, write down the children's questions on individual cards and leave these in the children's places so that they can find them quickly after lunch or play.

After lunch or play return to the classroom dressed as Florence Nightingale, with the pictures and the artefacts she would have used as part of her job. Tell the children that you are going to pretend to be Florence Nightingale and to answer their questions. Invite the first question and answer it as fully as you can, using the pictures and artefacts if relevant. Answer as many questions as you want to, remembering not to keep the children for too long.

The activity can be repeated as often as you like, until you have answered as many of the children's questions as you and they are happy with.

Afterwards, review the session and identify which questions told the children something useful about the period and which were less useful.

DIFFERENTIATION

Use an additional adult to help those children who have particular language difficulties. He or she can work with these children for five minutes to rehearse their particular question before the interview activity starts. Allow these children to speak near the beginning of the activity so that their questions are fresh in their minds. You may wish to work with groups of children while the other children record the artefacts that Florence Nightingale used during her work. This will allow you to work with different ability groups at their level.

Higher attaining children will be able to deal with technical language, and working with them as a group will allow you to develop their knowledge of new vocabulary.

WHERE NEXT

Repeat the activity for other famous people and events in history, for example Guy Fawkes, Bobby Moore and William Shakespeare.

Develop the idea and ask the children to interview older people they know and people who have experienced certain historical events in the recent past, such as the 60s to 90s.

ASSESSMENT

Note the children who work independently to identify suitable questions to ask, and those who needed support. Organise another similar activity so the children can practise the skills further if required, perhaps working in groups next time so that the lower attaining children have a greater opportunity to identify and ask questions.

LEARNING OUTCOMES

Most children will identify a range of questions to ask about a famous historical person. The usefulness of these will depend upon the children's general maturity and experience. Some questions will identify some reasons for her actions.

FURTHER HISTORY CHALLENGES

Who's who?
Give the children a sheet with information about five different famous people they have studied. Give them another sheet with the names of the famous people. Ask the children to identify questions which will enable them to match the correct set of information to the correct person.

The life and times of Person X
Ask the children to write questions they would ask other famous people. This requires them to find out some facts about the person before they can think of the questions. Give prompt sheets to lower attaining children to give them a start.

MEXICAN HEATWAVE

SUBJECT: GEOGRAPHY. QCA UNIT: 22 A CONTRASTING LOCALITY OVERSEAS – TOCUARO.

LEARNING OBJECTIVE

To make observations about where things are located and recognise changes in physical and human features.

THINKING OBJECTIVE

To ask geographical questions.

THINKING SKILLS

The children will look at maps and photographs of Mexico and compare two localities. They will build on their questioning skills by asking questions to find out how localities can change through human influences.

WHAT YOU NEED

A map of Mexico; photographs/postcards of popular tourist resorts on the Mexican Caribbean coast; board or flip chart.

WHAT TO DO
Introduce this lesson at the end of your unit of work on Tocuaro. This will allow the children to make comparisons between it and a Caribbean area and be informed enough to be able to ask questions.

Look at the map of Mexico with the children and locate the Caribbean coast. Move on to look at the photographs of tourist spots, for example Cozumel and Playa del Carmen, and find these on the map. Talk briefly about the physical features in these areas and compare these to the physical features in Tocuaro.

Reflect on the human features and way of life in Tocuaro before inviting the children to ask questions about what human features there might be in the tourist resorts. For example, *How many hotels are there? How many shops are there? What sort of jobs do people do here? Where do they live? How do they travel to work?* List the children's questions on the left-hand side of the board and reinforce understanding that all these questions relate to human features, things that have been built or made by people. Then, in groups, give the children two questions from the list to find answers to.

After about ten minutes gather the children back together and list the answers to their questions in a middle column on the board. Finally, add the answers to the same questions for Tocuaro on the right-hand side of the board.

Ask the children to compare the answers to their questions for the Caribbean coast and Tocuaro. What do the children notice? Are the answers the same or different? Are some the same, for example, that people walk to work in both locations?

DIFFERENTIATION
With lower attaining or younger children recall one particular aspect of life in Tocuaro and get them to ask questions to inform their research on how this compares in the tourist resorts. This should be an ordinary task, such as cooking or washing clothes.

Encourage middle and higher attaining children to use geographical language in their questions. They could think of a set of questions to find out about the weather in both Tocuaro and the coastal resorts, and carry out research in order to find the answers to these, noting any similarities and differences between the two.

WHERE NEXT
Ask the children to compare both localities with their own and with that of Katie Morag. They can raise questions to identify the similarities and differences. Use the answers to the questions to get the children to think about whether they would like to visit these places. Why?

ASSESSMENT
Use the children's questions to note whether they identify physical and human features. Organise further opportunities for them to ask questions about contrasting localities, guiding them towards noting the differences in the physical and human features.

LEARNING OUTCOMES
The children will learn to ask geographical questions about localities with which they are not familiar. They will use secondary sources to inform these questions and to identify how humans have brought about changes to the physical environment.

FURTHER GEOGRAPHY CHALLENGES
Where am I?
Ask the children to think of a list of questions about a favourite destination, which will lead the rest of the class to guess where it is. The questions should contain some information related to both physical and human features, such as the weather, places, work and shopping.
Can I do this?
Make a list of questions together to inform research about what people need to wear and what they can do in places around the world. For example, *Can I buy a loaf of bread locally or do I need to catch a bus? Do I need a hat to protect me from the sun? Do I need a scarf to keep me warm?*

VEGETABLE VARIETY

SUBJECT: DESIGN AND TECHNOLOGY. QCA UNIT: 1C EAT MORE FRUIT AND VEGETABLES.

LEARNING OBJECTIVE
To know that fruit and vegetables can be classified according to their sensory and other properties.

THINKING OBJECTIVE
To research and improve ideas.

THINKING SKILLS
The children will begin the activity by finding out the variety of vegetables found in stir-fries. They will then evaluate those they want to include in their own, giving reasons for their inclusions or

exceptions, before evaluating their choices and suggesting ideas for improvements.

WHAT YOU NEED
Empty packets of commercially made vegetable stir-fries; a variety of matching vegetables and some favourites of the children; a wok, vegetable knives, grater, chopping board, tablecloths, aprons; access to hand washing facilities; board or flip chart.

WHAT TO DO
A few days before you intend to do this activity, carry out a survey with the whole class to find out what the children's favourite vegetables are. Undertake a risk assessment and if you intend to eat the stir-fry at the end find out whether any children have food allergies.

Look at the commercial stir-fry packaging together and identify the vegetables on the pictures. Read the ingredients blurb and make a list of the vegetables on the board. Then show the children your selection of vegetables and find these in the list of ingredients. Ask the children why they think these vegetables were chosen. Ask, *Is it because of the taste? The colour? The texture? The way the vegetable has been cut?*

Ask the children if they want to include each vegetable in their own stir-fry. For all the vegetables chosen, ask the children, *Do we need to remove the skin or peel? How can we cut the vegetable? Shall we dice, slice or grate it? Why do you want to cut it that way? Will it make it easier to cook, eat or make the stir-fry look more interesting?*

In groups of six at a time, make a stir-fry together. Look at the pictures on the packaging again and together decide whether to cut and chop the vegetables in the same or in a different way. Choose those vegetables that the children want to include, chopping them as directed by the children. Mix the vegetables together in the wok and evaluate the texture and colour of the stir-fry. Ask, *Do you think other children will want to eat this? Does it look nice to eat? Are there any pieces that are difficult to pick up or are too big to eat? How can we improve the way our stir-fry looks or make it easier to eat?*

Compare the stir-fries with the pictures on the packaging. Have the children used their research when making their own stir-fry? What would they improve?

DIFFERENTIATION
This is a group activity so you can organise the children and target your questions accordingly. It will also give you good opportunity to supervise

and assess the level of the children's research skills as they decide whether and how to peel and cut the vegetables.

ASSESSMENT
After each group has finished, jot down the way they approached the task, any questions they raised and the contributions they made to discussions. Evaluate their comments to assess whether they have a clear understanding of how they used enquiry to inform their planning, design and evaluation of the stir-fries.

LEARNING OUTCOMES
The children will give reasons for vegetables suitable to include in a stir-fry based on the information they collected in an enquiry activity. They will express preferences, suggesting how improvements can be made.

WHERE NEXT
Ask the children to draw pictures of the stir-fries and say how each vegetable was cut by labelling each one.

Carry out a tasting activity and evaluate which is the class's favourite stir-fry. Why did the children like the one they chose the best?

Get the children to research the vegetables and fruits used in commercial salads and to use the information to create and improve their own salad variety.

FURTHER DESIGN AND TECHNOLOGY CHALLENGES
Chinese takeaway
Show the children a selection of Chinese vegetables and design a stir-fry together in the style of a dish from a Chinese takeaway. Bring in some Chinese takeaway menus for the children to identify the range of stir-fries available.

Anything you can do...
Set up an activity for the children to compare their stir-fry with a commercially produced one. Ask them to say which one looks the best, tastes the best and is the easiest to pick up with a fork or chopsticks. Ask them to write an evaluation, which requires them to say not only what could be improved, but also how they would make the improvements.

GOING ON HOLIDAY

SUBJECT: ICT. QCA UNIT: 1E QUESTIONS AND ANSWERS.

LEARNING OBJECTIVE
To learn how to plan a research base.

THINKING OBJECTIVE
To plan research.

THINKING SKILLS
The children will learn about the range of different types of questions and answers that can be asked and elicited. This activity allows them to put these together into a project so that they are using the range of questions and answers to feed into a computer.

WHAT YOU NEED
A computer and suitable database software; board or flip chart.

WHAT TO DO
Ask a volunteer to talk to the class about a recent holiday they enjoyed. Review why the child went there, what they did and whether they would recommend the destination to others.

Then make a list on the board of the children's favourite pastimes when they go on holiday. Ask, *What sort of accommodation do you like? What activities do you do? What would you want the weather to be like?* Together, transform these into questions together that they would ask a travel agent so that they could find a suitable holiday destination. Record these questions on the board.

Look together at the questions and note the different ways in which they can be answered. Point out that some have simple *Yes* or *No* answers, others have a specific factual answer. Ask, *Are there any questions that have more than one answer?* If there are, work with the children to make the question more specific, or turn it into a multiple-choice question. For example, the question *What activities does this destination offer?* might elicit several answers, so list a few choices that the children think of for an answer to be chosen from. Explain that if there are too many choices, the computer will have difficulty sorting the information to find the answer to the question.

Make a simple questionnaire form using the children's questions. Give a copy to each group of four children, and ask them to act out a question-and-answer session, with one child acting as the travel agent filling in the questionnaire.

Help the children enter the data into a simple database one group at a time. This could be organised as a numeracy group activity so that an adult can supervise while the other children are involved in independent numeracy work.

During a plenary session look at the database and show the children how to ask the computer a question. Put a question in and wait for the computer to find the answer. Then encourage the children to ask the computer their own questions. List these questions and write alongside whether or not the computer was able to answer the question. Ask the children why the computer did not certain questions. What have they forgotten to do? Were the questions precise enough?

DIFFERENTIATION
Use a prepared set of questions with lower attaining children. Ask them to use these questions as models for their own set of questions. This will allow them to follow their own interests and motivate their thinking. Higher attaining children could be asked to predict which questions from a list could be answered or not from the information that has been entered into a database. Make some of these very obvious.

WHERE NEXT
Repeat the activity, letting the children use other topics that have factual information. These topics could include homes, books and television programmes.

ASSESSMENT
Note the children who can ask a range of questions in different ways. Note the higher attaining children who can begin to predict whether or not a question can be answered and who refine their questions accordingly.

LEARNING OUTCOMES
Most children will become familiar with using a computer database and will be able to ask simple questions. Some will begin to realise that if the questions are not formed precisely and simply, or if information has not been entered, the computer will not answer the question.

FURTHER ICT CHALLENGES
Questionnaires
Look at different questionnaires and ask the children to highlight in different colours the different types of questions that they ask. How many different types can they find? What general information do the children think the questionnaire can be used to find out?

What will we find out?
Look at a database with the children and talk about the sort of information it contains. Give the children a list of questions and ask them to say whether or not they think they will be able to find the answers in the database.

Natural art

SUBJECT: ART AND DESIGN. QCA UNIT: 2B MOTHER NATURE, DESIGNER.

Learning objective
To learn that patterns in design can come from nature.

Thinking objective
To plan research and improve ideas.

Thinking skills
The children will conduct research on a range of crockery designs inspired by nature, using the Internet, pictures, paintings and actual crockery. They will find out about the different places where ideas can be found to help them with their decoration, and will continue to research ideas to improve their designs.

What you need
Plastic dishes (one for each child); cling film; PVA glue; newspaper and kitchen paper; collections of crockery, pictures and paintings with designs from nature on; painting materials; scissors; sketchbooks or computer; board or flip chart.

What to do
Show the class a range of crockery that has used designs inspired by nature for decoration. Talk about some of the ideas used by the designers and list these on the board for reference.

Tell the children you want them to make a papier mâché dish. Show them what to do, covering a small dish with cling film and using PVA glue mixed with water to add alternate layers of newspaper and kitchen paper. Over the days it takes for the dishes to dry, ask the children to start researching the pattern they will use to decorate their dish. Get them thinking first by asking questions, such as *What do you want your dish to look like when it is finished? What colour? With what are you going to decorate your dish? On what kinds of things can you base your designs? Where can you get some inspiration and ideas?*

They need to try out the colours they want to use against different backgrounds. They could use the computer for this if you wish, or could record their ideas in sketchbooks. Then, surround the children with designs that other potters have used and let the children research images for their own designs by looking through catalogues and magazines or perhaps using photographs from the Internet to spark their ideas. They could use Dazzle, or a similar computer program, to create stamps of their chosen designs and cut these out to use. The children could try out their ideas on a disposable dish to see whether they like their planned design before painting it onto their own dish. Encourage them to make improvements on their designs through further research.

When the dishes are dry, help the children to remove the papier mâché dish, remove the cling film, and paint both sides of their dish in their chosen colour. They can then paint, or glue cut-out paper designs, of their pattern from nature on their dish. Finally, show the children how to glaze their dish with a coating of PVA glue.

Differentiation
Stickers are useful decoration ideas for those children who have difficulty painting and/or cutting out their designs. This will allow a quality finish to the dishes. Remind them of their research and encourage them to decorate the dishes with a theme or things that have something in common.

Discuss with higher attainers how designers make sure that the pattern and designs are positioned precisely around the plates and dishes, and ask them to research some specific examples of this. They should then be encouraged to make their own designs precisely around the dish so that they are of equal distance apart and on the same level.

Where next
Research with the class different fabrics and wallpaper that have 'borrowed' designs from nature. Talk about the range of ideas developed. Work together to make a class fabric design to use as a tabletop cover to display the dishes on.

Ask the children to decorate flowerpots and ceramic tiles with designs from nature, such as flowers, leaves, trees, sun and stars. Remind them to base their designs on the things they found out when looking at a range of crockery.

Ask the children to research some pictures of artwork on canal boats and talk about the way that the artists have used flowers to brighten up everyday objects. Why did they do this?

Assessment
Watch the children as they research the designs used by different artists and note the range of places they look for their ideas. Look at the children's finished designs and talk about whether they have followed any of the ideas they collected, such as evenly spacing the designs around the dish, keeping things simple or combining two ideas to make one larger design. Note those children who can talk about the

visual qualities of their work once they have finished and say why they like what they have done, or those who can talk about the way they transferred details from their research into their own design.

LEARNING OUTCOMES

Most children will learn that a number of artists get ideas from nature for their designs and paintings. They will learn to research these through a range of different sources. Some will use natural objects for their own creative design ideas and use them successfully in their work. Most should be able to talk about what they like about their finished dishes and why.

FURTHER ART AND DESIGN CHALLENGES

Flowery things

Make a display that contains items with designs of flowers. Organise the display into colours and types of flowers. Then make a graph with the class to show how often the same flower and colour is used, to find out which is the most popular design and colour with designers.

Artistic nature

Get the children to research the work of famous artists and designers who use natural patterns and themes in their work, such as William Morris, Laura Ashley and Van Gogh. Give the children a range of art books and ask them to find all the pictures and sculptures that contain flowers, trees and other items from nature.

SWINGS AND ROUNDABOUTS

SUBJECT: MUSIC. QCA UNIT: 5 TAKING OFF.

LEARNING OBJECTIVE

To understand what is meant by pitch, and that changes in pitch can be used to describe action.

THINKING OBJECTIVE

To test out and improve ideas.

THINKING SKILLS

The children will use the different movements of playground equipment as a context to explore ideas and test out conclusions about the way tunes can move up and down. They will make improvements to their ideas by changing the direction and tempo of the pitch.

WHAT YOU NEED

Several identical sets of musical instruments, including xylophones, chime bars and glockenspiels, some with only the notes of the pentatonic scale and

which allow the children to explore pitch; pictures of different playground toys and equipment, including swings, slide, see-saw and climbing frame; board or flip chart.

WHAT TO DO

Talk to the children about a recent visit to the local park. What playground equipment do the children like to play on? Make a list of these or display the pictures you have of each one. Talk about how the children play on the equipment. Do they climb up and down, spin round and round, spring up and down and slide to the ground?

Play the first line of 'See Saw Marjory Daw' to the class. Talk about how the tune goes up and down. Which piece of playground equipment do the children think it best depicts? Does it sound like the see-saw? Does the tune go up in steps or jumps? Explain that it goes up in jumps, just like a see-saw goes up and down in jumps. If you are able, play the beginning of the tune on a xylophone so that the children can see the jumps between the notes as you play them. Ask the children to sing the tune using the new words *See-saw, up and down* and to use hand signals to show you how the tune moves.

Show the children the picture of the slide. Talk about how you climb up the steps before sliding down the slope. Ask, *What kind of sounds would you like to make to paint a picture of someone playing on the slide? Should the tune go up one step at a time or in jumps, or should the sound slide up? What sort of tune would paint a picture of someone sliding down?*

Choose an instrument and invite a child to create a sequence of notes to depict the movement of someone climbing up the steps of a slide. Once created, ask the child to repeat the sequence over and over again. Ask the class, *Does the sequence fit?* Explain that the child is repeating the same rhythmic pattern as an ostinato.

Next, invite someone to create a sound to depict the slide down the slide. Should this move a step at a time or should it slide? Invite the children to use a xylophone with a complete scale and a soft beater, and to make a sequence of rising sounds a step at a time and then a sliding sound afterwards to depict the movement of climbing up and sliding down. Talk with the class about the difference in the two parts. Tell the children that they are going to work in groups to make sounds for other pieces of playground equipment. Explain that they will need to use sounds to show the movement up and down, or round and round, depending on the equipment. Divide the children into four groups and give them the name of a piece of playground apparatus – see-saw, slide, climbing frame and swing. Give each group a set of instruments and a picture of the piece of equipment they will depict.

Let the children explore the sounds of their instruments first of all, before they begin to create their sound sequence. Move around the groups, reminding the children that once they have found a phrase they should repeat the pattern over and over. Prompt their working with questions, such as *Do you all need to play together, or can you take it in turns? Can three children play the up notes and three the down notes? Do the swing sounds move up and down smoothly? Do the see-saw sounds move up and down?* Suggest the climbing frame sounds are created so that they depict children climbing up and down at different times.

Bring the groups back together for a performance of their sequences. Invite the other groups to say what is good about the performances and whether the compositions sound like the playground equipment being represented.

DIFFERENTIATION

Write the sequences down using tonic solfa or names of the notes for the higher attaining children to follow. Some very able musicians will be able to test out their sequences on a tuned instrument to keep the groups going. The lower attaining group should either be mixed with other children or create an accompaniment for the slide.

WHERE NEXT

Use poems about a playground for the children to add their accompaniments to during choral speaking in literacy.

Let the children test out their ideas by asking classmates to say which piece of equipment they think the sequence depicts. Ask these children for their opinions, before the groups make adjustments and improvements to their compositions.

ASSESSMENT

Make a note of the children who are able to test out their ideas and make improvements in terms of the speed and direction of their sequences.

LEARNING OUTCOMES

Most children will be able to work together to try out ideas about how tunes move up and down in

order to paint a picture with pitch. They will make improvements to their ideas following discussion on how well they depict a particular piece of playground equipment.

FURTHER MUSIC CHALLENGES
Playing together

Organise the children into groups. Invite each group to choose one of the playground pictures, without telling the rest of the class which, and to create and perform a tune designed to help their classmates guess which piece of playground equipment has been chosen. Encourage the guessers with questions such as *Does it move up and down like a swing? Or does it move up in steps and then down like a slide?*

What does it sound like?

Play the tune 'Twinkle Twinkle Little Star' to the children and talk about how this tune moves up and down. Ask them, *Does the tune sound like stars twinkling?* Talk to the children about how they might add an accompaniment to make the tune sound more like stars twinkling. Let them explore, test and improve their ideas on the instruments they choose before performing the new version of the piece to the rest of the class.

TELLING STORIES

SUBJECT: RE. QCA UNIT: 2B WHY DID JESUS TELL STORIES?

LEARNING OBJECTIVE

To understand the content and meaning of the stories that Jesus told.

THINKING OBJECTIVE

To ask questions for given answers.

THINKING SKILLS

The children will be better able to recall and appreciate the meaning and content of parables they have learned through thinking about questions for an answer that they have already been given. They will work together in teams to identify possible stories and meanings before they ask a relevant question for the given answer. This will focus their minds on possible areas that the answers may refer to, drawing upon their knowledge and understanding of different parables and learning.

This activity can easily be adapted to assess any skill, knowledge and understanding and related to different religions and contexts. Similarly, it is a format through which the children's knowledge and understanding of a range of subjects can be assessed.

WHAT YOU NEED

A list of answers based on questions you want the children to ask about religious stories, parables and assessment content you want to cover; board or flip chart; different equipment for making sounds that the teams can use as buzzers, such as musical instruments or party blowers.

WHAT TO DO

Tell the children that they are going to play a game called 'This is the answer, what is the question?'. Explain that this game involves you giving them answers for which there could be a range of questions, and they have to work out which is the correct question. Choose answers about stories that Jesus told with which the children are familiar, which may include the Prodigal Son or the Feeding of the Five Thousand.

Start by giving the children an example. Write on the board the answer, *In a stable in Bethlehem*. Ask the children to suggest possible questions which might give them this answer. They may need to think of possible contexts where the answer may be found before suggesting questions. Record their suggestions and discuss each one. When you have collected a number of questions, ask the children, *Which question would best give the answer? (Where was Jesus born?* or a similar question would be relevant.) Accept all questions that are relevant, explaining why.

Then start the game. The children could play the game in teams so that they have the opportunity to confer. Divide the game into two different rounds, the first of which will require the children to think about the content of parables and their meaning, and the second for them to identify parables. Start the first round and give the children, for example, the answer *Because Jesus wanted the people to think about forgiveness*, to which the children could suggest the question, *Why did Jesus tell the story of the Prodigal Son?* Let the teams ask a question each before moving on to the next answer. Move on to giving answers based on parables the children have heard in the past that you want them to recall.

Move on to the second round, focusing on giving answers that require the children to name the parable to which they refer. For example, *Some seeds fell upon stony ground*. As you give each answer, encourage them to confer in their teams. When a team thinks they have a question, ask them to buzz in. Explain that only when a team is asked can they give their question and name the parable. Do not move on to the next answer until you are sure that all the teams have asked questions. There may be more than one relevant question for the same answer.

DIFFERENTIATION

Group the children in mixed ability teams to begin with. This will provide higher attaining children with competition from others of the same ability in different teams. It will give lower attaining children the opportunity to learn the rules of the game.

Repeat the activity, but this time put the higher attaining children together in one team and tell them you will only accept a multiple choice question from them each time.

You could make the game easier by telling the children the name of the parable at the beginning of each round or 'answer'. This will give them a context for their questions.

WHERE NEXT

Use the structure of the activity to guide the children in identifying questions about different religions and celebrations. Identify questions which when asked will identify the range of artefacts and/or places of worship used by different religions in their worship and ceremonies.

ASSESSMENT

This activity allows you to assess your class's overall knowledge and understanding of the parables they have studied. You may wish to play the game in ability groups to assess the knowledge and understanding of individuals through their suggestions of questions, and plan any additional follow up activities.

LEARNING OUTCOMES

The children will learn to ask questions to identify the content of the stories that Jesus told. The children will show that they understand that Jesus told stories with hidden meanings and messages to teach us about feelings.

FURTHER RE CHALLENGES

Answers and questions

Give the children another story from the Bible or a story from another religion studied recently. Ask them to make a list of answers to include in their own game of 'This is the answer, what is the question?'. Try out the game with their answers in another lesson.

Find the story

Give the children copies of different lists of answers, where each list refers to only one possible parable or story. Include the Bible reference at the bottom of each list. Invite the children to find the story to which the answers refer to and to write one relevant question which would guide the reader towards the right story.

Ball fun

Subject: PE. QCA unit: Games activities unit 1.

Learning objective
To throw a ball accurately in different ways.

Thinking objective
To plan research, predict outcomes and test conclusions.

Thinking skills
The children will think of a way to find out how far balls will travel when thrown in different ways. They will try out their ideas to find the answer to the query.

What you need
A large space for the children to work in, either the playground or the hall; enough balls of different sizes for the children to work with in groups of four; a way to measure or mark the distances balls will travel, such as skipping ropes if comparing the difference between distances, or trundle wheels and tape measures if measuring in metres; paper and writing materials.

What to do
Before the lesson talk to the children about the different ways to send a ball. Listen to their ideas before asking them to predict which way will send a ball the furthest distance. Why do they think this?

Explain that you want them to plan a way to find out how a ball will travel the furthest. Organise the children into groups of four, and give them time to talk and plan how they will go about this. They should consider what sort of throws they could use, how they will measure the distance, and so on. Ask each group to share their ideas with the rest of the class.

Take the children outside or to the hall. Let them warm up in pairs by asking them to throw the

different types of balls in your collection to each other. Explain that you want them to try to throw accurately too. After a few minutes gather the children together and ask them who has managed to send the ball over a large distance. Ask them how they did this and to demonstrate. Let the children explore this further in pairs. Then ask the class to go into their original groups and to modify the ideas they first thought of to throw the ball the furthest distance. Watch to see how they measure the distance the ball has travelled. Do they compare the distance each time they throw, or do they measure the distance in metres?

Compare the results on return to the classroom to see if each group found the same thing in terms of which throw sent which type of ball furthest. Did their testing give the conclusions they expected?

Differentiation
Help lower attaining children organise themselves and to think about how they will know which throw sent the ball the furthest. Talk with them to make sure they are clear about what they are finding out. Expect higher attaining children to record the distances in a table and to check their results by carrying out the test more than once. Discuss with them how many times they think they should do this to test out their conclusions thoroughly.

Where next
Ask the children to repeat their tests with balls of different sizes from those they used before, planning and predicting outcomes before testing. Do each of the balls still travel as far?

Assessment
Note those children who can plan carefully how to find an answer to the query. Listen as they talk, to notice whether their ideas focus on how effective a throw will be, rather than simply how hard they can throw it.

Learning outcomes
The children will think about how to plan a test to find an answer to a query. They will work together in groups to discuss their ideas and this will involve predicting and thinking about how to measure what they find out.

Further PE challenges
Kick or throw

Ask the children to plan a research and test out their ideas as to whether a ball will travel the furthest when thrown or kicked. Give the children different sizes and types of balls to try out.

CREATIVE THINKING SKILLS

INTRODUCTION

Creative thinking is not just about creating poems, pieces of art, music, dance and gymnastic sequences, although these do provide good opportunities for children to think creatively. It is also about identifying possible solutions to problems or to get over difficulties when, for example, trying to depict a special moment in their lives. By thinking creatively children can learn to identify why an author has chosen the theme that they have or used a particular style of writing in their work. This will allow the children to consider these things when creating their own projects, thus making their learning richer and more meaningful.

Children should be given lots of opportunities to develop their own creative learning. Often we give them one strategy for solving a particular problem. The activities in Chapter 2 in this book ask the children to give reasons for their ideas and strategies. This chapter focuses on the children deciding for themselves why certain things have been organised as they have, and on finding possible alternatives to solve a problem. Questions are used in the activities to enable you to guide their thinking throughout and to get them to think imaginatively and laterally, the roots of creative thinking. A key to asking questions when trying to develop creative thinking is to give the children time to answer. For example, do not expect an answer within less than ten seconds.

The activities outlined here, while written within specific contexts, are organised so that the children can work together in groups. This allows them to collaborate and bounce ideas off each other, sparking further creativity. A key skill outlined in the National Curriculum involves the children working with others to meet a challenge. Part of the development of this key skill involves the children learning to appreciate the experience of others, considering different perspectives and benefitting from what others think. The topic contexts of the activities in this chapter can be adapted for all subjects.

The way you organise children's learning is crucial to give the children the opportunity to think about how they will organise their own learning. Group work gives them suitable opportunities to consider and negotiate which ideas will be accepted and developed. Thought sharing is one way to get the children to volunteer ideas in an uninhibited way. If all ideas are accepted, everyone is encouraged to contribute. The ideas may be discarded at a later stage but the process means that good reasons have to be given for this. The creative thinking skills are:

◎ creating ideas
◎ imaginative thinking
◎ finding alternative innovative outcomes/lateral thinking
◎ hypothesising
◎ extending ideas.

INTRODUCING CREATIVE THINKING SKILLS

Subject and QCA unit, NLS or NNS objective	Activity title	Thinking objective	Activity	Page
English NLS objective: To use graphic knowledge to make sense of what they read	Thinking	To extend ideas	Adding thought bubbles for the characters in each of the pictures in *Kipper* to convey what characters may be like	80
Maths NNS objective: To describe features of familiar shapes	Floor tiles	To extend ideas and think laterally	Making different tessellation patterns using squares in different positions and rotations	80
Science QCA unit: 1D Light and dark	See through	To hypothesise	Investigating which materials are transparent	81
History QCA unit: 2 What were homes like a long time ago?	Household objects	To think laterally	Looking at household objects from the past and deciding how they were used compared with modern versions	81
Geography QCA unit: 1 Around our school – the local area	How do I get there?	To hypothesise	Looking at a map of the local area and deciding how to get to different places of interest	82
Design and technology QCA unit: 2D Joseph's coat	Mexican magic	To generate ideas	Designing and sewing a rug with Mexican designs	83
ICT QCA unit: 2A Writing stories: communicating information using text	Attractive words	To extend ideas	Using a thesaurus to replace adjectives with more interesting adjectives on screen	83
Art and design QCA unit: 1B Investigating materials	Garden weaving	To think creatively	Designing a decorative trellis frame for a garden	84
Music QCA unit: 2 Sounds interesting	Crawling and flying around	To think imaginatively	Composing a piece of music to depict the movements of minibeasts	85
RE QCA unit: 1F What can we learn from visiting a church?	All things bright and beautiful	To extend ideas	Designing a flower arrangement for a church	85
PE QCA unit: Dance activities unit 1	Minibeast ball	To think imaginatively	Making up dances to depict the movements of different minibeasts	86

THINKING

SUBJECT: ENGLISH. NLS OBJECTIVE: TO USE GRAPHIC KNOWLEDGE TO WORK OUT, PREDICT AND CHECK MEANING TO MAKE SENSE OF WHAT THEY READ.

LEARNING OBJECTIVE

To use graphic knowledge to make sense of what they read and to describe what a story character may be like.

THINKING OBJECTIVE

To extend ideas.

THINKING SKILLS

The children will extend their ideas about how they can use pictures to help them understand what is happening in a story. They will consider what certain characters may be thinking by their body positions and facial expressions. This will help the children to learn to search for meaning beyond the literal and to appreciate the subtle humour that is produced in some texts.

WHAT YOU NEED

Kipper by Mick Inkpen (Hodder Children's Books); large paper thought bubbles (one for each group of children); felt-tipped pens; Blu-Tack; enlarged copies of the illustrations on the last page and pages 5 and 6, and copies of each subsequent illustration.

WHAT TO DO

Read *Kipper* to the children. Revisit the illustration in which the ducks watch as Kipper tries to stand on one leg. Ask the children to look carefully at the ducks' expressions and wonder what they may be thinking. Ask, *What sort of expressions are the ducks wearing? How are they looking at Kipper? Does this give us a clue to what they may be thinking?*

Organise the children into groups and give each group an illustration from the book. Have enough groups to cover all the illustrations in the book, except the final one, allocating each group one character in their illustration to write a thought bubble for. Prompt the children to look carefully at their character's expression. Explain that they should consider in their groups lots of things that the character may be saying before deciding together on the one they like best. Tell them they should then write this in a thought bubble and Blu-Tack it to the picture.

Display the pictures as a storyboard and ask the groups to share their ideas. Then attach the final illustration and finish by creating a class thought bubble for each of the characters in it.

FLOOR TILES

SUBJECT: MATHS. NNS OBJECTIVE: TO USE MATHEMATICAL LANGUAGE TO DESCRIBE FEATURES OF FAMILIAR SHAPES.

LEARNING OBJECTIVES

To identify a square when in various positions and rotations; to understand that squares will fit together without leaving any spaces.

THINKING OBJECTIVE

To extend ideas and think laterally.

THINKING SKILLS

The children will extend their ideas by thinking about a square in different positions or rotations. They usually make patterns with the square standing on its edge, and this activity will help them to recognise squares when standing on their points or corners. By thinking laterally, the children will explore the range of patterns that can be produced if the square is turned on its point, or if squares do not meet at the corners every time. They will also use mathematical language when describing the squares. This activity works equally well with other shapes you may wish the children to learn about, depending on their age and ability.

WHAT YOU NEED

Squares all the same size, some plastic ones for the main teaching activity and some cut from poster or tissue paper for the group activity; large sheets of paper; Blu-Tack; glue; whiteboard.

WHAT TO DO

Stick one of the plastic squares to the whiteboard in its upright position and ask the children to name the shape. Talk with them about what makes a square unique. Place another square next to the first so that the edges and corners meet. Talk about how the two squares fit together. Continue until you have covered a good piece of the board with squares. You could get two children to do this if you wish. Ask the children whether they think that if you carry on fitting the squares together in this way they will cover the whiteboard without leaving any spaces.

Remove all the squares from the board and repeat the tessellation activity, but this time rotate the first square and place it at an angle. Do the children think that the squares will still be able to fit together? Invite someone to add another square so that the edges fit together. Do the squares still fit together even though they are rotated? Do the children think that you can cover the board so that there are no spaces left between the squares? Continue until a good piece of the board is covered. Do they think they can cover it all now?

Make one last pattern together, but this time, place the second square so that the edges of the squares meet but the corners do not. Ask the children, *Do they still fit together?* Invite a volunteer to come up to the board and continue the pattern. Ask the children whether there are any spaces between. Ask, *Do the squares still fit together even though the corners do not meet?*

Give the children some poster or tissue paper squares and some glue or Blu-Tack. Working in pairs or small groups, challenge them to make different patterns by fitting the squares together in different ways without leaving any spaces. Ask them questions like, *How many ways can you turn the square? What happens if you put the squares halfway along the side of each one? Do they still fit together? Can you think of another way to put the squares together so that they still fit, but make a different pattern?* Compare the children's patterns and count how many different ones there are. Do the children think there are any more patterns that can be made?

SEE THROUGH

SUBJECT: SCIENCE. QCA UNIT: 1D
LIGHT AND DARK.

LEARNING OBJECTIVE
To consider the properties of materials using the sense of sight.

THINKING OBJECTIVE
To hypothesise.

THINKING SKILLS
The children will speculate on what will happen and why, before setting out on an investigation. They will learn that predicting is more than guess work.

WHAT YOU NEED
Several windows; sheets of tissue, crepe and cellophane paper; sheets of plastic; transparent materials, such as bubble wrap, polythene wraps, empty drinks bottles, clear nail varnish; a light sensor or similar.

WHAT TO DO
Tell the children that they are going to find out which materials will let through the most light. Show them the different papers in your collection and ask the children to predict which papers will block out or let through the most light. Ask, *Which one will let through the most light? How do you know? How will you measure this?*

Get the children to cover different windows with the different papers. Then ask them to measure which one lets through the most and the least light. Ask, *Why does the cellophane let through more light than the other papers? Why does the crepe paper let through least light?*

Look together at the collection of transparent materials and ask the children to predict which one will let through the most light. Show the children how to place the different materials over sheets of plastic, and ask them to find out which lets through the most light and which lets through the least. Were the children right? Can they say why certain transparent materials let through more light than other transparent materials?

HOUSEHOLD OBJECTS

SUBJECT: HISTORY. QCA UNIT: 2 WHAT WERE HOMES LIKE A LONG TIME AGO?

LEARNING OBJECTIVE
To understand the way people used to live through exploring a range of everyday objects from the past.

THINKING OBJECTIVE
To think laterally.

THINKING SKILLS
The children will be confronted with objects from the past which they will need to think laterally about in order to deduce what they used to be used for. They can move on to consider how inefficient everyday household objects once were and think about how inventors made them more efficient as time passed. They will consider the effects this has had on the way people live, in terms of making domestic tasks easier and less time consuming.

WHAT YOU NEED
A modern steam iron, a flat iron; an electric drill, a hand drill; a hand whisk, an electric whisk.

WHAT TO DO
Show the children the flat iron and ask them what they think it is. Ask questions, such as *What does it look like? How was it used? What could it be used for today? How did people make it hot? How long would this take? How would it stay hot?* Show the children the modern iron and ask them to compare the two,

noting the similarities and differences. Ask, *Which would be the quickest and most efficient to use? Why? How long would it take to do the ironing with the flat iron?* Can the children think about what else people would have been able to do on the days that they did the ironing.

Tell the children about the fabrics that were available at the time of the flat iron, how heavy they were and how creased they got. Ask, *Why did an inventor include steam in the electric irons?* Ask the children to think what people used instead of steam before this. Can they think of things that people did to make the clothes damp if they were dry, or do they think that people did the ironing when things were still wet?

Repeat this questioning process with the drills and whisks. Let the children try out the hand whisks to whisk cornflour and water. Time how long it takes and talk about how tired the hand becomes. Repeat the process with an electric whisk. Which of the two would the children like to have if they had lots of whisking to do? Can the children think of other things that have been invented to make things easier and quicker to do?

How do I get there?

SUBJECT: GEOGRAPHY. QCA UNIT: 1 AROUND OUR SCHOOL – THE LOCAL AREA.

Learning objective
To learn to use directional vocabulary when describing routes to different places.

Thinking objective
To hypothesise.

Thinking skills
This activity goes beyond the children describing one route, using directions and making decisions about which is the most appropriate way to travel. The children will begin to consider which way to turn when following directions and routes on a map of an area with which they are familiar. They will hypothesise whether it is quicker or shorter to travel by foot, car or bus by comparing different routes on a map. You can relate this work to the Katie Morag stories by considering the quickest and fastest route to get from and to different places on the Isle of Struay.

What you need
A large map of the local area; smaller copies of the map showing local roads and footpaths; different coloured highlighters or felt-tipped pens.

What to do
Talk about the children's routes to school. Mark on the large map in green the different walking routes, and in red the routes travelled by car. Then compare the different ways. Ask, *Are they the same? Do those who walk come a different way?*

Choose a local feature, for example a shopping centre, swimming pool, park, monument or bus stop. Together, plot the walking route from the school to that place. Then plot the route that you would take if you went by bus. Introduce directional vocabulary as you talk about the routes with the children. For example, as you reach a T-junction on the map, ask the children, *Do you turn left or right? When you get to the end of this road, which way do you turn?* Demonstrate this by following the route with your finger or a large pointer, gesturing with your other arm the direction. Ask the children if this is the quickest or most direct route. How do they know? Ask, *Would a car use the same route? Which way would it go? Would it be quicker to go by car or to walk? Why? What about the bus?*

Give each pair of children a photocopy of the large map. Challenge them to find the local feature you drew the route from the school to and to mark it with a cross. Next, ask them to find the school and mark this with a cross. Ask the children in their pairs to think about the way they would walk to a chosen place from the school. They should then compare this with the journey they would travel if they went by bus or car.

With the class, compare two different routes that pairs of children found to the same place. Draw the routes on the large map, in a different coloured pen from those used before, for the children to consider. Ask, *How are the routes different?* Encourage directional language in the children's responses. Can the children think of another way to walk to this place or has the best/quickest/safest way been found?

Mexican magic

SUBJECT: DESIGN AND TECHNOLOGY. QCA UNIT: 2D JOSEPH'S COAT.

Learning objective

To use existing fabric designs as inspiration for creating their own pattern on a Mexican rug.

Thinking objective

To generate ideas.

Thinking skills

The children will use the geometric designs and bright colours used in Mexican art as inspiration to design and make a rug in that style. They will work independently to create their own designs, then use a simple cross stitch and running stitch technique to transfer this onto a class rug.

What you need

Examples of Mexican geometric designs; squared paper and drawing materials; ribbon and braids in bright colours; embroidery silks; glue; Binca cut into a large rectangle (for the class rug) and smaller individual squares (small enough that the children can finish them quickly); scissors; needles.

What to do

Look with the children at the geometric designs and stitch work used in Mexican patterns on rugs or fabric. Ask, *What do you notice about the designs in this picture? What colours have the artists used in this design? How have they used ribbons to add decoration? How are the designs organised? Are they symmetrical?*

Explain that you are going to work together to make a small version of a Mexican rug, using cross-stitch squares and decorating it with brightly coloured ribbons and braid.

Show them the large rectangle of Binca and explain that this will form the base of the rug. Show the children the smaller squares and tell them that these will be their individual part of the rug.

Give each child a piece of squared paper so they can design their geometric cross stitch pattern in bright colours. Tell them they should base their designs on the Mexican patterns they have seen. When these are completed, ask them to transfer their patterns by sewing them on a Binca square. Then arrange each child's finished square around the edge of the rectangular Binca base and attach them with a running stitch. Ask the children to sew or glue brightly coloured braid around the outside of the rectangle and on the inside edge of the squares. Finally, get them to embroider, or make a pattern with ribbons, in the centre of the rug.

Evaluate the finished rug. Do the children like seeing their ideas on it? What do they particularly like about this? Are they pleased with the finished rug? Why?

Attractive words

SUBJECT: ICT. QCA UNIT: 2A WRITING STORIES: COMMUNICATING INFORMATION USING TEXT.

Learning objective

To know that text can be entered and corrected using a computer.

Thinking objective

To extend ideas.

Thinking skills

The children will learn to extend their ideas and not to accept the first word that they see or think of when describing a person, setting or action. They will consider carefully whether the word fits and best describes the word picture they want to create.

What you need

A copy of a short story for each pair of children, either one you have written yourself, or preferably one that has been written during a class story writing activity and which contains words such as *then*, *went* and *nice*; thesauruses, highlighter pens; computers.

What to do

Read through the story together and comment on the number of times that *then*, *went* and *nice* have been used. Organise the children into pairs and give each pair a copy of the story. Allocate them *then*, *went* or *nice* and ask them to highlight it when they see it in the story. Explain that you want them to replace the word with a more interesting one each time it appears. Tell them the new word should describe the setting, person or action better than the existing one. Show them a thesaurus and explain what this is, or ask them to think of a book that they could use to help them find more interesting words which mean a similar thing.

Ask them to choose one word they would like to use as a replacement first and ask them questions about their choice. Ask, *Do you think this is an interesting word or could you find something better to use? Does this word reflect what you want to say? Does it describe what the character is like, the setting, or the way the person moves precisely enough?* After five minutes, choose one of the highlighted words, for example *nice*, and list all the words the children have found to use instead.

Go to the computer, load the story and show the class how to highlight, delete and replace *nice* with their more interesting words from the list. The children should then work in their pairs to highlight and replace the words they have chosen, saving and printing their story after they have finished. They could use the computer thesaurus to add others if you have this facility and it is interesting enough!

Read samples of the children's stories to the class and talk about whether they have made it sound more interesting. Work together to choose ideas from different children's stories to make one class version.

GARDEN WEAVING

SUBJECT: ART AND DESIGN. QCA UNIT: 1B INVESTIGATING MATERIALS.

LEARNING OBJECTIVES
To ask and answer questions about the starting points for their work; to develop their ideas.

THINKING OBJECTIVE
To think creatively.

THINKING SKILLS
The children will think carefully about the aesthetic look of a finished frame before planting their trellis. They will need to think about the practicalities of using the right plants to create interesting effects of colour, shape, form and texture. The children will realise that people have different likes and dislikes in colour and shape and will need to consider for whom and why they are making the trellis, whether to create a particular atmosphere, a place to sit or a place to look at. The children will think about the people that will see and use the trellis, and

understand the importance of taking everyone's views and feelings into account.

WHAT YOU NEED
A collection of plant catalogues and/or climbing plants; a garden trellis or simple topiary frame; pots and planting compost; a digital camera; board or flip chart; paper and drawing materials.

WHAT TO DO
Before you start, check your LEA policy on which plants are safe to grow in school, and check for any allergies amongst the children. It will be useful for the children to have taken part in some weaving activities before embarking on this activity.

Remind the children of any materials they have used in weaving activities, if appropriate. Explain that today they are going to start to explore how to make a living weaving with plants and a trellis, explaining what the latter is if necessary. Look together at pictures in catalogues, at plants you bring into the school, or visit a local garden centre and use a digital camera to take pictures of different types of trellis and climbing plants. Make a list on the board of the different colours, shapes and sizes of plants that are available. Ask the children, *Which plants can we use to weave in and out of the garden frame? What colours will we choose? Will we plant them in the ground, in pots or in beds?*

Discuss the things that you will need to make the living weaving. Make a list of the children's suggestions on the board. Add details of colour, shape and size. Ask the children to design their own living weaving on paper. Tell them they should choose a trellis, pots and plants and show what they think their finished weaving will look like. Question them as they work to get them to think about the colour and shape of the plants, and also the scent, textures and form of the finished arrangement. This will challenge them to consider the three-dimensional feel of the frame and to think about using plants of different heights, which will give the weave depth.

When the children have finished, evaluate the designs as a class and choose the ones you like best. Negotiate with the children which one they will develop, and set this up, either outside or in the classroom. As the plants grow, let the children weave them carefully in and out of the garden trellis.

CRAWLING AND FLYING AROUND

SUBJECT: MUSIC. QCA UNIT: 2 SOUNDS INTERESTING.

LEARNING OBJECTIVE
To explore instruments and recreate the sounds of different minibeasts.

THINKING OBJECTIVE
To think imaginatively.

THINKING SKILLS
Very few minibeasts make a sound picked up by the human ear when they move, so the children will need to use their imaginations to compose sounds that represent them. They will evaluate and make improvements to their compositions, thus extending their ideas further.

WHAT YOU NEED
A range of instruments for the children to play; a tape recorderboard or flip chart; four different coloured felt-tipped pens.

WHAT TO DO
Ask the children to tell you as many different minibeasts as they can think of and record these on the board. Together, identify four that look and move very differently, for example a caterpillar, grasshopper, ladybird and spider. Focus on each one and talk about how they move, such as quickly or slowly, whether they run, fly, walk or jump. Perhaps they can do a mixture of these movements.

Then tell the children you want them to relate the movements of each minibeast to musical sounds. Split the class into four groups and allocate each group a minibeast. Explain that as minibeasts don't make sounds that we can hear, the children will need to use their imagination to compose sounds they think represent their minibeast. Tell them they should consider whether the sounds should be fast or slow, loud or quiet, long or short. Should some minibeasts

have more than one sound to increase the texture? Do any of the minibeasts make a particular shape when they move which should be reflected in the matching musical phrase? You could even challenge the children to compose a repeating rhythmical pattern for their minibeast.

Let the children explore the range of instruments and compose several short sound phrases which depict the way their minibeast moves. After two minutes, ask each group to perform their compositions to the rest of the class. Ask the class to choose a favourite phrase for each minibeast and make suggestions on how it could be developed further. Give the groups some time to do this.

When each group is ready, put the four minibeast phrases together in a class performance. Vary the performance by getting the groups to play the sounds separately, in pairs and all together. Use a different coloured felt-tipped pen to represent each minibeast and create a score, recording when each instrument plays in the piece. Also make a tape recording of performances.

ALL THINGS BRIGHT AND BEAUTIFUL

SUBJECT: RE. QCA UNIT: UNIT 1F – WHAT CAN WE LEARN FROM VISITING A CHURCH?

LEARNING OBJECTIVE
To understand why many Christians want their church to look beautiful.

THINKING OBJECTIVE
To extend ideas.

THINKING SKILLS
The idea that Christians want their churches to look beautiful is brought to life through celebrations and festivals. However, the practice of using flowers to decorate the church is often a more regular one. This activity seeks to extend this idea to everyday occasions in the Christian calendar. The activity can be extended to consider how other religions decorate their places of worship and those that do not.

WHAT YOU NEED
Enough containers, oasis flowers and greenery for children to work in groups of four to make their own flower arrangement.

WHAT TO DO
Talk to the children about the reasons why Christians decorate their churches throughout the year. Explain

that they want to create an atmosphere of welcome and respect to people who visit, to encourage them to take part in worship and treat the building with reverence. Talk about the times when flowers are particularly used to decorate a church. The children may suggest weddings, christenings, Easter and Harvest Festival times.

Talk about the feelings that churches promote, such as happiness, kindness, friendship, honesty and truth. Explain that these are all positive feelings. Choose happiness and ask the children to think about the kinds of colours and shapes that could be used when decorating the church to represent this. Ask, *Would you want big or small arrangements, or both? Would you use bright or dull colours? Would you choose lots of flowers or just a few?*

Show the children the flowers in your collection and talk about the different colours and shapes. Individually, ask the children to draw a design to incorporate some of the flowers into a flower arrangement to depict happiness in a church. After ten minutes invite the children to discuss their ideas with a partner and then in groups of four, asking them to agree on a group flower arrangement. Give out the oasis and containers to the groups, and present the flowers so that the children can choose their combinations.

Decorate the classroom with the happiness flower arrangements. Talk about the flowers the children have chosen and why they have made the shapes that they have. Agree that all the arrangements depict happiness and would welcome worshippers into a church.

MINIBEAST BALL

SUBJECT: PE. QCA UNIT: DANCE ACTIVITIES UNIT 1.

LEARNING OBJECTIVE
To put together a dance with a clear beginning, middle and end.

THINKING OBJECTIVE
To think imaginatively.

THINKING SKILLS
The children will use the information about how a real creature moves to spark their imagination to create a suitable dance sequence. They will consider the shape, direction and speed of the different minibeasts that they have chosen to depict in their own compositions. The music they composed in the lesson 'Crawling and flying around' (see page 85), will spark their imagination by giving their creatures some character.

WHAT YOU NEED
A recording of the children's composition from 'Crawling and flying around'; a tape recorder; a video which shows different minibeasts moving, preferably a spider, ladybird, caterpillar and grasshopper; a video player and television; different pieces of music for the children to move to.

WHAT TO DO
Play the children the video extract and talk about the different movements of the minibeasts. Ask the children questions, such as *How do the creatures move? Do they use legs, wings or some other part of their body?*

Remind the children of 'Crawling and flying around', where they created the sounds of minibeasts, and explain that you want them to move in the way that one of those minibeasts would move. Questions here will help the children focus on how to copy the minibeasts: *Does a caterpillar move quickly or slowly? Does it move in a straight line? Does it crawl, run, fly or move in a different way? How would you show how the caterpillar moves? Would you be high off the ground or close to the ground? What shape would you make?*

Give the children time to choose a minibeast to depict and to think about what kind of movement to perform. Let them try out ideas with a partner before deciding. Let them practise the movements to get them absolutely right. As the children work, talk about the direction, speed and shape of their movements and encourage them to build these aspects into their moves. Challenge them to give their creature a character, for example by turning the caterpillar's head to look around, by changing the speed of the spider's movements as it darts across the room, by creating patterns as the ladybird flies from one place to the next, or getting the grasshopper to jump in all directions both fast and slow.

Listen to the recording of the children's compositions and talk about when each minibeast is present. Tell the children that you want them to perform their movements in time to the music. Structure the entrances and exits of the different minibeasts and decide from where and to where the children will start and finish their movements. Play the tape, giving the children direction when to start and finish their dance until they can listen and respond independently.

Once the order and structure of the children's movements is secure, get them to perform to different kinds of music, for example a piece of modern dance music, a classical piece or traditional aborigine music.

EXTENDING CREATIVE THINKING SKILLS

Subject and QCA unit, NLS or NNS objective	Activity title	Thinking objective	Activity	Page
English NLS objective: To discuss and compare story themes	A new title	To extend creative ideas	Deciding why an author chose a book title and suggesting alternative titles that reflect the content of the story	88
Maths NNS objective: To estimate, measure and compare lengths	Wrapping boxes	To think laterally and find alternative innovative outcomes	Wrapping boxes of varying shapes using different sizes of paper	89
Science QCA unit: 2E Forces and movement	Flying saucers	To form hypotheses	Investigating which frisbee travels the furthest and learning about fair testing	90
History QCA unit: 1 How are our toys different from those in the past?	Spinning around	To think imaginatively and creatively	Playing with old toys, learning about how they were once played with and devising modern games for them	91
Geography QCA unit: 1 Around our school – the local area	A new name	To hypothesise	Looking at the local area and why buildings and features are named as they are	92
Design and technology QCA unit: 1D Homes	Flowerpot mobiles	To think laterally and creatively and find innovative outcomes	Making a mobile using different kinds of flowerpots	93
ICT QCA unit: 2B Creating pictures	Spot the difference	To think imaginatively	Making two spot-the-difference pictures, which are slightly different in several ways	95
Art QCA unit: 1A Self portrait	Comic book heroes	To extend creative ideas	Exploring and creating different features that give cartoon characters their personalities	96
Music QCA unit: 6 What's the score?	Dancing drums	To develop ideas	Composing a drum beat and rhythm to dance to	97
RE QCA unit: 2C Celebrations	Wrapping presents	To create something for someone else	Wrapping presents appropriately to portray feelings	99
PE QCA unit: Dance activities unit 2	Monster stomp	To explore and extend ideas	Composing a dance to portray the movement of imaginary monsters	100

A NEW TITLE

SUBJECT: ENGLISH. NLS OBJECTIVES: TO DISCUSS A RANGE OF STORY THEMES; TO DISCUSS AND COMPARE STORY THEMES.

LEARNING OBJECTIVE
To discuss story themes.

THINKING OBJECTIVE
To extend creative ideas.

THINKING SKILLS
The children will consider carefully why authors choose and create the titles they do for their stories. They will then use this information to develop their own ideas. The story suggested here allows the children to think beyond the literal if they are able and this will encourage them to extend their own ideas to include a title which is not literal.

WHAT YOU NEED
Alfie's Feet by Shirley Hughes (Red Fox); books which have titles that closely match the content of the story inside, such as *Mrs Wishy Washy* by Joy Cowley (Shortland) and *We're Going on a Bear Hunt* by Michael Rosen (Walker Books), some of which are familiar to the children and some which are not; board or flip chart.

WHAT TO DO
Read *Alfie's Feet* to the children, either all in one lesson, or finish it during this lesson having started to read it in earlier literacy lessons during the week. As you read the story talk about what is happening: *Why did Alfie want a pair of wellingtons? What did he like doing? How did Alfie's feet feel in the wellingtons? Why did they feel funny? Why did his mum write 'R' and 'L' on the wellingtons?*

Focus on the title of the book. Ask the children, *Why do you think Shirley Hughes called the book 'Alfie's Feet'?* Identify with the children the main idea in the story. Help them to understand that it is about Alfie learning to put his shoes on the right feet. Talk about how the children's shoes feel when they put them on the wrong feet. Discuss how the children know which foot to put which shoe on – what strategies do they use to remember? Ask, *Could the book be called something different? What can you suggest?* Give the children an idea if they cannot think of a title themselves, for example *New Shoes*, or *Alfie's Wellingtons*. Ask, *Why could the story be called this instead?* Talk about how there is a clue to the context of the story in the title. Extend the children's ideas by including ideas which are not directly linked to

the context, such as *Wrong Feet* or *Back to Front*. Talk about how these titles could be suitable as well.

Look at some other book titles and briefly discuss what the story is about. Ask, *Does the title give the reader a good idea of what the story is about?* Ask the children to suggest alternative titles again. Listen to their suggestions, record them on the board and ask the children to choose the ones they like best.

DIFFERENTIATION
Lower attaining children should work with an additional adult recalling the content of familiar stories, using the titles as prompts. Ask a group of higher attainers to record for themselves what they think an unfamiliar story is about, by reading the title. Ask them to find out whether they were correct by reading one story each.

WHERE NEXT
Get the children to look at other books by Shirley Hughes and ask them to talk about the titles. Can they find reasons why she chooses the titles she does and suggest suitable alternatives?

ASSESSMENT
Note the children who understand that the title of the book gives a clue to the story content. Some children will discuss the meaning of certain words and phrases and the intention of the author. Note the children who begin to think creatively about their own titles when they next write a story.

LEARNING OUTCOMES
The children will begin to make links between book titles and the content. They will learn to extend this skill and to think more carefully about their own story titles when writing.

FURTHER ENGLISH CHALLENGES
Search for the title
Leave a selection of books for the children to read. Challenge them to find the title in the text. From their knowledge of the story, can they think of another suitable title that is also included in the text?
Poetic licence
Give the children copies of short poems with the title taken out. Challenge the children to provide a

suitable title. Compare this with the original and talk about how and why their version is different from the poet's.

WRAPPING BOXES

SUBJECT: MATHS. NNS OBJECTIVE: TO ESTIMATE, MEASURE AND COMPARE LENGTHS.

LEARNING OBJECTIVE
To develop an awareness of measures by comparing lengths of paper against shapes.

THINKING OBJECTIVE
To think laterally and find alternative innovative outcomes.

THINKING SKILLS
The children will be presented with sets of boxes of different sizes and several pieces of paper in which to wrap them. They will need to decide which piece of paper fits which box and give reasons why. This will require them to compare the length of the paper to the length of the sides of each box. This will lead them to think about whether the paper will be large enough.

With the Further maths challenge 'Wrapping up boxes', where the paper only fits if the box is placed at an angle, this will make the activity more difficult and will challenge higher attaining and some middle attaining children (expect them to find an alternative way to solve the problem of wrapping the boxes).

WHAT YOU NEED
Collections of cube- and cuboid-shaped boxes of different sizes (one should be small, one large and enough of other sizes for each group of children to have a selection); a range of wrapping papers either in different colours or patterns which are not too fiddly for the children to handle, each one cut to fit only one box; sticky tape; scissors.

WHAT TO DO
Show the children the boxes and the different sizes of paper. Select a box and ask the children which wrapping papers are big enough to wrap the box in. Some children will try this out by placing the box on each piece of paper and seeing which will fit around it. With these children focus their thinking by asking, *What can you tell me about the length of this piece of paper? How does it compare with the length of the sides of this box?*

Select a second box which is small and ask the children to choose the best sized sheet of paper. Are they all too big? What could the children do to make the paper fit the box?

Repeat this, but this time use a box that is too big for any of the pieces of paper. What can the children suggest now?

In groups, get the children to look at the boxes in their collection and to decide which piece of paper has been cut to fit which box. Explain that you have cut the papers so that all the boxes can be wrapped. Watch to see how the children approach the task, prompting them with questions only if they get stuck. When the children have matched all the boxes to the correct piece of paper, invite some children to wrap the boxes. You may need an additional adult to help depending on the number of boxes you have.

DIFFERENTIATION
Reinforce the concept with lower attaining children by giving them boxes and paper where it is obvious which piece of paper fits each box. Move on to boxes which are much smaller than the paper and which requires them to cut it to the correct size. Children who are successful with the set of boxes in the activity should attempt the Further maths challenges straight away, which require them to turn some of the boxes at an angle to make the paper cover, or to use more than one piece of paper.

WHERE NEXT
Set up another group of boxes and wrapping paper for the children to wrap independently. Leave a collection of ribbons and bows for the children to decorate their wrapped boxes.

Use containers of different shapes for the children to investigate in the same way. If they need help, explain that the shapes are easier to wrap if placed inside a box shape first.

ASSESSMENT
Note the children who need lots of prompting and help, and those who go about solving the problem independently. This group are ready to work with standard measures to work out the lengths of paper related to the lengths of the sides of the boxes.

LEARNING OUTCOMES
The children will learn to think through a problem laterally, identifying strategies in order to solve it. They will learn to persevere to find the answer to the

problem and to understand that there is often more than one way to solve the same problem.

FURTHER MATHS CHALLENGES

Wrapping up boxes
Show the children the group of boxes again, and this time use sheets of wrapping paper cut to a size so that the boxes can be wrapped only if placed diagonally on the paper and are wrapped corner to corner. Explain that each piece of paper has been cut so that it is just big enough to wrap up one of the boxes and there are enough pieces to wrap the boxes again. Leave the children to investigate the pieces of paper and boxes in groups. They may try to solve the puzzle by trial and error. If they do not realise after a while that they need to wrap the boxes so that the corners of the wrapping paper meet, ask them questions, such as *Does the box have to be straight with the paper? Does it help if you turn the box?* When one group of children has solved the puzzle, invite them to explain what they did. Challenge the children again to match the pieces of paper to their corresponding boxes, which only fit when the box is turned at an angle, and then to wrap the boxes.

Big boxes
Use large boxes and challenge the children to wrap these with the least number of sheets of paper possible. Which group used the least number and still managed to cover the box? Ask the children to estimate the number of sheets they think they will need. Were they right? Did they use more or less than they first thought? As the activity progresses note if the children become more accurate with their estimates.

FLYING SAUCERS

SUBJECT: SCIENCE. QCA UNIT: 2E FORCES AND MOVEMENT.

LEARNING OBJECTIVES
To learn when and why a scientific test is not fair; to recognise the importance of fair testing when collecting results.

THINKING OBJECTIVE
To form hypotheses.

THINKING SKILLS
The children will learn that to hypothesise they are building on their prediction skills. To hypothesise, the children need to have some prior knowledge of a process so that they can build on their learning. This activity allows the children to refine their predictions so that they are using the results of an investigation to hypothesise what they think is happening and why.

They will think about how to retest different frisbees in a fairer way by looking carefully at the results of their original test and evaluating how they carried this out. The scientific enquiry skills of measuring and recording results in tables and graphs will be used to inform future hypotheses.

WHAT YOU NEED
A large, safe space; if possible enough frisbees of different sizes and designs for each child or pair of children in the class (or organise the children into groups so that each group tests a frisbee one at a time in a different order); metre rules or trundle wheels; chalk; board or flip chart.

WHAT TO DO
Show the children the frisbees and allow them to try these out by throwing them across a large space. Make sure that the children all stand in a line and throw the frisbees in the same direction. Reinforce the importance of not starting to move forward to measure until everyone has stopped throwing.

Return to the classroom and explain that you want to find out which frisbee will travel the furthest. Can the children predict which the children think will go the furthest and to suggest why. Help them with questions if necessary, such as *Will the large round frisbee travel further than the small round frisbee?* Then collect the children's ideas about how they might go about finding out. If no one suggests it, explain that they could go outside and measure how far the frisbees are thrown. Other things to consider include everyone standing at the same place to launch their frisbee, measuring how far each frisbee travels whether using standard or non-standard measures (let the children decide which) and how to record the information. Then go outside and test the frisbees. Reinforce the safety rules and make sure there is ample supervision to ensure that these are followed. Ask a couple of children to help you record how far each frisbee travels.

Return to the classroom and compare the distance that each frisbee travelled. Ask, *Is it possible to say which frisbee travelled the furthest? Why not?* Discuss with the children how the test was not fair. Ask them to suggest reasons why they think it wasn't fair. These may include different units of measurements used, different children throwing, different shapes and weights of frisbees. Discuss how they think they could make the test fair. Does this affect the children's earlier hypotheses about which frisbee travels the furthest and why?

DIFFERENTIATION
Some children may already have an idea of fair testing. When the others have started their investigations, work with this group for about five minutes agreeing how they will make the test as fair as possible. Allow them to carry out the more controlled test.

WHERE NEXT
Carry out another test, focusing on deciding whether results are reliable. Get the children to note whether a test is fair by asking them to list any reasons why it was unfair. An investigation where the children melt ice would be suitable.

ASSESSMENT
Complete a science skill assessment as the children carry out the testing. Make particular note of the children who know that the test is unfair so that they can consider how to make it as fair as possible.

LEARNING OUTCOMES
The children will form hypotheses and conclusions during the activity. This will develop a climate for investigation, and a natural, inquisitive and questioning approach to their work.

FURTHER SCIENCE CHALLENGES
Paper aeroplanes
Ask the children to design and make a paper aeroplane to travel the furthest. They should use a range of papers of different sizes and develop different ways of folding and joining these. Some children may want to stick the wings onto the body. When the children have made their aeroplanes and planned their test, allow them to carry it out. Which aeroplane travels the furthest distance? How do the children know? Did they all start at the same place when testing their aeroplanes? Did they measure the distance accurately? Finally, ask them to assess whether their test was fair.
Testing vehicles
Give the children some information on different vehicles, organised as a graph or a table, and ask

them questions about the data, such as *Which vehicle travels the furthest and fastest? How do you know?* Ask the children how they think the investigation was carried out to gain the information. Do they know if the tests were fair?

SPINNING AROUND

SUBJECT: HISTORY. QCA UNIT: 1A HOW ARE OUR TOYS DIFFERENT FROM THOSE IN THE PAST?

LEARNING OBJECTIVE
To learn that toys have changed over time and that this indicates changes in the way that people live now compared to the past.

THINKING OBJECTIVE
To think imaginatively and creatively.

THINKING SKILLS
By exploring a range of toys that spin, with a particular focus on the hoola hoop, the children will think imaginatively about how toys were used in different periods in the past. They will create their own ideas of how to play with these toys and use their imaginations to develop games and competitions.

WHAT YOU NEED
Hoola hoops (one for each child); a range of toys that spin or go round, such as a top, skipping ropes, helicopters, windmills, robots, roundabouts, construction kits and car tracks, ensuring that there is a range of old and modern toys.

WHAT TO DO
Show the children the range of toys in your collection and talk about how old they may be. Together, sort them according to whether they are modern or old. Then refine the sorting into whether the children think they were played with by their parents or grandparents, and label these with a rough time period. This will depend on the age and ability of the children and may range from, *Before my parents/I was born, When my grandparents/parents were children* to, *During the 40s, 50s, 60s...* Ask, *Are there more toys in the modern group? Why do you think this is the case?* This will lead the children to understand that there is a greater range and number of modern toys than those from long ago, and that these changes affect the way we live now in comparison to the way people lived in the past.

Let the children explore the different toys (except the hoola hoops) to find out how they work. Can the children think of a game to play with some of the toys, perhaps to find out who can make the spinning top spin for the longest time. When the children have had enough time exploring each of the toys, talk about how each one worked and ask them to share some of the games they have discovered with the toys.

Show the children a hoola hoop and explain that this was a popular toy in the late 1950s and early 60s. Talk about its shape and the material from which it is made. Show them how the hoops were played with and let them try to hoola hoop themselves. Explain that children spent a long time developing this skill and persevered until they had accomplished it. Ask, *Do you think it was the first time that children played with a hoop? Do you think children played with these at the beginning of the 20th century? How do you know? Did they play with them in a different way? Were they made from a different material?*

Show the class how children in the early part of the 20th century used to play with hoops by rolling them along the floor and chasing them to try to keep up. Show the children how a stick was used to move and steer the hoop. Let the children explore these ideas for a few minutes. Ask questions, such as *Do you think it was easy or hard to bowl hoops along with a stick? Why was this? Is it because the ground is uneven? What would the ground have been like in the early 1900s? Do you think the roads were covered in tarmac and were smooth? What were the roads made from? How would this affect the way the hoop travelled?*

DIFFERENTIATION
Ask very directed questions to those children who are unable to say which are the old and modern toys. For example, *What is this toy made from? Is this a modern material or was it about when your grandparents were small? What colour is it? Were toys as colourful as this when your grandparents were small?*

WHERE NEXT
Look at other modern and old toy collections with the class, for example baby toys or toys with wheels. Ask them to think how the older toys used to be played with and to compare these with the modern ones.

Show the children skateboards from the 70s and a modern skateboard, and ask them to note the similarities and differences. Ask, *How are they played with today that is different from the past?*

ASSESSMENT
Note the children who show a knowledge and understanding of aspects of the past, and who are able to think creatively about how artefacts can be used. Some children may notice similarities and differences in terms of whether certain things had been invented at different historical times.

LEARNING OUTCOMES
Most children will note the similarities and differences between some toys of today and those in the past. They will think creatively about how toys they are not familiar with were once played with and adapting their use by making up modern games to play with them. They will note that things change over time and that those changes affect the way people live.

FURTHER HISTORY CHALLENGES
Hoola hoops
Ask the children to create games with the hoops to play at the school fête. Perhaps the winner is the person who can keep the hoola hoop going for the longest time, or can roll it along the ground the furthest. This may encourage parents and grandparents to show off their expertise to the children.

A NEW NAME

SUBJECT: GEOGRAPHY. QCA UNIT: 1 AROUND OUR SCHOOL – THE LOCAL AREA.

LEARNING OBJECTIVE
To make observations about features and their location in the local environment.

THINKING OBJECTIVE
To hypothesise.

THINKING SKILLS
During the children's study of the local area, they will look at where things are located and why. The children will be building on these observations to hypothesise why certain buildings and areas have the names they do. They will use the evidence to think of other suitable names for the buildings and areas in the locality.

WHAT YOU NEED
A large map of the area you intend to study; photographs of buildings and features in the locality; Blu-Tack; a large space to display the map if doing this as a class lesson.

WHAT TO DO

Look at the map of the locality with the children and talk about all the different features they can see. Talk about why some things are located where they are. For example, why the bus stop is by the village shop, a car park by a supermarket and a park by the river. Look at the photographs of the buildings in the locality and ask the children to locate their position on the map. Attach them to the map with Blu-Tack. Talk about why they are located where they are, asking the children questions, for example *Is it next to a particular feature, such as a river, pond, the sea or a road? Is it located on a corner, in an area away from the main road or at a crossroads? Is there a designated roadway to the building or is it behind the High Street in a small cul-de-sac?*

Talk about the names of the buildings and get the children to try and form hypotheses about why they are called what they are. Ask, *Are they called after their owners now or in the past? Are they so called because of their location? Are they called this because the area is famous for something in particular (for example, is the Racing Horse Arms near a racecourse?)?*

Finally, get the children to look at the map, or consider the local area, and come up with areas, places and other buildings that have relevant names. Can they form hypotheses about these? Or ask the children to use their knowledge of the locality to give buildings and features relevant names, giving reasons for their choices.

DIFFERENTIATION

Extend the activity for those who are able by looking at more obscure names. For example, Bluebell Cottage may be so named because of the bluebells that bloom close by in spring. Ask them to look at how the area has changed and what they think has brought about those changes. Have any names been changed as a result? Ask lower attainers very direct questions, such as *What is the name of this building? What is the name of the family that own it?* in order to lead them to the answers.

WHERE NEXT

Look with the children at the picture of the Isle of Struay in *The Big Katie Morag Storybook* by Mairi Hedderwick (Red Fox). Discuss the names the author has given to the different areas, features and buildings. Talk about the possible reasons for these names and ask the children to suggest some alternative names for the houses that belong to the islanders.

ASSESSMENT

Assess the children's ability to suggest why the names for certain places have been chosen. Note those who are using this learning to understand how the area has changed and the reasons for this.

LEARNING OUTCOMES

Most children will suggest why buildings and places are called what they are and use geographical features to base their own suggestions for names on.

FURTHER GEOGRAPHY CHALLENGES

Treasure Island

Give the children a large outline of an island, and ask them to add features and one or two buildings. Tell them to think carefully about where they are placing these in relation to the physical features of the island. Ask them to think of a hypothesis for giving the areas a name. The children should be encouraged to give reasons for their choice of names and locations of the buildings and features.

School names

Look together at a plan of the school and ask the children to give each classroom a name. Discuss the possibilities before letting the children make signs for each one. Finish by thinking of names for other rooms in the building and for the features outside.

FLOWERPOT MOBILES

SUBJECT: DESIGN AND TECHNOLOGY. QCA UNIT 1D HOMES.

LEARNING OBJECTIVES

To select materials, techniques and tools to make a mobile; to join materials in different ways to suit the purpose of the model.

THINKING OBJECTIVE

To think laterally and creatively and find innovative outcomes.

THINKING SKILLS

The children will be given the task of deciding for themselves how to use string and dowelling to make flowerpots hang straight in a mobile. They will investigate a problem, think of possible solutions and try these solutions out. They will need to think laterally, to look at the problem from different viewpoints to find the best solution. The children will learn to think creatively to find ways to attach flowerpots to string and to consider difficulties such as balance and form.

WHAT YOU NEED

A collection of flowerpots of different colours, shapes and sizes with one hole in the bottom (these could be decorated flowerpots from a previous art and design lesson); dowelling cut to different lengths; string; wire coat-hangers if desired.

WHAT TO DO

Explain to the children that they are going to make a mobile with flowerpots to hang in the school garden or the classroom. Tell the children they need to design how they want the mobile to look. Ask them, *Should we organise them in a line, in a row, or from top to bottom? Which pot do we want at the top? Which pots will hang from the longest piece of string and which from the shortest? How many will we have in each row?*

Talk about how the flowerpots can be attached to the string. Ask the children, *What will happen when we try to tie the string around the pot? How can we prevent the pot falling off the string? How can we stop the pot from being lopsided?* Give the children a pot and some string and let them explore independently first, and then discuss the possibility of tying the end of the string to a small piece of stick and passing the string through the hole at the base of the flowerpot. The stick will go across the hole rather than through it, thus allowing the children to suspend the flowerpot in a straight line from the string.

Go on to make the class mobile, either by hanging the flowerpots along one piece of wood in a line or joining two pieces together in a cross shape. Sometimes metal coat-hangers make suitable structures, too. Help the children build the mobile structure. Try not to show them what to do, but question them to help them find a solution themselves.

When the mobile is complete, talk through how you thought about the problem from several angles before making it. Make sure the children realise that instead of simply using the string to tie the flowerpot directly onto the mobile, they tied a small stick to the string first before attaching the flowerpot to the mobile.

DIFFERENTIATION

Some children will need a lot of support to help them understand how the stick keeps the flowerpot in a straight line and that if string is tied around the pot it will hang lopsided. Hang two alongside each other to show this clearly. Alternatively, the children can work in pairs until each mobile is finished. Higher attaining children should be challenged to join the flowerpots in a line vertically. Ask them to think of a way of doing this.

WHERE NEXT

Show the children a range of lampshades and talk about how these are connected to the fitting to make them hang in a balanced way.

ASSESSMENT

Assess the strategies that the children use to solve the problems. Note which children persevere and try out different ways of tying the string to the flowerpots to make them hang straight. Do some children abandon the string and try to join the pots using different materials? Ask the children if they are happy with the finished model or do they want to make improvements?

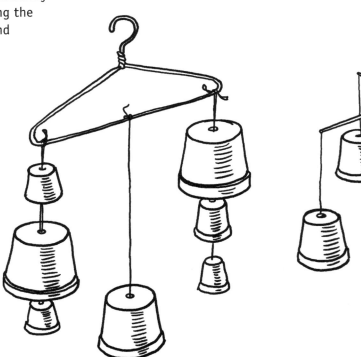

LEARNING OUTCOMES

The children will learn to think through a problem and to try out different strategies in order to solve it. They will use a range of design and technology skills to make models.

FURTHER DESIGN AND TECHNOLOGY CHALLENGES

Bill and Ben

Give the children a variety of flowerpots and invite them to make models of Bill and Ben the Flowerpot Men. Note the children who use the same techniques to join the flowerpots together as in the main activity, so that they are in a straight line. Challenge some children to make a character that stands or sits. How did they manage to join the pots to make them stable? Some children may decide to make sculptures by arranging the pots in different ways to make a model or representation.

Pot containers

Ask the children to decorate a flowerpot each and devise different uses for them, such as pencil holders, flag stands or toy garages. Challenge the children to join several together to make multipurpose storage jars for their school equipment. Suggest they make sections for paper clips, pencils, erasers, rulers and sharpeners. Ask the children how they will join the pots.

SPOT THE DIFFERENCE

SUBJECT: ICT. QCA UNIT: 2B CREATING PICTURES.

LEARNING OBJECTIVE

To create pictures using ICT.

THINKING OBJECTIVE

To think imaginatively.

THINKING SKILLS

Using their imagination the children will alter existing pictures to create a spot-the-difference game. The imaginative way that they change the features on the page will make each piece of work unique even if you decide to let all the children start from the same picture. They will also develop more precise and focused observation skills, which will help them to look more closely when collecting and interpreting information in many subjects.

WHAT YOU NEED

Computers; a clip art package or similar; two similar pictures with some differences which the children will be able to spot, enlarged so that the whole class can see; a prepared picture for the children to copy and create differences on; paper; glue.

WHAT TO DO

Show the children the spot-the-difference pictures. Ask them to look carefully to find as many differences as they can. Then tell the children that they are going to make their own spot-the-difference pictures for their friends on a computer.

As a class, look through the clip art files and show the children how to insert two pictures onto one page, for example a tree and a flower. A garden picture is usually effective, as you can insert small creatures, trees and flowers. Tell the children they can also change colours or resize and reposition images on the page. Either revisit briefly any skills that you need to, or organise the next part of the lesson as a show-and-do activity.

Working in pairs at each computer if you have an ICT suite, or on a rota working with an additional adult if possible, ask the children to create a picture by inserting smaller images onto the page. Give them the freedom to develop their own ideas and to decide on their own context for the picture.

Explain that when the children have created their picture they should save this to file. Show them how to do this if necessary and give the children a prompt sheet. Give the children time to produce their pictures. This may take a number of sessions, and depending on your access to computers, a number of weeks. When the pictures are finished and saved, tell the children to print out a copy.

Alternatively, you may wish to provide a starting picture for the children to copy and make changes to. In small groups, ask the children to discuss the possible changes they could make. Go round the groups asking questions to encourage this discussion, for example *How can you make changes to this part of the picture? Can you change the colour of one part or do you need to change the whole thing? How much smaller do you want to make this feature? Will this make it too hard/too easy for children to notice?* Tell the groups to come to a decision together about the changes they will make and that these shouldn't be more than six.

Either the same day or in the next lesson, show the children how to retrieve the picture. Let them make their planned changes and ask them to save the picture. Print out copies of both pictures each group now has and get each group to stick their pictures side by side on a sheet of paper.

Display the spot-the-difference pictures and ask the other children in the class to find the differences, or include the pictures as an activity in the school magazine if you have one.

DIFFERENTIATION

Sit children of similar ability next to each other. This will allow you to keep your eye on those who need extra help, and intervene as necessary with support. Make sure that the children are not tempted to change everything. Sit higher attaining children together so that they can help each other and discuss ideas independently. This will work whether you have a suite of computers or one or two in the classroom. Plan the lessons according to the amount of support less skilled children will have.

WHERE NEXT

Ask the children to make another set of pictures using a different context as an assessment task.

Set up activity sheets in the writing or reading area for the children to complete the spot-the-difference sheets independently. Grade the sheets according to difficulty and challenge the children to continue until they can complete the most difficult. Encourage the children to work in pairs if they get stuck so that they can help each other.

ASSESSMENT

Note the children who use the full range of tools to make changes to their pictures, trying things out and discarding them until they are happy with the one that they want. Note the progress the children make in improving the focus of their observation skills. Also note those children who design and make their own imaginative pictures and those who copy your idea.

LEARNING OUTCOMES

Most children will generate ideas and amend them before deciding on the finished piece of work. Some will need help to choose images to make their picture and to keep some things the same. Some children will extend their ideas by changing smaller details in the picture, thus making the differences harder for others to find.

FURTHER ICT CHALLENGES
Find the difference
Extend the activity to include other types of puzzles, for example creating word searches and hidden picture pieces which will require other children to look closely. Ask the children to make their own suggestions and to organise these independently. Enlist the help of parents to find suitable materials from books and magazines. How many different types of puzzles can the class come up with?

COMIC BOOK HEROES

SUBJECT: ART AND DESIGN. QCA UNIT: 1A SELF PORTRAIT.

LEARNING OBJECTIVE
To suggest ideas about how to represent others.

THINKING OBJECTIVE
To extend creative ideas.

THINKING SKILLS
The children will extend their knowledge and understanding of facial features by looking closely at how they can develop the shape, direction and style of line to create different expressions. This extension of ideas is a critical part of creative thinking and goes beyond just adding features. The children will be using a range of skills to extend their ideas beyond just creating.

WHAT YOU NEED
A short video clip of a favourite cartoon character, for example Mickey Mouse, Bob the Builder or Scooby Doo; a collection of comics, books and cards with the same and other cartoon characters in; illustrations of the wolf from 'Little Red Riding Hood'.

WHAT TO DO
Show the class the video clip and talk about the character's personality. Ask, *What sort of character is he? How do we know?* Show them a picture of the same character and focus on how the artist has drawn him, asking, *What sort of features does he have? Does he have big or small eyes, ears, mouth or nose? What sort of expressions does he have? Does he smile a lot or frown?*

In small groups, ask the children to find pictures of other cartoon characters in the comics and books. Get them to choose one of these to look at in their group to focus their thinking. Go round the groups posing questions to help them, such as *Is he a happy character or sad? How do we know? What shape are*

THINKING SKILLS: AGES 5–7

96

the eyes? Are they open, closed or half-closed? Are they drawn in a straight line or at an angle? Ask them to find a character with different features, such as different teeth, tongue or ears, and to think about how the artist has portrayed the character by the way he or she has drawn the features.

Look together at different illustrations of the wolf from Little Red Riding Hood. Ask, *What sort of expression does he wear? Does he look cunning? How has the illustrator made him look cunning?*

Give the children, or ask them to trace, an outline of a wolf and let them design their own wolf expressions. Tell them to focus on one feature at a time, prompting them to think about the size, shape and position of the eyes. Ask, *How can we make the eyes express cunning? Should we draw them in a line? Curved or at an angle?* Before they work on the mouth area ask, *Will the wolf be grinning? What about the teeth and tongue – should they be seen?*

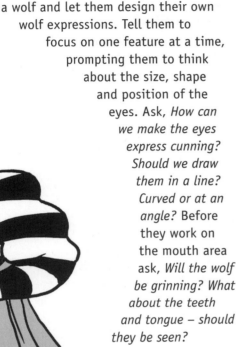

DIFFERENTIATION
Concentrate on finding the cartoon characters in books with lower attaining children and ask them to choose one to copy. Let them talk about the features they have drawn. Extend the activity with those who are more able by asking them to devise their own cartoon character. Let them choose whether their character will be happy, sad or wicked.

WHERE NEXT
Repeat the activity for the wolf in 'The Three Little Pigs', or the crocodile in *The Enormous Crocodile* by Roald Dahl (Puffin).

ASSESSMENT
Note the children who are beginning to think about the position, shape and direction of the features on their pictures independently. Those who are not yet doing this should be given the opportunity to talk about their own and others' work and to describe what they think and feel about this.

LEARNING OUTCOMES
Some children will begin to use the visual information they have collected about characters to extend their own ideas in their drawings and paintings. They will all have the opportunity to explore ideas and to create their own ideas for portraying different cartoon and/or story characters.

FURTHER ART AND DESIGN CHALLENGES
Thoughtful individuals
Look together at the images in a cartoon book, such as *Bob the Builder* and talk about the characters. Ask, *How has the artist brought the characters to life? What are they thinking? How do we know? What is it about the features and expressions that give us a clue?* Ask the children to add speech bubbles and to write in what each of the characters could be thinking. Repeat this with photographs of the children taking part in various activities and set up a storyboard to display these.

Colourful characters
Look at the colours artists have used for different cartoon characters. Get the children to paint pictures of superheroes and villains, adding suitable facial expressions. They could also choose colours which they think portrays each character's function.

DANCING DRUMS

SUBJECT: MUSIC. QCA UNIT: 6 WHAT'S THE SCORE?

LEARNING OBJECTIVE
To understand how symbols can be used to represent sounds.

THINKING OBJECTIVE
To develop ideas.

THINKING SKILLS
The children will be building on work from other QCA units about dynamics, duration and rhythm to create their own composition. The focus will be on developing this through the writing of a musical score. They will consider how the musical elements are used to portray a particular outcome, and find a way to convey this using symbols to instruct their friends to perform the piece exactly as they want it to sound.

WHAT YOU NEED
A collection of drums both commercial and home-made that make a range of sounds (enough for three drums per group of children); an extract from a drumming composition, such as the third track of Disney's millennium celebration music, *A Tapestry of*

Nations, which contains an exciting passage, or use African or Japanese drumming compositions; CD or tape player; board or flip chart.

WHAT TO DO

Play the children a piece of drum music from Africa, or a piece of modern drum music. Which parts do the children like best? Ask, *How does the composer make sure that the people performing play the piece exactly as he/she wants it to sound?* See if any of the children suggest the use of symbols, and if not, ask, *Does the composer use symbols?* Briefly show the children some musical symbols that the composer may have used.

Listen to the extract again and identify any repeating patterns in the music. Ask the children to clap these. Pose questions about the rhythmic patterns, such as *Are the sound of the rhythms the same pitch and tone throughout? Are the rhythms played on the same drum? Are the sounds open or closed, long or short?*

Put three drums in a row and demonstrate the different sounds they make. Show how the sounds can be made different by beating on the centre or edge of the drums. Explain to the children that you want them to compose some repeating patterns on the three drums. Demonstrate by performing the same repeating pattern on each drum individually, and then including two and finally three of the drums. Ask the children which pattern they liked best and why. Repeat this and keep it in your head for later.

In groups, let the children explore three drums of their choice and tell them you want them to create a rhythmic pattern. Reinforce the rules of taking turns and listening to each other. Perhaps they can evaluate which pattern they like best by giving each other composition marks out of ten. When each group has chosen their rhythmic phrase, let them practise it over again to make sure they can remember it exactly! Then ask each group to perform their piece to the class.

As a class, talk about how the children can record their rhythms to instruct others to play it in exactly the same way. Repeat the composition you performed earlier and show how to record it on the board. Make a mark for every drumbeat in the pattern, perhaps making the faster beats smaller or closer together. Let the children decide how to depict their own rhythmic pattern. Next, talk about how loud you want the piece to be played. Again, add to your example on the board the correct musical symbols to show where it should be loud and quiet. Ask the children to do the same for their composition.

Finish by asking the groups to swap scores and perform each other's pieces. Ask the children whether their piece was played exactly as they composed it and then to make any necessary adjustments to their notation.

DIFFERENTIATION

All children will have the opportunity to explore the different sounds that drums make to create their own ideas. You may need to work with some children when composing their pieces to make sure that the rhythms have some kind of structure, for example a repeating pattern.

WHERE NEXT

Create a longer composition by putting the children's ideas together onto one tape.

Listen to the different drum beats and talk about how the music makes the children feel. Ask, *How has the composer created this? Has he changed the dynamics, tempo or rhythms?*

ASSESSMENT

Move around the groups as the children explore the drums to help them create ideas. Note those who have built some structure into the piece and those who are just banging the drums in a haphazard fashion. Note the children who have included loud and quiet parts to add effect, and those who are beginning to organise the sounds into some kind of structure.

LEARNING OUTCOMES

The children will learn to explore the different sounds made by one type of instrument and use this to create their own composition. They will use their knowledge and understanding of musical elements to structure their compositions and to record these using symbols to instruct others how to play it.

FURTHER MUSIC CHALLENGES
Jungle beat

Build up a longer composition over a number of weeks. Organise the class into groups and ask each group to choose four rhythms, giving each rhythm a number. They should sequence the rhythms in the order that they like, writing this down. Ask them to repeat this so that each group has two different sequences of the four rhythms to make a final piece. As a class, perform each group's final piece twice to make a composition long enough to use in developing a class dance sequence in PE.

Kitchen drums

Go on a drum safari with the children to find everyday things that will create good drum sounds. Ask the children to use these to perform their drum composition. Evaluate which substitute drum the class like best. Did the children find any objects that did not make good drums? Why do they think this is? Use this knowledge to make or improve the children's home-made drums.

WRAPPING PRESENTS

SUBJECT: RE. QCA UNIT: 2C CELEBRATIONS.

LEARNING OBJECTIVE

To learn that celebrations often involve giving gifts to commemorate the occasion.

THINKING OBJECTIVE

To create something for someone else which celebrates their achievements.

THINKING SKILLS

The starting point for this activity is evaluation, and it will give the children a good idea about the importance of people's feelings when creating something for someone else. The main focus will be on thinking around the problems to produce something suitable, which will reflect what we think of other's achievements. This is set within the celebrations theme because people often celebrate a particular achievement in some way, including special assemblies in school. If you do not already hold such an assembly, you may wish to think about doing so.

Be sensitive to the different religious groups in your school. Follow your school's policy for RE carefully. Take the make up of your particular school into account when choosing the resources for festival work outlined in the thinking challenges.

WHAT YOU NEED

A range of wrapping papers, lengths of ribbon, bows, gift tags; sticky tape; scissors; sturdy boxes of varying sizes; sticky labels; coloured card; felt-tipped pens; a present or box wrapped in newspaper; a collection of stickers, some new and some old and tatty; two certificates, one new and one old; board or flip chart.

WHAT TO DO

Tell the class that you want to make a list of as many special occasions that people celebrate as they can think of. Include birthdays, weddings, christenings and name-giving ceremonies. As the children make their suggestions record them as two lists on the board, one for celebrations and the other for festivals.

Look at the list of celebrations together and talk about other things people may celebrate, such as winning the World Cup, a gold medal in the Olympics or passing a driving test. Point out that these are all occasions when people have achieved something special and the celebrations are a way of saying, *Well done*. Talk about the celebration assemblies you may hold in school. What type of things do you congratulate people for? What are the children who have achieved something special given to note this achievement? (Perhaps a sticker or certificate.) Explain that the way the reward is presented also tells the person receiving it what we think of them.

Show the children your present wrapped in newspaper and talk about what someone may think if you gave them a present wrapped in this way. Talk about what you might use instead. Look at two certificates, one very attractive and new, the other plain and tired looking, and talk about what the recipient would think about each one.

Repeat this with the stickers in your collection. Sort them into two groups according to whether the children think they convey the right messages to the receiver. For each sticker ask, *Would they think their achievement was being celebrated? Would they think they had achieved something special if they were presented with this?*

Give the children felt-tipped pens, white sticky labels and coloured card to design and make certificates and/or stickers which they think convey the message *Well done* in the best way. Also, set up a table with a range of wrapping paper, ribbons, bows, gift tags and sticky tape for the children to wrap up pretend presents in a way that would make a recipient feel appreciated. Make sure that the range of available resources gives a wide choice so that if you organise the activities as a round robin, the last group has an equally wide choice to choose from.

Look at the children's finished certificates, stickers and presents and talk about the message each one gives to the receiver. You could use a computer to reproduce some of these to use in your celebration assemblies.

DIFFERENTIATION

Help the children with their ideas. Talk about the kinds of symbols to use, and colours and sizes. Put spellings on the board or on card for any children that need to copy so that they do not make spelling mistakes. Let some children use a simple paint program on computers to create their designs. Some children may want to design and make different things to recognise achievement. Make resources available for this if you are able or if not, ask for a detailed design so that you have time to gather the resources together.

WHERE NEXT

Get the children to design cups and trophies to present to 'winning' tables for good behaviour.

Discuss which celebrations are religious and which are not.

ASSESSMENT

Note the children who use suitable symbols in their designs and who think of original ways to say, *Well done.*

LEARNING OUTCOMES

The children will begin to develop a respect for the feelings and views of others. They will co-operate to devise a reward which recognises achievement.

FURTHER RE CHALLENGES

Religious celebrations

Design and make a class card to celebrate a current festival, for example Divali, Easter, Eid or Hanukkah. Let the children decide for themselves the resources they will need to make the card suitable for the purpose.

Wrapping paper

Ask the children to design and make wrapping paper in which to wrap presents appropriate to give at the different religious festivals and other celebrations during the year. Include gold and silver pens, glittery stickers and brightly coloured base paper.

MONSTER STOMP

SUBJECT: PE. QCA UNIT: DANCE ACTIVITIES UNIT 2.

LEARNING OBJECTIVE

To compose and perform dance phrases that express and communicate ideas and feelings.

THINKING OBJECTIVE

To explore and extend ideas.

THINKING SKILLS

The children will create ideas in response to a story and a piece of music. They will respond to a piece of music by tailoring their movements to the drama created by the way the music speeds up to its climax. This will act as the structure to the dance piece.

WHAT YOU NEED

Not Now, Bernard by David McKee (Andersen Press); music from *Hall of the Mountain King* by Savatage (or similar dramatic piece with 16 bars of repeating music); dice; board or flip chart.

WHAT TO DO

Before the dance session, read *Not Now, Bernard* to the children and talk about the monster in the story. Ask, *What does it look like? How does it move?*

At the start of the session, use music from *Hall of the Mountain King* for a warm-up. Let the children freely explore a range of movements in response to the music for about two minutes. Talk about how the music makes the children feel. Does it sound light or creepy, cheerful or menacing? Revisit the conversation you had about the monster's movements. Talk about the strength of the children's monster movements by asking, *Do your movements have a clear starting and finishing point? How have you achieved this? How can you make your movements more dramatic? How is your monster moving – slowly, quickly or a mixture of the two? Is your monster short or tall? Is he moving carefully and quietly, or is he doing more of a stomping movement?*

Then ask the children to move to the music again, making improvements to their movements and sharing ideas with each other on how to make their dance more interesting.

Observe half of the class at a time and let the children who are watching choose four of their favourite movements. Get the whole class to practise these movements a few times until you are sure they can remember each one. Give each movement a number, and play a game by calling out a number and expecting the children to perform the correct movement.

Over the next two sessions, take each movement in turn and develop this with the children. Develop each movement differently, so that when they are put together the finished sequence will have contrast in style, movement and shape. Talk with the children about the dynamics and levels, and encourage them to add any turns and changes of direction necessary. When the children are happy with the four movements, ask them to put all four together into a 16-bar (64 beats and 4 bars per sequence) phrase, which is repeated until the climax of the music is reached.

In the next session, put the children into groups to discuss the 16-bar phrase. Go round the groups to facilitate discussion, asking, *Are you happy with the order of the movements? Do you want to repeat the same order over and over, or do you want to vary it?* Let the children practise their own 16-bar phrases in the order they want to carry out the movements, before asking them to repeat their phrase in front of the class. Evaluate these and then allow all the groups some time to make improvements to their phrases. As they rehearse, move round the groups prompting them with questions which will help them to extend their ideas.

When the groups have had enough time, bring them back together to perform their phrases to the rest of the class. Then ask the groups to perform their phrases in a sequence to form a class dance. Develop the final part of the sequence. Discuss with the children what happens at the end of the piece of music. Ask, *Is the music calm or is it dramatic? What do you think may be happening?* Ask them to show this individually through dance. Ask, *Will you make more frantic movements? How will you finish? Will this involve twists and turns? What shape will you hold to make a final balance?* Choose a few good examples and get the children to agree on their favourite to finish their class dance with.

To finish, get the children to perform the whole dance again, adding the end movement where they can all join in together. The children can practise the dance for a performance.

DIFFERENTIATION
Extend the activity for those who are more able by dividing the groups into pairs. Let each child perform a movement in turn before performing the movements in their pairs.

Suggest ideas if the children don't suggest anything themselves, and give them the chance to explore, discuss, evaluate and improve the ideas.

WHERE NEXT
Develop the children's dance over the next few weeks by getting them to concentrate on particular dance skills, such as developing different heights, strengths of movement and shapes. Use the same structure to create new dance ideas for topics in other subjects.

ASSESSMENT
Note how the children use the elements of dance to help them create imaginative and interesting movements. Which children use the ideas of others to extend their own imagination and improve the drama in their performance?

LEARNING OUTCOMES
Most children will perform basic actions, copy and repeat these to compose a sequence, thus developing some creative ideas. Some children will develop and extend their ideas by beginning to link the movements with feelings and moods.

FURTHER PE CHALLENGES
Pick 'n' mix dancing
In a literacy lesson, explore the range of feelings that the children may experience if they see something they like or dislike. Write the words they think of on cards. During dance, hold up the word cards one at a time and ask the children to create movements, shapes and actions that depict the words.
Travelling light
During a music lesson play the children extracts from Tchaikovsky's *The Nutcracker Suite*, which contains music at different speeds and dynamics. Ask the children to write down all the movement words they think of as they listen to the music, for example running, marching, stamping, tiptoeing. Transfer the words to cards and use these as prompts for the children to compose a dance of different types of movements. Play the extracts and allow the children to respond, creating dance movements which reflect the mood of the music.

EVALUATION SKILLS

INTRODUCTION

Evaluative thinking involves children being involved in the assessment of their own learning. This is one of the key skills in the National Curriculum, which acknowledges that the children should be clear about what they need to do in order to improve their work. Links to the key communication skills, particularly speaking and listening, are clear, and one way forward is for teachers to include this aspect in lesson planning. Opportunities for the children to reflect, review and critically evaluate their learning during and after lessons are needed. This leads to them identifying for themselves ways to improve their learning and performance. They can plan for themselves the next steps in their learning through choosing particular parts to work on, based on a clear assessment of their skills, knowledge and understanding.

Evaluative thinking links closely to all the other key thinking skills. For example, the children will be evaluating information they have collected and organising it so that it makes sense; they will make decisions on the usefulness and quality of that information in relation to the purpose of the task; they will use enquiry skills to raise and answer questions about what they are doing in terms of its value; and they will think creatively to solve any problems or queries that arise. Although evaluative thinking is the culmination of other thinking skills used during an activity, it is sometimes necessary for the children to evaluate what they have before they start work. This involvement of the skill during the planning stages of the activity will allow the children to direct and organise the steps of their own learning.

The lessons in this chapter focus on the children considering carefully what they are doing and what they have done and identifying for themselves where they need to improve. The organisation of learning allows them to bounce ideas off each other and to plan ahead for the next steps in learning. Questions form prompts for their thinking. Teacher assessment informs this process. You need to be clear about the children's level of performance and where you want the children to go next. Rather than telling the children what is good about their performance and directing them to the next activity and task, the activities here use questions to help the children do this for themselves. Group work supports this process well, as the children are able to use each other's ideas and comments.

Learning styles and the climate for learning are important. The activities here provide for the many different ways children learn. They all start with the children performing something, which forms the basis for evaluation. Therefore, the children are developing these skills within a personal context. The skills are:
⊙ evaluating information – judging value, usefulness and quality
⊙ suggesting improvements
⊙ developing criteria for judging.

INTRODUCING EVALUATION SKILLS

Subject and QCA unit, NLS or NNS objective	Activity title	Thinking objective	Activity	Page
English NLS objective: To write simple lists	Tomato sandwich	To evaluate instructions and suggest improvements	Deciding whether instructions are clear enough to make a sandwich from	104
Maths NNS objective: To measure using suitable units and equipment	How far round?	To evaluate equipment (judging usefulness)	Selecting resources to measure along and around a range of objects	105
Science QCA unit: 1B Growing plants	Peas and beans	To evaluate and compile information	Investigating conditions of growth in order to grow healthy plants	105
History QCA unit: 17 What are we remembering on Remembrance Day?	Poppy Day	To evaluate information	Considering what evidence tells us about Remembrance Day services	106
Geography QCA unit: 1 Around our school – the local area	Litterbug busters	To evaluate sites for litter bins	Evaluating the best places to put litter bins	107
Design and technology QCA unit: 1B Playgrounds	Monkey house	To evaluate playground apparatus	Designing a climbing frame for toddlers and young children	108
ICT QCA unit: 2D Routes: controlling a floor turtle	Getting there	To evaluate instructions (judging usefulness) and make improvements	Following and editing directions to see if they lead to the planned destination	109
Art and design QCA unit: 1C What is sculpture?	How does it make you feel?	To evaluate art (judging value)	Looking at and handling pieces of sculpture to talk about what feelings they evoke	110
Music QCA unit: 7 Rain, rain, go away	Feelings	To evaluate music (judging quality)	Listening to a range of music and talking about the images and feelings the pieces conjure up	110
RE QCA unit: 1A What does it mean to belong?	Here I am	To evaluate information (judging value)	Deciding how people know they belong to a group, organisation or club	111
PE QCA unit: Games activities unit 1	Targets	To evaluate skills (judging quality)	Practising throwing skills using a range of equipment and targets	112

THINKING SKILLS: AGES 5–7

TOMATO SANDWICH

SUBJECT: ENGLISH. NLS OBJECTIVE: TO WRITE SIMPLE LISTS.

LEARNING OBJECTIVE
To write instructions as a list.

THINKING OBJECTIVE
To evaluate instructions and suggest improvements.

THINKING SKILLS
The children will read instructions and evaluate whether they think they are clear and comprehensive enough. They will check this opinion by watching the instructions being carried out. They will then make improvements by inserting any missing items and instructions they identify.

WHAT YOU NEED
Sandwich-making instructions which omit the knife and slicing of the tomatoes (see What to do); all the items identified in your sandwich-making instructions, along with the omitted knife; paper and writing materials; board or flip chart.

WHAT TO DO
Before the lesson, prepare the sandwich-making instructions. Write them in two sections – *What you need* and *What to do*. List all the items needed to make a tomato sandwich, except a knife. On the *What to do* list, omit the instruction to slice the tomato. Write the other instructions as a simple list.

TOMATO SANDWICH

WHAT YOU NEED
2 SLICES OF BREAD
BUTTER FOR SPREADING
A TOMATO

WHAT TO DO
1. SPREAD THE BUTTER ON THE BREAD.
2. PUT THE TOMATO ON ONE SLICE OF BREAD.
3. PLACE THE OTHER SLICE OF BREAD ON TOP.

At the beginning of the lesson, tell the children that they are going to look at making sandwiches. Give each child a copy of the instructions and ask whether by looking at the title they can guess what kind of sandwich you will be making. Read through the *What you need* section and ask the children whether they

think all the necessary resources have been included. Ask them to add anything they think is missing. Look at the *What to do* section together. Read each point on the list and evaluate whether all the instructions that are needed are included. Consider the children's suggestions on what may be missing from the *What you need* list and the *What to do* section.

Evaluate the children's thoughts by making a sandwich, following the instructions. Either confirm or bring to their attention the missing knife and the instruction to slice the tomato. Do this by playfully placing a whole tomato between the two slices of bread. Ask the children to edit their list of instructions accordingly.

Tell the children to write a list of instructions to make a different kind of sandwich. Invite some children to share these with the class, asking the rest of the children to express an opinion about the quality of the instructions. Can they suggest how to make them better?

How far round?

SUBJECT: MATHS. NNS OBJECTIVE: TO MEASURE USING SUITABLE UNITS AND EQUIPMENT.

LEARNING OBJECTIVE
To measure different lengths using a range of equipment.

THINKING OBJECTIVE
To evaluate equipment (judging usefulness).

THINKING SKILLS
The children will be applying their measuring skills to decide for themselves which piece of equipment to use to measure different things. They may have already measured different parts of their body in science and this activity will act as reinforcement, or as an introduction to that work. The key to this lesson is the evaluation of which piece of equipment is the most useful to measure around and along different things.

WHAT YOU NEED
Enough tape measures, rulers, metre rules, trundle wheels, string, ribbon, straws and lengths of wood for each group of children to have at least one; objects and areas of the classroom to measure; pedometer; paper and writing materials.

WHAT TO DO
Talk to the children about their last measuring activity and remind them what they did, to reinforce this previous learning. Then look at the scale on a metre stick and talk about what measurement each unit represents. Compare this to the scale on a tape measure and trundle wheel. Demonstrate counting on in ones, twos, fives and tens to familiarise the children with these steps.

Stretch a length of ribbon or string along the metre rule and ask the children to measure how long it is by reading the appropriate point on the scale. Invite a few children to do this, checking that they start in the right place at the beginning of the ruler. Reinforce that they should measure from zero on all measuring devices.

Organise the children into groups and give each group a range of objects and areas of the classroom to measure. Include some round objects and some large areas that are best measured with a metre rule, or even better a trundle wheel. Provide a range of equipment for the children to select from and which is suitable to measure all the objects in your collection. Let the children decide for themselves how to record the measurements, or if they are not ready to do this they can record them in a table.

When the groups have completed their measuring talk about which piece of equipment they used to measure which objects. Why did they choose the equipment they did? Why did they use the tape measure to measure around the teapot, for instance? Ask questions to focus the children's thinking, such as *Which is the best measuring ruler to use? Why is this the best? How is it different from others? What unit of measurement did you use? Why did you decide to use metres/centimetres?*

When the children are clear about why they chose certain measuring equipment for certain distances, talk about the everyday uses of measuring length and the equipment chosen by the people who use them. For example, measuring the distance between the school and home to find out whether to provide a bus to school; measuring the height and width of a door to find out if it will fit the door frame. Show the children a pedometer and talk about how this measures how far people walk.

Follow up the activity with independent tasks. For example, asking the children to measure different objects, areas or distances in centimetres, metres or kilometres/miles; asking them to find a way to measure round objects with a straight ruler.

Peas and beans

SUBJECT: SCIENCE. QCA UNIT: 1B GROWING PLANTS.

LEARNING OBJECTIVE
To learn that seeds and plants need certain conditions to grow.

THINKING OBJECTIVE
To evaluate and compile information.

THINKING SKILLS
The children will look closely at the evidence they gain from growing plants in different environments and evaluate the information they collect to make decisions about what they need to do to improve the growth rate of the plants.

WHAT YOU NEED

Four grow bags; bean and pea seeds; a watering can; a light place and a dark place to grow the plants.

WHAT TO DO

Show the children the seeds and the grow bags and tell them they are going to try to grow peas and beans. Following the instructions on the packets, allow the children to plant the pea and bean seeds in the grow bags. Then place one of each bag in a light area and one of each in a dark area. Make sure the children water the plants as directed on the packet and monitor the growth of each set of seeds into small plants. Record the growth as a table. What do the children notice about the colour, size and condition of each set of plantlets? Ask, *What does this information tell us?*

Move both sets of plants into the light area and record the changes that take place in those that have previously been kept in the dark. Ask the children, *What does this tell us about growing plants and light? Does this information point to any conclusions?*

Fail to water one set of plants for a few days. Ask the children to monitor the growth and note the changes, and again ask them questions about what the information they record tells them about plants and growing. (Begin to water the plants again before they wither.) Similarly, put one set of plants outside and ask the children the same questions.

Finally, get the children to use the information to put together a list of *Dos* and *Don'ts* for growing seeds and use it as a guide to plant new seeds.

POPPY DAY

SUBJECT: HISTORY. QCA UNIT: 17 WHAT ARE WE REMEMBERING ON REMEMBRANCE DAY?

LEARNING OBJECTIVE

To learn about an event in the past that is still commemorated today.

THINKING OBJECTIVE

To evaluate information.

THINKING SKILLS

The children will look carefully at evidence to see what it tells us about an event in the past – here which evidence is useful for telling us why we commemorate Remembrance Day. The activity can be adopted as an approach for evaluating information surrounding any historical event. It will help the children to develop an understanding of the past and a sense of time.

WHAT YOU NEED

Poppies; photographs and a video extract of a Remembrance Day service; video player and TV; board or flip chart; paper and writing materials.

WHAT TO DO

Talk about any historical events the children have already learned about. Then move on to talking about Remembrance Day and explain that it commemorates the end of major wars, such as the First and Second World Wars. Explain that people still take time to remember these wars today through a special service of remembrance each year.

Explore the meaning of remembrance with the children and talk about how we remember and commemorate certain things, for example birthdays with presents and cards, holidays with photographs. Talk about how Remembrance Day is observed by different organisations.

Look at the poppy and ask the children what this tells us. How does this remind us of the events that happened in the First World War? Visit the local war memorial if you have one nearby, or show the children photographs of one. Ask, *What part does this play in the special service of Remembrance Day?* Show the class the video extract of a Remembrance Day service and talk about the importance of the war memorial in the service.

Revisit the information that the children have looked at so far in learning about Remembrance Day (the poppy, the war memorial). Ask, *Do these things help us to know about what happens on this special day? Do they remind us of what happened in the wars that have taken place in this and the last century?*

Ask the children to suggest all the people who are involved in special services around the country on Remembrance Day. Make a list of these on the board. Ask, *What does this tell us about the importance placed upon Remembrance Day?*

Ask the children to write down each piece of information or evidence they have looked at today. Invite them to add their thoughts about how this helps them to find out about the history behind Remembrance Day.

LITTERBUG BUSTERS

SUBJECT: GEOGRAPHY. QCA UNIT: 1 AROUND OUR SCHOOL – THE LOCAL AREA.

LEARNING OBJECTIVE
To recognise how the local environment may be improved.

THINKING OBJECTIVE
To evaluate sites for litter bins.

THINKING SKILLS
The children will think carefully about how the inclusion of litter bins will help keep the environment tidy. They will evaluate where best to place to them in order to get people to use them when they are really needed.

WHAT YOU NEED
A camera; a large map of a local attraction, beauty spot, seaside resort or theme park (it needs to clearly show shops, cafes and takeaway stalls); smaller copies of the map; small pictures of litter bins (enough for each group of children); glue.

WHAT TO DO
Take the children on a walk around the local area and carry out a survey to identify and record all the places where you found litter bins. Photograph these and add the pictures to a map of the area on return to the classroom. Why do the children think the bins are placed in the positions they are? Make a mental note of the criteria they think of.

Show the children the map of a local beauty spot or attraction. Talk about the physical and human features they can see on the map. Then ask them to look carefully for all the places in which they think litter would be generated. (Perhaps somewhere that is a good place for a picnic, or anywhere where they could buy an ice cream, a drink or a meal. Is there a sweet shop where people can buy a small snack?) Evaluate together whether these would be good spots to place litter bins. Check their evaluation skills by asking, *Why?*

Organise the children into groups and give each group a smaller version of the map. Ask them to stick the pictures of small litter bins onto the places on the map where they think there will be the most litter. Ask, *Will the introduction of these bins improve the environment? How can we get people to use them? How often will they need to be emptied?*

Monkey house

Subject: Design and technology. QCA unit: 1B Playgrounds.

Learning objective
To design a climbing frame suitable for a toddler or small child.

Thinking objective
To evaluate playground apparatus.

Thinking skills
The children will evaluate whether particular items of equipment in a playground are suitable for a toddler. They will give reasons for their opinions and evaluation. They will go on to use this information to design a suitable climbing frame for a toddler or small child.

What you need
A large plan of a local playground; photographs of each item of equipment; a photograph of a climbing frame; books, posters or other material showing climbing frames.

What to do
Follow your school's policy for visits and risk assessments, and go to the local playground to look at or test out the range of equipment first. Then, ensuring that the children are aware of the school's rules and regulations about what they are allowed to use and what they are not, take them to the playground and let them investigate the equipment. Take photographs of the different pieces of apparatus and on return to the classroom add these to the correct spot on the plan of the playground.

Talk with the children about which pieces they liked and why. Identify those pieces which would be suitable for a toddler or small child to play on. Make sure the children evaluate the apparatus in terms of size, safety and the difficulty level of climbing on or operating.

Focus on a climbing frame (showing a picture if there was not one in the playground). Talk about the size of the bars, the attachments and whether it is suitable for a small child.

Ask the children in groups to collect pictures of climbing frames and talk about which ones would be the most interesting and suitable for small children, and why. Ask, *Which ones are too big, too high off the*

ground or with bars that are too large? Why do toddlers need different types and sizes of things to climb on? Should the bars be closer together?

Still in their groups ask the children to make their own designs for a climbing frame that would be suitable for a toddler or small child. Tell them to consider what they have learned in the lesson so far, and focus their thinking by asking, *What kind of things would a toddler need? How high should the climbing frame be? How small do the bars need to be?* When they have completed their designs ask them why they have chosen the things that they have, and why they have put them in the places that they have: *Do the toddlers have somewhere to climb through, under and over? What about ladders and a slide? What colours do you want to use? Why are these colours best?*

Choose the designs you like best and show these to the whole class, explaining the features that are good in them. Could the class choose parts from all the designs to make one climbing frame?

Getting there

SUBJECT: ICT. QCA UNIT: 2D ROUTES: CONTROLLING A FLOOR TURTLE.

Learning objective

To develop and record a set of instructions to get from one place to another.

Thinking objective

To evaluate instructions (judging usefulness) and make improvements.

Thinking skills

The children will look closely at a set of instructions and judge whether they give enough guidance to get them from a start point to the correct finishing place. They will then consider how they can make improvements to the instructions so that they are as precise as possible.

What you need

A large set of instructions that direct you from one place to another in the classroom or hall, or wherever you are doing the activity; paper and writing materials.

What to do

Sit the children in a circle. Display the instructions so that everyone can see them clearly. Read the instructions aloud and ask the children if they can say where they think they will end up if they follow the instructions. Can they be sure about this? Are the instructions precise enough?

Invite one child to act as a robot. This will allow the children to see the effect of the instructions first hand and will help them carry out the evaluation. Read the first instruction, such as *Move forward two paces*. Evaluate whether the instruction is clear enough. For instance, does it say where the starting point is? Does it tell you which way to face? What about the size of the paces the person takes – is one person's step the same length as another's? Should the instruction say: *Move to the door* instead? What would be wrong with this if you were writing the instruction for a real robot? (Explain that a robot only understands precise units of measurement and directions and would need more precise instructions, such as *Move forward 2 units, turn 90 degrees*.) Agree what the unit and an approximate length each pace in the instructions should be. Read the next instruction, such as *Turn left*, and ask if this is clear. Continue with each instruction, repeating the questioning process to evaluate its effectiveness each time. Give the children ample opportunity to consider alternatives or use more precise language. Edit the instructions as you work through the list, until you have a revised set.

Allow the children to work in pairs to write instructions to get from one place to another within the school building and grounds. Let them test these out and edit them. You may need an additional adult to help with supervision. When the children have finished, choose one pair and follow their instructions as a class. Ask the person who wrote the instructions whether you have all arrived at the correct place.

If not, consider why. If appropriate, return to the classroom, copy and edit the instructions and try them out again. Are they better this time? Why? Make sure the children understand that this is because they are now more precise.

HOW DOES IT MAKE YOU FEEL?

SUBJECT: ART AND DESIGN. QCA UNIT 1C WHAT IS SCULPTURE?

LEARNING OBJECTIVE
To say what they think and feel about art.

THINKING OBJECTIVE
To evaluate art (judging value).

THINKING SKILLS
The children will think about what they feel about different pieces of sculpture or paintings and why. They will have the opportunity to handle sculptures so that they can consider the texture as well as the colour and shape. They will consider how the texture can evoke feelings about the object. They will also understand that not all people will feel the same way as they do about a particular piece.

WHAT YOU NEED
Books and postcards of sculptures or paintings (see What to do); paintings and pieces of sculpture (or animal figures); plastic-coated garden wire or pipe cleaners; clay; paper and drawing materials.

WHAT TO DO
If possible, take the children on a visit to a museum or gallery and let them look first-hand at paintings and sculptures, otherwise show them any suitable examples you may have in school, or use photographs from books. Include works about daily life, for example paintings and sculptures of families and of people at work and at rest. Talk about the expressions on the people's faces. What do the children think the people are feeling? Why? How can they tell? Discuss with the children what the painter or sculptor wanted people to think about when they look at the work. How do we know? What does each painting or sculpture make the children think about and how does it make the children feel? Do all the children feel the same way? Explore why some children like a particular piece while others do not.

Back in the classroom, show the children sculptures which you are happy for them to handle, such as small animal figurines. Talk about the different materials used by the sculptors. Ask, *How do the sculptures feel? Does the texture affect the way you feel about the figure? Which one do you like best? Why? Is it perhaps because it reminds you of a happy event?*

Ask the children to make simple sculptures from pipe cleaners, plastic-coated garden wire, clay or natural materials. Children who find it difficult to add the facial expressions with wire could make drawings of these.

FEELINGS

SUBJECT: MUSIC. QCA UNIT: 7 RAIN, RAIN, GO AWAY.

LEARNING OBJECTIVE
To think about how sounds can be used descriptively.

THINKING OBJECTIVE
To evaluate music (judging quality).

THINKING SKILLS
The children will evaluate how a composer creates a particular mood through changes of speed, pitch, rhythm and dynamics. They will also talk about how the music makes them feel, beginning to use the relevant musical vocabulary.

WHAT YOU NEED
Extracts from *Hall of the Mountain King* by Savatage, 'The Sorcerer's Apprentice' by Dukas, 'The March of the Toreadors' from *Carmen* by Bizet, 'Clair de Lune' by Debussy; alternatively link this lesson to work with *Carnival of the Animals* by Saint-Saëns or *Peter and the Wolf* by Prokofiev, or use popular music, such as a compilation of Beatles songs; board or flip chart.

WHAT TO DO
Listen to the pieces of music in turn and ask the children questions about each, such as *What does this piece of music make you think of? Why is this? How does it make you feel?* List the feelings that the children name.

Talk about how the composer makes the music sound the way it does. Get the children to try to identify all the elements of the music. Talk about the dynamics by discussing how loud or quiet the music is. Ask questions such as, *What mood does this create? Is there more than one sound? Are the sounds low or high, fast or slow? Is there a repeating pattern?* Relate this to the tempo, pitch and texture. Look back at the list of feelings you recorded and see if the children can link particular elements in the music with the feelings it evokes.

Instead, or in another lesson, listen to extracts from *Carnival of the Animals* or *Peter and the Wolf* and ask the children to try to work out what animals are being depicted. How are the children making their decisions? Is it because the tune is slow and low? Does it make them think of a particular animal because it contains lots of jumps?

You could use the music in a dance lesson to reinforce the ideas. Let the children respond to the music with movement and talk about why they moved in the way that they did.

HERE I AM

SUBJECT: RE. QCA UNIT: 1A WHAT DOES IT MEAN TO BELONG?

LEARNING OBJECTIVE
To learn about the concept of belonging.

THINKING OBJECTIVE
To evaluate information (judging value).

THINKING SKILLS
In this activity the children will consider how belonging to the school is expressed, by the use of the school crest and colour of the uniform for example. They will discuss how the meaning behind this sense of belonging to the school is made clear to other people, before going on to think about how other organisations use crests and colours to show their belonging.

WHAT YOU NEED
A copy of the school crest; items that include the school crest, such as letterheaded paper, a compliment slip, school sweatshirt, the school brochure; board or flip chart.

WHAT TO DO
Look at the school crest with the children and discuss its different parts. Ask the children, *Does it have a picture or symbol? What does this mean? Are there any words? What do they say?*

Show the children the things in your collection that carry the school crest. Can they find the crest on each of these? Talk about why it is included on these items. Ask questions, such as *Why does the crest appear as a letterhead? Why is it at the very top of the page and bigger than the school address?*

Look at the school brochure cover. Ask, *Why is the crest big? What colour is it? Why is it in these colours?* Talk about how the size and colours make the crest stand out and this is because it shows what the school stands for, what it means to belong to the school and how important this is.

Look at the school sweatshirt and bring the criteria of colour into the discussion. Ask, *Why is the sweatshirt the colour it is? What colour is the crest?* Can the children think of other clubs and organisations that use colour to show that their members belong?

Ask the children to evaluate all the information they have discovered about how belonging is shown in the school, and list these on the board. Ask them to judge their own sense of value and belonging after looking at this information.

TARGETS

SUBJECT: PE. QCA UNIT: GAMES ACTIVITIES – UNIT 1.

LEARNING OBJECTIVE

To develop throwing skills.

THINKING OBJECTIVE

To evaluate skills (judging quality).

THINKING SKILLS

The children will begin to recognise the best throwing technique to use for different items of equipment. They will begin to make adjustments to their own throwing techniques in response to these evaluations.

WHAT YOU NEED

Various targets – a wall with large and small circles drawn on, hoops, baskets or bins; large and small balls, beanbags and quoits; skipping ropes.

WHAT TO DO

Follow your usual warm-up activities and then give the children a few minutes to practise throwing large and small balls into the air, against the wall and bouncing them on the ground. Ask the children to work in pairs to send balls to each other, concentrating on sending the ball to their partner's hands. Ask them to try this at a range of distances, and while standing still and moving.

Call the children back together and talk about the different kinds of throws they used. Did they use underarm throws all the time? Did those who were standing further away from each other use overarm throws?

Show the children how to send the balls to each other by bouncing them. Explain that this is sometimes useful when trying to get a ball to a partner when someone else is trying to get the ball, as in games like Piggy in the Middle. Let the children try this technique out for five minutes and then ask them questions, such as *Was this successful? How important was it to have an accurate aim to get the ball to your partner?*

Tell the children that you want them to practise and improve the accuracy of their aim by finding the best way to throw different apparatus at different targets. Tell them that each time they hit the target they score a point. Quickly show the children the range of targets (these can be drawn on the wall and on the ground, be hoops on the ground and baskets) and equipment you want them to throw. Use skipping ropes to mark where the children should stand. Organise the children into groups to practise their throwing skills for a while at the targets, until you are sure they know how to try to score. Encourage children needing more of a challenge to stand further back.

Encourage the children to talk to each other about why certain throws were more successful than others. Ask them, *What did she do to hit the target? How did she manage to throw the ball that far?* As they are practising, talk with each group about any difficulties they are experiencing. From time to time share these evaluations with the whole class. Ask the children how this information can help them improve their own throw. Does it help perhaps if they finish with the throwing hand towards the wall? Ask, *Is it easier to throw underarm or overarm? Is it easier to roll the quoits rather than throw them? What if you throw them so that they land flat? Does this make the throw more accurate than if they land upright? Is it easier to use beanbags when throwing at a target on the ground? Why? Is it because they do not roll when they hit the ground?*

When you return to the classroom, talk about the difficulties the children had hitting the targets. Which piece of throwing apparatus was best for throwing at a target on the wall, on the ground, over a distance, into a basket? Agree on a best match of throwing apparatus and target, explaining why this is the best match.

EXTENDING EVALUATION SKILLS

Subject and QCA unit, NLS or NNS objective	Activity Title	Thinking objective	Activity	Page
English NLS objective: To locate parts of text that give information	Dinosaur facts	To evaluate information and develop criteria for judging	Evaluating whether an information text is useful for answering questions	114
Maths NNS objective: Sorting, classifying and organising information in simple ways	Sweet facts	To evaluate mathematical information (judging usefulness)	Evaluating whether data they have collected gives the information they need	115
Science QCA unit: 1C Sorting and using materials	Mirror, mirror	To evaluate (judging quality)	Investigating a range of materials to see which will reflect and make a mirror	117
History QCA unit: 4 Why do we remember Florence Nightingale?	Captain Cook	To evaluate and interpret evidence	Finding out about Captain Cook from a range of sources of evidence	118
Geography QCA unit: 2 How can we make our local area safer?	Crossing safely	To evaluate information	Identifying on a map of the local area where it is safe to cross the road and where it is not	120
Design and technology QCA unit: 1D homes	A model street	To evaluate materials	Making models of flats and houses, and joining them together to make a model street	121
ICT QCA unit: 2A Writing stories: communicating information using text	Poster magic	To evaluate work and make improvements	Creating a poster and editing to improve it	123
Art and design QCA unit: 1B Investigating materials	Does it look right?	To evaluate preferences and suggest improvements to a design	Designing and making stitched table mats, considering colour, shape and pattern	124
Music QCA unit: 2 Sounds interesting	The castle cellar	To evaluate instruments (judging usefulness)	Adding sound effects to a poem and evaluating the different ways sounds are produced to create effects	126
RE QCA unit: 2B Why did Jesus tell stories?	What sort of person am I?	To evaluate stories	Examining respectful behaviour	127
PE QCA unit: Gymnastic activities unit 1	Does it fit?	To compare and evaluate apparatus	Evaluating which pieces of apparatus best support gymastic sequences	129

DINOSAUR FACTS

SUBJECT: ENGLISH. NLS OBJECTIVE: TO LOCATE PARTS OF TEXT THAT GIVE INFORMATION.

LEARNING OBJECTIVE
To read to find facts, and to begin to understand that the reader selects according to need.

THINKING OBJECTIVE
To evaluate information and develop criteria for judging.

THINKING SKILLS
The children will be presented with information on a known topic, but the focus will be on evaluating whether the information they have is useful or not. The children will start by asking questions about the topic to identify what they want to find out. They will look carefully at the information given to decide, based on their own criteria, whether it is useful or not. Only then will they try to answer their own questions.

WHAT YOU NEED
A poster or fact sheet on a chosen topic; Internet access; a collection of books on the chosen topic; paper and writing materials; board or flip chart.

WHAT TO DO
Show the children the poster or fact sheet you have chosen to use, for example of a tyrannosaurus, and ask what they can see. Encourage them to describe the dinosaur and to talk about its particular features. In response to their descriptions ask, *How do you know?* Try to get them to tell you that the information has come from the poster.

Develop a set of questions that the children would like to know about this dinosaur and write these as a list on the board. Let the children think of their own questions, but they could include:
- How big was it?
- What did it eat?
- How did it move?
- Where did it live?
- How long ago did it live?

Ask the children to evaluate the poster and decide whether it contains the information needed to answer each of the questions. Go through the list of questions and get them to try to answer each in turn. If the children have difficulty answering any of the questions due to insufficient information on the poster, ask them how useful they think the poster is for finding the answers to the questions. Ask, *Is there enough information on the poster?*

Organise the children into groups and give each group a copy of the questions. Give them a selection of books or let them use the Internet, to try to find the answers to their questions. Finish by asking them to evaluate which resource was most useful for answering the questions.

DIFFERENTIATION
Extend the activity by asking more able children to find additional material in the library. This will involve them using a library catalogue system, and contents and index pages. The material they choose should be useful to their purpose and they should only return with the books if they provide answers to some or all of the questions.

Ask another adult to work with the lower attaining children, researching one dinosaur on a CD-ROM or in a book where facts are written simply as labels or short paragraphs. The children should evaluate whether the information is useful or not while the adult reads to them.

WHERE NEXT
Use other reference material you have available and repeat the activity on a different topic. Prepare the questions beforehand, or ask the children to devise their own, before letting them go ahead to evaluate the information sources.

ASSESSMENT
Note the children who stray from the task. Some may enjoy looking at the material because of its interest, rather than evaluating it in specific terms. Note this and organise a similar task to include this topic in the future.

LEARNING OUTCOMES
The children will learn to evaluate the usefulness of literary material in terms of predetermined criteria. They will make decisions about which is the most useful to the task. Some children will develop research skills of locating information using an index and contents page, and learning to use a library index system.

FURTHER ENGLISH CHALLENGES

Useful or not

Give the children a set of questions about any topic that you are working on at the moment. In groups, give them a set of information material, some of which contains the information they will need and some which does not. Ask the children to evaluate each piece of material and say which contains the

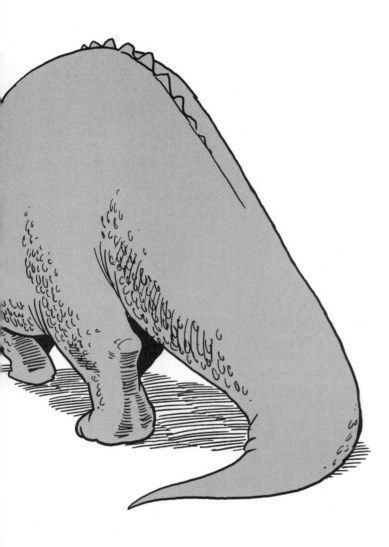

information they are looking for. Are there any which duplicate the information found in another source? Which one holds the most useful information?

How, what, where, when, who and why?

Organise a research activity in geography, history or science that requires the children to find suitable sources of information to answer questions raised in an enquiry lesson.

SWEET FACTS

SUBJECT: MATHEMATICS. NNS OBJECTIVE: SORTING, CLASSIFYING AND ORGANISING INFORMATION IN SIMPLE WAYS.

LEARNING OBJECTIVE

To present information as a chart or graph.

THINKING OBJECTIVE

To evaluate mathematical information (judging usefulness).

THINKING SKILLS

The children will be involved in a common sorting and graphing activity, but rather than answering a set of questions based on this information directly, they will be evaluating whether the information allows them to answer their set of questions. They will appreciate that not all information is always useful for finding answers to certain questions, because the information that has been collected is limited.

WHAT YOU NEED

Packets of the same sweets (the sweets must be different colours); a large sheet of paper or foil; a prepared sheet of questions about sweets (one copy per child); paper and writing materials; board or flip chart.

WHAT TO DO

Explain to the children that they are going to evaluate whether information always gives answers to questions. Give the children a copy of the questions at this point. Include some questions for which the information collected will not give the answer, such as *Which one tastes the best? Do all the packets contain the same number of sweets?*

Show the children a packet of sweets and ask them to say what they think is inside. Ask who likes sweets and be prepared for the noise! Tell the children that they need to find out how many sweets of each colour there are in the packet to help them to answer the questions. Invite them to suggest how they might discover this and how they might record the results.

Empty the contents of the sweet packet onto a clean sheet of paper or foil and ask two children to quickly sort the sweets into sets according to colour. Complete a tally chart on the board as fast as you can in response. Look at the first colour on your chart. Count the number of sweets and either record it as a tally total or fill in a graph, depending on the children's level of understanding.

Ask the children to look at your sheet of questions again. Tell the children that they are going to find out whether the information you have recorded about the different numbers of coloured sweets gives them the answers to your questions. Read out the first question. For example, *How many red sweets are there?* or *Which coloured sweet is found most often in your packet?* or *Which sweet tastes the best?* Ask the children to look at the graph or tally chart and decide if the question can be answered. If it can, tell them to write *Yes* next to the question, if not to write *No*. Continue with the next question or two, until you are sure the children understand what to do.

Form the class into groups and ask them to repeat the activity, working their way down the list of questions. Work with any groups that need support to reinforce their understanding of how they are evaluating the information they have collected for its usefulness.

Finally, go through the list of questions again and evaluate whether the children agree on which questions can be answered. Ask, *How can we find the answer to those questions that cannot be answered? Is there a better way of finding out?*

DIFFERENTIATION
Allow higher attaining groups to carry out their own investigation into how many sweets are in each packet. Some children will be able to compare their answers and reach conclusions about whether there is always the same number of red sweets in each packet, or whether there are always the most of the same colour each time.

Encourage some children to identify their own questions they want answered before recording the numbers of each colour in their own packets of sweets. They should then answer *Yes* or *No* in evaluating whether the information is useful enough to allow them to find the answer to their questions.

Make the lower attaining children your focus group so that you can reinforce the purpose of the activity.

WHERE NEXT
This activity can also be done with Liquorice Allsorts and can include questions about 3-D shapes.

ASSESSMENT
Note the children who understand that they are able to answer the questions because of the clear way the information is presented, and that they can answer questions only about the colour of the sweets because this is the information they collected.

LEARNING OUTCOMES
The children will practise their skills in collecting and suggesting how to present data. They will begin to evaluate the information they have collected by noting whether certain questions can be answered by using it.

FURTHER MATHS CHALLENGES
Sweet challenge
Give each child a fun-sized packet of sweets and ask them to find out whether they have the same number,

colour and size of sweets in their packet as the other children in their group. How did they collect and record the information? Was this way useful? Did it help them to find the answer to the question?

Giant sweets
Give each child a larger packet of sweets and ask them to estimate and then find out how many sweets are in each packet. How did they find out? Did they guess, and then count each sweet individually? Was this a useful way of estimating? How many children used what they found out from the smaller fun-sized packets in the 'Sweet challenge' activity to make

more accurate estimates? When the children realise that this is a useful way to support their estimates give them a different sized packet of sweets and ask them to estimate how many sweets this packet contains. Did they use the smaller packets to help solve the problem? Was this a useful way?

MIRROR, MIRROR

SUBJECT: SCIENCE. QCA UNIT: 1C SORTING AND USING MATERIALS.

LEARNING OBJECTIVE
To investigate properties of materials.

THINKING OBJECTIVE
To evaluate (judging quality).

THINKING SKILLS
The children will evaluate a range of materials and, along with reasoning skills, evaluate the quality of each material and whether each one can be used as a mirror. They will need to reason which materials are shiny and some children will begin to realise that it is because the surface reflects light. The Further

science challenges will provide the opportunity to make some surfaces shinier by applying polish, which will show a reflection, and to explore what happens to the reflection when the 'mirrors' are bent in different ways.

WHAT YOU NEED
A collection of objects made from different materials, some which reflect light, such as sheets of foil, polished wood and metal, plastic sheeting, car windscreen sun shieds, and some which don't.

WHAT TO DO
Put out a range of materials, some which are shiny and some which are not. Sort the materials together, according to their properties. Start with familiar properties so that the children can start from what they already know. Then ask the children to name other ways of sorting the materials. If no one suggests it, sort the materials according to whether they are shiny. Ask, *What do these objects have in common? Are they all smooth? Are the things that are not shiny all rough?*

Look at the shiny things in your materials collection. Can the children see their reflection in any of them? Ask, *How well can you see your reflection? Is it good enough to see to comb your hair in?* Explain that the object is shiny and shows a reflection because the material is reflecting a lot of light. Get the children to evaluate the materials and their ability to reflect light, and to sort them into groups of poor reflectors, medium reflectors and good reflectors.

Repeat the evaluating and sorting activity with a different set of shiny materials. Use unusual shaped and coloured objects to tease the children's evaluations, such as a spoon, kitchen pots and pans, coloured metals. Ask, *Does the red foil give a red reflection? Why does your reflection look bent in the spoon?*

DIFFERENTIATION
Ask those who are ready for extension to investigate reflections in water. Put water into different containers, including one container that is clear, and ask the children to predict whether they will see their reflection in each. Will they see their reflection in the clear container? Why not? Explain that unless the container is placed on a dark non-transparent surface, the light will pass through the container and not be reflected back because the container is transparent.

Work with lower attainers to explore metal materials first to establish the concept of shininess. When you are sure they understand, move onto other non-metallic materials to explore.

WHERE NEXT
Link the concept to road safety issues, such as being seen in the dark. Look at a range of clothing and

other items that have reflective strips attached. Get the children to evaluate these in terms of their light-reflecting quality.

Look at bicycle reflectors and talk about how these can be seen in the dark. Let the children play with a range of these using torches in a dark place. Ask them to evaluate the ability of the bike reflectors to reflect light.

ASSESSMENT

Note the children who understand why some materials make good mirrors. Watch the children and question them about their choices. Are they choosing a particular material because it is shinier and smoother?

LEARNING OUTCOMES

The children will learn to evaluate the things with which they are working to help inform their choices and decisions. They will sort materials according to their properties.

FURTHER SCIENCE CHALLENGES

Mirror, mirror on the wall

Give the children a range of materials, such as wood, rigid plastic sheets, tin foil and metal, and a tin of polish. Challenge them to polish the surface to make a mirror. You will need to supervise this activity carefully and make sure that the children use the polish safely. Check to see if the children choose suitable materials. Ask the children to evaluate which make the best mirrors by putting the materials in order from the one that makes the best mirror to the one which is the least effective. Talk about why.

Hall of mirrors

Make a hall of mirrors with large sheets of card covered in foil or windscreen sunshields, and bend them in different directions. Remind the children about their explorations with the spoons and pots and pans in the main activity, and ask them to predict what they will look like when they look at themselves in the 'mirrors' that are bent in different directions. Perhaps some children have been in a hall of mirrors at a funfair. Make a note of the predictions and test this out afterwards. Ask the children to describe the different ways that they look as the mirrors are bent in different directions. Can any of the children suggest why this happens? Ask them to arrange the mirrors in what they think are the best order to create more fun – measured by whoops and laughter. Evaluate the quality of these mirrors as a class – which give a good reflection and which offer the most fun.

CAPTAIN COOK

SUBJECT: HISTORY. QCA UNIT: UNIT 4 WHY DO WE REMEMBER FLORENCE NIGHTINGALE?

LEARNING OBJECTIVE

To learn about a famous person from the past.

THINKING OBJECTIVE

To evaluate and interpret evidence.

THINKING SKILLS

The children will look at a range of sources of evidence to find out about Captain Cook and his voyage to Australia. They will evaluate which evidence is most useful and reliable for finding out particular things about him and his travels.

What you need

A narrative of Captain Cook's travels to Australia; a map of the world; reference books, Internet access; a portrait of Captain Cook; paper and writing materials; board or flip chart.

What to do

Tell the children the story of Captain Cook's voyages and how he was one of the first Europeans to sail to Australia. Use the portrait of Captain Cook and plot his progress on a map to add interest. Tell the children that he sailed between England and Australia between 1768 and 1771. Talk about his ship *Endeavour* and the kind of ship that it was. Ask the children how they think people know this information. What sources of evidence might they have used to find out?

Talk about the range of evidence available that would give this information. Suggest sources of infomation we have now that would not have been available at the time, such as photographs, accounts recorded on television and radio. Can the children suggest any evidence that may have been recorded at the time, such as paintings and drawings by people who travelled with Captain Cook.

Make a list on the board of some of the things the children might want to know about this man and his adventures. For example,
⊙ What was the name of his ship?
⊙ What did Captain Cook look like?
⊙ How many people were in his crew?
⊙ What did they eat and drink when at sea?
⊙ Did anyone catch any nasty diseases?

Split the class into groups and give each group a question from the list to research. Ask them to list the evidence that would be useful in finding the answers. For example, to find out the name of Cook's ship the children could use pictures drawn by people on the ship, stories told by people he met and worked with, the ship's log – from reference books and the Internet. To find out whether anyone caught any diseases, the ship's log would probably be the most useful piece of evidence. By working in groups the children should support and spark ideas off one another. Follow up some of the lines of enquiry that the children suggest. Find out which piece of evidence was most useful in answering each question. Why?

Differentiation

Work with lower attaining children on one piece of evidence and help them evaluate all the information that can be gleaned from this. For example, look at a picture of Captain Cook and talk about what he is wearing, what he looks like and the kind of things he used. Ask, *Does he have a watch? Why not? Does he wear the same kind of clothes as men do today? How are they different?* Evaluate with the children whether this portrait was useful to help them find out a bit more about Captain Cook. How was it most useful – to tell us what he looked like or to tell us about his voyage to Australia?

Ask higher attainers to list all the sources of evidence that are available today that were not available at the time of Captain Cook. These will include reference books and the Internet and will rely on people's recollections and interpretations of what happened. Are these sources of information more or less reliable than the artefacts from the time of Captain Cook?

Where next

Repeat the activity with other famous people and events.

Assessment

Look at the children's ability to evaluate the range of evidence available today and at the time of Captain Cook. Who has managed to interpret the evidence to find out what they wanted to know?

Learning outcomes

The children will learn about someone who is famous. They will consider and evaluate many sources of evidence, deciding which are useful and which are not so useful in helping them find particular information about the person.

Further history challenges

Where in the world?
Use the evidence the children have found to track the voyages of Captain Cook as he sailed around the world. Ask, *How do we know he went to these places?* List all the sources of evidence the children evaluate as reliable in finding out this information, and display these alongside a large map of the world and a picture of Cook's ship.

CROSSING SAFELY

SUBJECT: GEOGRAPHY. QCA UNIT: 2 HOW CAN WE MAKE OUR LOCAL AREA SAFER?

LEARNING OBJECTIVE
To identify safe places to cross roads on a map of the local area.

THINKING OBJECTIVE
To evaluate information.

THINKING SKILLS
The children will consider places in the local area where it is safe to cross the roads. They will evaluate the places in terms of whether they have been specifically designed to keep pedestrians safe from traffic. Talk about dangers of crossing the road without an adult to reinforce safety rules. We certainly do not want to encourage the children to go out by themselves.

WHAT YOU NEED
A large map or plan of the local area (this can be a commercially bought one or one that the children have made themselves during a previous lesson); the same map divided into smaller sections for group work (include the local High Street, a local supermarket including car park, different routes to school, the local park and so on); information from a traffic survey of the local area.

WHAT TO DO
Show the children some of the information in the traffic survey and identify together where the busiest place is for local traffic. Ask, *Is there anywhere where it is usually quiet? Where is it almost always busy? Where is it dangerous to cross the road?* Interpret the information together to find out whether certain roads are busier at certain times of the day.

Then show the children the large map of the local area and ask them to identify a few instances where there are crossing points for pedestrians, such as underpasses, pelican crossings, zebra crossings or places where crossing patrol people cross the children. Ask, *Why do you think these special crossing places have been put where they have? How many safe places to cross can you see on the map? Why is this place safe?* Mark these safe places together on the map. Talk also about how to use the different crossing places in terms of waiting for the green man, looking both ways and listening, waiting for an adult to stop the traffic before crossing, and so on.

Explain to the children that you want them to find all the places in the local area where it is safe to cross the road. Divide the children into smaller groups and give each group a different section of the map to concentrate on. Ask them to talk about and negotiate where they think safe places to cross the road are. Work with one group, but from time to time monitor the other groups so that they are clear about what is expected. Ask them why they have chosen a particular place and so on.

Invite each group to tell the rest of the class the reasons why they have chosen the places they have on their section of the map. Transfer the children's ideas to the large map and put this on the wall so that the children can see all the places where they have suggested it is safe to cross roads. Identify all the places where it is definitely not safe to cross the road and indicate these on the map with red crosses or pedestrian symbols with a line through.

If appropriate talk about when and where crossing patrol is on duty outside the school. Why is the person here at these particular times?

DIFFERENTIATION
Ask higher attaining children to identify on their map where it would be a good idea to have extra crossings. What information do they have to back up their evaluation?

WHERE NEXT
Look at photographs of different areas that show roads and places that the children are likely to need to get to, for example the local park, library, shops or school itself. Ask the children to evaluate whether and where it is safe to cross in each place. Ask them to discuss and put the photographs into a list of *safe* and *not safe*.

Discuss the different safety measures that could be developed in the places in the local area where the children identified that it was not safe to cross certain roads.

Write a class safety code for crossing the road. Make sure you include the need to be with an adult. Look at a picture map of the Isle of Struay from one of the Katie Morag stories and talk about where it could be dangerous to cross the road. What might the dangers be and how can Katie overcome these?

ASSESSMENT

Record which children can evaluate whether it is safe to cross a particular road or not, and tell you why. Talk to the children about the places they have identified as safe crossing points and assess their level of understanding about the need to always have an adult when crossing the road. Note which children can evaluate where good places would be for pedestrian crossings and at what times of the day it would be most desirable to have crossing patrol on duty outside the school.

LEARNING OUTCOMES

The children will record information and ideas accurately on a plan or map to show specific information they have evaluated about the local area.

FURTHER GEOGRAPHY CHALLENGES

Make it safe

Give the children photographs of different places to look at. Include places of local interest and those with which they are not familiar. Make sure that each one shows a place where it is not safe to cross without some kind of traffic control. Ask the children

to glue each photograph to a piece of paper and to evaluate in groups where they think any traffic controlling measures need to be introduced to calm the traffic.

Traffic calming

Talk to the children about the different traffic-calming measures that have been introduced in some parts of the country, such as traffic lights, speed bumps, roundabouts, one-way systems and speed restrictions. Ask the children to choose and evaluate which may be the best solution to calming traffic in their locality. Encourage them to give reasons for their choices.

A MODEL STREET

SUBJECT: DESIGN AND TECHNOLOGY. QCA UNIT: 1D HOMES.

LEARNING OBJECTIVE

To assemble and join models of houses.

THINKING OBJECTIVE

To evaluate materials.

THINKING SKILLS

This activity focuses on the children choosing their own resources by evaluating which are most suitable for the task. This approach can be used in other subjects including art and design, music and PE. Instead of giving the children a range of materials from which to choose, give them more freedom to direct their own learning by asking them to identify materials for themselves when they plan their model. They should nevertheless be guided into choosing those that will make their models as realistic as possible. Link the work to learning about 3-D shapes in maths.

WHAT YOU NEED

Photographs of houses and flats; large sheets of paper and felt-tipped pens; a range of materials for making, including boxes, card, paper, sheets of plastic, wood and transparent materials; a range of tools for cutting and joining, including scissors, snips, glue, masking tape and staplers; a range of materials for finishing, including fabrics, paint, recycled materials; construction kits; a large flat space to display the finished model street.

WHAT TO DO

Model the design process with the children. Show them the photographs and talk to them about the houses and flats shown. Tell them that you want them to design a block of flats as a class. Draw the front view on a large sheet of paper, discussing with the children all the time if this is what they want. Ask them to say what kind of windows they would like – Georgian style, plain or with leaded criss-cross patterns.

Decide together how to make the building. Ask the children, *Should we use boxes or card? How will we join them together to make the block of flats? What materials will we use to make the windows, doors and roof tiles? What properties should the material for making the window panes have?* Label the design with the children's suggestions.

Then let the children work individually or in pairs to design and make their own model house. As they work, talk about the things they will use to make each part. Talk with them about how they will join the pieces together and how they will add features such as tiles, chimneys, television aerials, doors and windows. Some may decide to paint the detail onto their design. Evaluate the finished models together and talk about whether the finished models look like the original designs.

Explain to the children that now you want them to make a street with the houses they have made. Revisit the work you have done, if appropriate, discussing the different types of houses and homes. Ask the class to decide how many detached and semi-detached houses they would like to have in their street. Ask questions to focus the children on methods of making the street, such as *How will you join the houses together to make a street? Will the buildings be close together? Will they be separated by flats, garages or shops?*

Once the children have decided what their street will look like, place the models of the houses in a row on the display surface. Allow the children to try out different arrangements until they are happy with the street. Add to the street by asking the children to make models of other buildings, for example a block of flats, garden sheds and garages. They could make gardens for some of the houses, too.

DIFFERENTIATION

Talk to those who need help choosing which materials would be suitable for windows, brickwork, gutters and doors. Display photographs of buildings in the centre of the table for the children to refer to as they make their models and draw their attention to the materials which would be suitable for making each part of their model house.

WHERE NEXT

Get the children to select suitable materials from which to make street furniture for the finished model. Let the children use their personal observations of the things that are found in their own street to stimulate their ideas.

ASSESSMENT

Note the children who choose suitable materials for the different parts of their model house. Make a particular note of those who give good reasons for their choices, for example choosing transparent materials for the windows. For those who find this difficult, focus on developing their skills in the Further design and technology challenge 'Cinderella's castle'.

LEARNING OUTCOMES

The children will construct a model based on their own design. They will evaluate the suitability of which materials to

use before starting the making task. Many will be able to give reasons for their choices. They will use their evaluation skills to construct a street with their models, making improvements so that the finished model is as realistic as possible.

FURTHER DESIGN AND TECHNOLOGY CHALLENGES

Skyscraper city

Ask the children to work in groups to build skyscrapers. Allow them to use construction kits, such as constructo straws, mobilo or quadro for the frame. They can make the windows by attaching cut-out frames filled with transparent paper. They could make card fascias by photocopying brickwork patterns onto brick-coloured paper and attaching these to the structure to make the walls.

Evaluate the finished skyscrapers. Do they stand up straight? Which kits are the most effective for this? Are they all suitable? Can anyone think of any other kind of material which would make skyscrapers and would stand up better? Challenge the children to make a skyscraper from wood and card. How will they join the wooden frame to make the structure strong enough to be very tall?

Cinderella's castle

Let the children choose different types of buildings to make from 3-D shapes. Look at an image of Cinderella's castle from a film or illustration. Florida travel brochures will have good pictures in them, or you could find one on the Internet. The children should identify and find suitable materials and shapes, and join them together to make the castle. Encourage them to make a hinged door for the front of the castle and to add floors so that they can act out the story as a castle role-play activity using small toys.

POSTER MAGIC

SUBJECT: ICT. QCA UNIT: 2A WRITING STORIES: COMMUNICATING INFORMATION USING TEXT.

LEARNING OBJECTIVES

To use ICT to communicate ideas through text; to enter text and correct it.

THINKING OBJECTIVE

To evaluate work and make improvements.

THINKING SKILLS

The children will discuss the intended audience for a poster they will create, and evaluate whether the finished poster is easy to read and conveys the intended message. They will make improvements to their work by editing on screen, discussing with a partner and considering how the computer makes it easier to make changes.

WHAT YOU NEED

A commercial poster; a prepared computer file containing a border, pictures and boxes for the text; a spelling sheet containing the information for your chosen context; interactive whiteboard (optional).

WHAT TO DO

Spend a few moments looking at the poster with the children. Discuss the text, pictures and the way that the information is displayed.

Talk to the children about the class poster you want them to create. This could be a healthy eating poster, a poster to reinforce the class rules or to advertise a forthcoming school event.

As a class, open your prepared file at the computer. Focus the children's attention on planning how the poster should look by asking questions, such as *Where do you think the title should go? How big should this be?* Show the children how to use the font icon to select the type and size they want. Type in the title of the event and try it in different font styles, sizes and colours. Ask the children to decide which one they would like to use. Next, think about the other information that the audience will need to know. Get the children to key this into the document and read it through together.

Let the children evaluate the poster and edit the title and information as they wish, perhaps adding a picture or symbols. Save the work and print out a copy. Add a sentence at the bottom to summarise the key message of the poster. For example, *Eat fresh fruit and vegetables to keep yourself healthy.* Show the children how to edit the sentence to make it correct if necessary by using the shift key for capitals and arrow keys to move the cursor to the correct place.

Gather the children together so that they can see the computer screen or interactive whiteboard, or wait until you return to the classroom with paper copies. Talk through the poster that the children have created and note good things about it. Ask, *Can the text be seen easily from a distance? Is it easy to read? What about the choice of colour? Are you happy with the way you have organised the pictures and text?*

Allow the children to make any changes and improvements by altering the text on screen. Save the second version and compare the two to note and evaluate the improvements. Is the poster clearer now? Talk about the benefits of using the computer for this process.

DIFFERENTIATION

Invite higher attaining children to use clip art to add additional pictures to the poster and to move the existing items around.

Ask an additional adult to work with lower attaining children so that they can talk about the poster they have created. Prompt the adult with questions so that they can get the children to evaluate for themselves and identify how they can make any improvements.

WHERE NEXT

Get the children to use the same computer skills to make celebration cards, calendars and labels. Give the children a particular purpose and audience so that they can evaluate whether the finished design fulfils its intention.

ASSESSMENT

Listen to the children's comments as they work. Note those who consider the importance of seeing the text clearly. How many changes do they want to make? Which children are aware of how much easier and more time-saving it is to make changes using a computer than when writing and drawing by hand.

LEARNING OUTCOMES

The children will develop text and layout on screen and recognise that they can make changes to improve it. They will evaluate whether the poster's message is clear for its intended audience.

FURTHER ICT CHALLENGES

Elephant magic

Draw an outline of an elephant on a whiteboard and challenge the children to decorate it by drawing lines to make a colourful pattern. Encourage the children to evaluate their work as they progress, to make any changes which will improve the finished picture. Challenge higher attainers to add spots and stripes in different colours to add interest to the design.

Sweet delight

Provide the children with an outline picture of a sweet wrapper. Challenge them to add colour to the sweet and the background before finding a suitable colour in which to write the name of the sweet. Evaluate the designs to make sure that the name stands out clearly to the buyer.

DOES IT LOOK RIGHT?

SUBJECT: ART AND DESIGN. QCA UNIT: 1B INVESTIGATING MATERIALS.

LEARNING OBJECTIVE

To consider colour and shape in creating a stitch-work design.

THINKING OBJECTIVE
To evaluate personal likes and dislikes, and to suggest improvements to a design.

THINKING SKILLS
The children will consider their likes and dislikes before using this information to design their own table mat. They will use suitable colours to create a design on paper, which will allow them to see what the finished mat will look like before they start. They will continue to evaluate their mat as they sew and make any changes they think will improve the finished product.

WHAT YOU NEED
A prepared sampler of stitches; Binca; a selection of embroidery threads; crayons or pencils to match the colours of the threads in the selection; dotted paper.

WHAT TO DO
Use the ideas in the illustration on the left to prepare the sampler of stitches. Talk to the children about which stitches they like and get them to talk about the colours and shapes of the stitches. Ask them to say why they like the particular ones that they do. Explain to the children that you want them to design and make their own table mat, using decorative stitches.

Show the children the different threads you have available. Pass them round and invite the children to say which they think would be best for their finished table mat. Ask them to give reasons for their choices.

Give each child a piece of Binca and ask them to start thinking about what their table mat will look like. Tell them to decide whether they are going to have rows of stitches, whether they intend to go around the outside, then move further towards the centre with each row of stitches, or whether they want to divide their piece of Binca into smaller squares. Perhaps they want a mixture of these. They should be encouraged to think about this before embarking on their design. Give them a piece of dotted paper and ask them to design their own stitch pattern and colours to use. When they have finished, talk about the stitches and colours they have chosen. Ask, *What do you think of the colour combinations? Have you used an interesting range of stitches? Why do you like this stitch next to this one?* Perhaps the children have chosen their favourite colour or the favourite of a special person to whom they intend to give the finished mat.

Start the children off on their individual sewing. Talk to each child about their design and make sure that they do not want to make any improvements or alterations to their design before starting. Having an additional adult would help here. Organise several sessions for the children to complete their designs before allowing them to start sewing.

DIFFERENTIATION
Talk to the children who have difficulty with colour, shape and pattern or prompt any adult working with the children to help them select their next stitch from the sampler. Allow those who are able, to choose their own stitch and colour independently. Ask them to give reasons for their choices as you start them off, using questions as prompts.

WHERE NEXT
Repeat the activity, asking the children to make bookmarks, perhaps for a school charity event or for the children to use in their individual reading books.

Talk with the children about mats and other designs that use cross-stitch to make the pictures and patterns. Encourage the children to say whether they like particular patterns or not, giving reasons for their opinions in terms of colour and shape.

ASSESSMENT
Note the children who go beyond exploring ideas to investigating different combinations of colour and pattern. Which children think of more complicated designs, which use a range of different sizes and shapes of stitches to add interest and make improvements to their work? Which children design some kind of structure to the overall design such as four symmetrical sections? Which children are continually looking at their work and making changes to improve the design?

LEARNING OUTCOMES
Most children will learn about the visual and tactile elements of colour, pattern and texture. They will use this knowledge to design and make stitch-work pieces. They will review what they have done and say how they can improve their designs.

FURTHER ART AND DESIGN CHALLENGES

Trellis stitch

Tell the children you want them to design and make a garden fresco panel for the school garden. Show them a trellis panel which you can use as a basis for weaving different materials. The children's designs could include feathers, ribbons, natural materials and string. Invite the children to create a large version of the stitches they used on their sewing in the main activity, including running and cross stitch. Evaluate the finished trellis to see if it is as attractive as the original design.

Copycat

Make drawings of a stitch-work pattern for the children to copy by sewing. Allow the children to choose different colours if they wish. Afterwards, compare the different versions of the patterns and ask the children to say which one they like best and why.

126 THE CASTLE CELLAR

SUBJECT: MUSIC. QCA UNIT: 2 SOUNDS INTERESTING.

LEARNING OBJECTIVE

To explore different sound sources.

THINKING OBJECTIVE

To evaluate instruments (judging usefulness).

THINKING SKILLS

The children will evaluate the usefulness of an instrument in creating a desired sound. They will decide whether an instrument can be played in a different way to change the sound to create a particular mood. They will express thoughts and feelings about the sounds created and say how these can be improved to create a better effect.

WHAT YOU NEED

The poem 'This is the key to the castle' by Dave Calder, published in *Twinkle, Twinkle Chocolate Bar* compiled by John Foster (Oxford University Press); sets of instruments for each group of children (a range that will give the children the opportunity to develop and combine different types of sounds as well as changes in dynamics, pitch and tempo).

WHAT TO DO

Read 'This is the key to the castle' to the children and ask them to suggest the kind of sound effects they could make to accompany the poem. Look briefly at the instruments and quickly remind the children of the sounds that they make. Spend no more than five minutes on this.

Put the children into small groups and tell them to choose an instrument each to add sound effects to the first part of the poem. Let them go off and practise the effects they want to make, exchanging their instruments if they wish. After about ten minutes bring the children back together and listen to each group in turn. After each group performance, ask the other children to say which instruments effectively portray the different objects in the poem, such as the cellar, the stairs or the rat, in the poem. Can anyone suggest a different way to play each instrument to make the sound effect more striking?

When each group have performed, choose the best sounds to depict each object and choose half the class to perform the final combination of sounds alongside a reading of the poem.

Ask general questions about the instruments and their sounds to finish, such as *Which instrument makes a bright/warm/dull/dingy sound? Which instruments are good for making sounds that move up and down?*

How can you make sounds go faster or slower on different instruments?

DIFFERENTIATION

Extend the activity for more confident musicians by introducing silence as an element. Talk about how this contributes to the mood and effect of a piece of music. Make sure that children with hearing difficulties have their particular needs met as outlined in the individual education plan. Organise a spot where these children can work where there is little or no background noise.

WHERE NEXT

Record the music pictorially, showing how the instruments will be played to create the desired effect. Ask the children to evaluate whether the score relates this to the performer. How will the changes in pitch, duration, dynamics and tempo be shown?

ASSESSMENT

Listen to the children as they work in their groups, noting down their evaluation comments about why they have chosen a particular instrument. Notice whether they are relating their choice to the effect they want to create or because they like to play this particular instrument. Note the children who put more than one instrument together to create different textures of sound. Encourage the children to use musical language when they are explaining to you why they chose to use the instrument(s) that they have.

LEARNING OUTCOMES

Most children will learn that sounds can be made in different ways and that the same instrument can produce different kinds of sound. They will work together to contribute ideas and evaluate their part in creating a class composition. They will evaluate how different musical elements can be organised to reflect a particular mood.

FURTHER MUSIC CHALLENGES

A sound story

Read a story with a jungle setting and challenge the children to think about all the sounds that are likely to be heard. Working in groups so the children can evaluate their composition together, get them to compose a sound picture to tell the story of a walk through the jungle. Let the children choose from a full range of instruments, including culturally diverse ones. Help those who need it by playing some jungle sounds from a television or radio programme, or use a taped story which contains sound effects.

In a dark, dark house

Read *Funnybones* by Janet and Allan Ahlberg (Puffin) to the children and ask them to identify all the sounds that they are likely to hear as the skeletons go about their business. Invite the children to evaluate different instruments that would be most suitable to create a sound picture of the story.

WHAT SORT OF PERSON AM I?

SUBJECT: RE. QCA UNIT: 2B WHY DID JESUS TELL STORIES?

LEARNING OBJECTIVE

To behave respectfully to the values and concerns of others.

THINKING OBJECTIVE

To evaluate stories.

THINKING SKILLS

The children will consider how different characters in familiar stories make each other feel. They will evaluate certain behaviour and decide how this impacts on others. They will relate this to their own experience and reflect upon the times when someone's behaviour has made them feel a particular way. Finally, they will relate this to what they have learned about why Jesus told stories or their work on the Jewish faith.

WHAT YOU NEED

Pictures of cartoon and story characters, particularly those from 'Snow White' and 'Cinderella'; a classroom toy; stories from the Bible or the Torah; board or flip chart.

WHAT TO DO

Organise the children into a circle. Spend a few moments (as a circle time activity if you wish) naming and talking about the children's favourite story character and why they like that particular one. Ask, *Is the character kind? Has he or she done something useful?* Talk to the children about the characteristics of some of the figures they are familiar with, for example the manner of the Ugly Sisters and their treatment of Cinderella. Ask the children to compare this with the way Buttons behaved towards her. Ask, *Which character showed a respect for Cinderella's feelings? Which characters showed no respect?*

Pass your usual toy round the circle and invite the children to contribute an idea for a story book character, or someone from personal experience, who is particularly kind, brave or who has done something for someone else in order to support them. Allow those children who want to contribute to hold the toy while they talk, while those who do not want to make a contribution can pass the toy onto the next person. If there is time, ask the children to also name a character that has been cruel or unkind.

Choose a different story, for example 'Snow White', and list all the characters in that story on the board. Ask the children to decide whether each character has a respect for the feelings of other characters in the story. How do the children know? Ask, *How should the character change his behaviour to show a respect for the feelings of others?*

Read a suitable story from the Bible, such as The Good Samaritan, or about Moses from the Torah. Ask the children to evaluate the characters and identify those who have been kind and those who have not. Talk about what the story is saying and the message it is giving.

Finish with a circle activity getting the children to talk about their own personal experiences of times when someone has been kind. Explain to the children that they are evaluating a suitable story that they can tell others to explain a particular message about kindness.

DIFFERENTIATION
Extend the activity for those who are more able by listing the titles of stories with which the children are familiar and asking them to evaluate the main 'message' from each one. Work with lower attaining children on one story and identify how each character behaves. Ask, *How does this make the others feel? How should the character behave instead?*

WHERE NEXT
Make a list of all the stories the children can think of which teach them about how they should behave towards others. Include those from the Bible or from other religions the children have studied. Make a judgement about how well the stories teach us about how to behave and respect the feelings of others.

Relate respect and behaviour to the children's own experience by talking about issues in school, for example a classmate who is kind, or times when they have had problems with other children. Check that they all know what to do if they have problems in school and address any issues raised. Hold meetings to talk about behaviour on the playground and how the children can make this time better for everyone, such as not excluding people from games.

ASSESSMENT
Listen to the children's contributions and note those who are aware that stories often tell a message which

helps us to understand how to treat and respect others' feelings and beliefs.

LEARNING OUTCOMES
Most children will learn that many stories teach us how to behave towards each other. They will evaluate stories from the Bible or Torah and use them to help decide for themselves how they should behave.

FURTHER RE CHALLENGES
Character charades
Set up a role-play area for the children to act out their favourite stories. Choose a particular message each week and ask the children to think of a story that reflects this message. Concentrate on one story each week so that the children can develop a good understanding of the characters. Challenge

the children to make up a mime and to show through their body language and expression the kind of person they are depicting. Invite them to perform the mime to the other children during circle time, for them to guess the name of the character and the message they are conveying. When all those who want to take part have finished, ask the children to evaluate which character it was easiest to guess and why. Did the mime depict the message chosen that week and if so why? How did the children use body language to depict the different characters?

Who am I?

Ask the children to choose part of a story they know that Jesus told, or one from the Torah, depending on the unit you are studying. Develop a class play with no words, which shows the behaviour of the character and what that part of the story teaches. The audience should try to guess the character and story, and evaluate whether the actions tell us the intended message. Talk about how the children guessed the character and story. How did the actors portray the feelings and characters? Did they make it easy because of the expressions they used or by their actions?

DOES IT FIT?

SUBJECT: PE. QCA UNIT: GYMNASTIC ACTIVITIES UNIT 1.

LEARNING OBJECTIVE

To perform movement phrases using a range of body actions and body parts.

THINKING OBJECTIVE

To compare and evaluate apparatus.

THINKING SKILLS

The children will evaluate which apparatus best supports a particular gymnastic sequence. They will make improvements to the quality of their sequence in response to evaluations of how well the apparatus suits it.

WHAT YOU NEED

A range of gymnastic apparatus, such as benches, tables, mats and planks.

WHAT TO DO

In a preparatory PE lesson compose a sequence of moves on the floor which incorporates a travel, turn, jump and balance. Use this as a warm-up activity to remind the children of their movements.

At the beginning of this lesson set up apparatus that will provide a range of opportunities for the children to develop the same sequence at different levels, with flat and sloped surfaces for balancing and opportunities to roll and balance. Allow the children to try out their movements on a chosen piece of apparatus. As they practise their moves, ask them to consider which piece is best suited for the sequence that they developed the week before on the floor.

As the children work, talk to individuals about the suitability of the apparatus to support their sequence. Stop at opportune moments and ask the children to suggest how they could improve the quality of their moves. Encourage them to evaluate carefully which piece of apparatus best suits the sequence. Ask them if they have tried a different piece of apparatus and can compare and evaluate which is best. Ask them why they chose a particular piece over another.

Ask small groups to demonstrate their sequences to each other so that the children can evaluate whether their classmates have chosen the best piece of apparatus. Can the audience suggest a better piece and explain why? Can the children make improvements if they start in a different place? If they finish in a different place, will this make the ending more interesting?

DIFFERENTIATION

Use a wide enough range of low-level and higher-level apparatus to meet the needs of all children. Establish how those with mobility difficulties can use low-level apparatus, which will allow them to balance on the floor, crawl through, along, over or under. Challenge the better gymnasts to evaluate how they can perform their sequences on more challenging apparatus, such as wall bars. Include sequences which have several possible starting and finishing points, and which will allow them to move in different directions at different speeds.

WHERE NEXT

Allow the children to work on each section of the sequence with different types of apparatus in turn. They should evaluate which piece of apparatus is best for the beginning, middle and end of their sequence, and design a combination which will support all sections of the sequence's performance.

ASSESSMENT

Note those who can evaluate which piece of apparatus is best and who can identify a good starting and finishing point to support the quality of their sequences. Note whether some children change their sequences to suit different types and arrangements of apparatus.

LEARNING OUTCOMES

Most children will learn to decide for themselves the most useful type and arrangement of apparatus to suit their sequences.

FURTHER PE CHALLENGES

Apparatus for friends

Set up a large magnetic board or similar, and pictures of the range of apparatus you have. Invite the children to create different combinations of apparatus for other people, using the pictures. Make sure that the children identify the starting and finishing points

of the sequence. Can they think of a more creative place to begin? Can they think of a better way to link some of the movements together? Ask them to say why they have chosen the pieces of apparatus they have and why they have arranged them in this way.

Changing moves

Put out four sets of apparatus which are all very different. Include some which are low level (mats, benches and tables), wall bars with a low balance beam, ladders and tables with some attached at an angle, high tables and mats with no benches or planks between. Allow the children to perform their sequence on the different apparatus. Ask other children to evaluate which is best and to suggest any changes to adapt the sequences to the different types and arrangement of apparatus. How can the children make improvements to the quality of their sequences? Can they vary the levels, direction or speed?

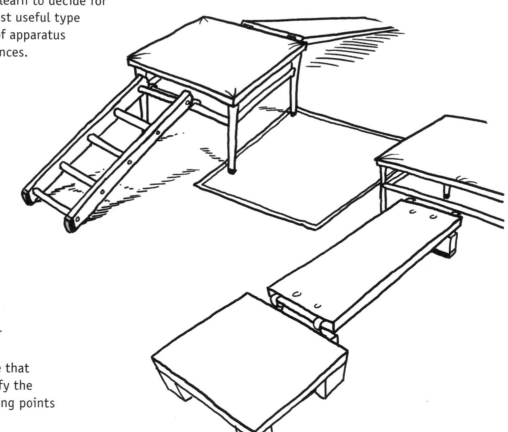

CROSS-CURRICULAR PROJECTS

INTRODUCTION

This chapter draws together the full range of thinking skills into activities which can be taught as a complete project. The chapter offers two themed projects – 'Oh, we do like to be beside the seaside' and 'Hansel and Gretel' – within which the subject areas can be taught. Although one main thinking strategy is identified in each activity, often more than one is being used. For example, in the activity 'Famous authors' in the 'Hansel and Gretel' project (see page 152), the focus is on information processing as the children locate and collect information, but they also use creative thinking skills to extend ideas, and draw upon enquiry skills by asking questions.

The purpose of this chapter is to highlight the thinking skills, and it is the questioning and organisation of learning which carries most importance. Each activity is flexible enough to address several learning objectives. As the purpose is to show how to organise lessons to address the children's development of thinking skills, you may wish to focus on a different learning objective in some lessons.

OH, WE DO LIKE TO BE BESIDE THE SEASIDE

The activities in this project provide a context through which to teach the knowledge and skills identified in the QCA Schemes of Work. To establish links with subjects across the curriculum and to give the project a real feel, you could turn your classroom into a seaside role-play area, creating different areas which could develop all the activities in the project.

Suggestions for role-play areas include:
- Turn your book area into a beach space. Place a Punch and Judy show in the corner and suitable seaside seating around it. This could be garden furniture, beanbags and beach mats.
- Use windbreaks as fencing to separate the different seaside areas. A tent in a camping area could provide a quiet place for children to read. Include a large parasol to create 'shade'.
- Display some holiday fiction and allow the children to choose which books they would like to read.
- To one side of the classroom place a large sand tray, preferably on the floor (you may want this to be surrounded by cupboards so that children don't trip over it), but it could be on a table or a stand, and fill it with different things from which the children can make sand castles and sand sculptures.
- Create a writing area where the children can go to write postcards. A post office is an interesting context to make this area into.
- Make a souvenir shop in the area of the classroom where the children do maths. Or create a seaside café in one area – the children will have fun doing any work in a café. A travel agent is also a good choice of role-play area.

HANSEL AND GRETEL

Many curriculum ideas have been developed which are set within traditional stories. In this project a deliberate attempt has been made to get away from the usual stories that are used. 'Hansel and Gretel' has been chosen because, although some teachers use it to teach children about saying *No* to strangers, it is one which has not traditionally been chosen for other subjects despite being read to children for many years.

The activities in this project can be covered over a week or a longer period. Advice in the National Literacy Strategy now means that teachers often look at one text in detail over a week, and the supporting lessons in this project show how learning in a range of subjects can be promoted through one context. The activities are deliberately planned so that the same subject and thinking focus can be adapted and set within another story context if you wish.

OH, WE DO LIKE TO BE BESIDE THE SEASIDE

Subject and QCA unit, NLS or NNS objective	Activity title	Thinking objective	Activity	Page
English NLS objective: To assemble information from experience ICT QCA unit: 2C Finding information	Write a postcard home	To evaluate the usefulness of information	Interpreting information and using computers to write a postcard about a holiday.	133
Maths NNS objective: To recognise coins and use £ and p notation	Souvenir hunters	To evaluate information and judge monetary value	To write different amounts of money using £ and p notation within a context	134
Science QCA unit: 2D Grouping and changing materials	The seaside café	To predict outcomes, anticipate consequences and test conclusions	Carrying out an investigation into how food items change when exposed to heat	136
History QCA unit: 1 How are our toys different from those in the past?	Seaside toys	To ask and answer questions	Noting the similarities and differences between toys in the past and those used today	137
Geography QCA unit: 4 Going to the seaside	Beaches	To locate and analyse information	Identifying and describing human and physical features on a map and matching them to pictures	138
Design and technology QCA unit: 2C Winding up	The Punch and Judy Show	To analyse mechanisms	Making a moveable curtain for a puppet theatre	139
ICT QCA unit: 2C Finding information	Sandcastle flags	To locate and collect information; to analyse flags	Using search techniques to find flags from the UK and around the world	141
Art and design QCA unit: 1C What is sculpture?	Sand sculptures	To think imaginatively	Exploring natural materials and incorporating these into a design for a sculpture or collage	143
Music QCA unit: 3 The long and the short of it	Donkey rides	To evaluate rhythms (judging usefulness)	Exploring how sound pictures are created by listening to and creating music	144
PE QCA unit: Games activities unit 2	Frisbee frolics	To think creatively; to evaluate performance (judging quality)	Creating new beach games with familiar beach toys	145

WRITE A POSTCARD HOME

SUBJECT: ENGLISH. NLS OBJECTIVE: TO ASSEMBLE
INFORMATION FROM THEIR OWN EXPERIENCE.
SUBJECT: ICT. QCA UNIT: 2C FINDING INFORMATION.

LEARNING OBJECTIVES

To interpret information to write a postcard home
about a holiday; to use computers to research and
present information.

THINKING OBJECTIVE

To evaluate the usefulness of information.

THINKING SKILLS

The children will be evaluating the usefulness of
information to inform decisions about what to
include in postcards about a holiday destination. Use
questions to encourage the children to think about
their intended reader, what is interesting and how to
compact lots of information into a small amount of
space.

WHAT YOU NEED

Postcards from a UK seaside
destination; weather statistics for
a week, including the hours of
sunshine, the type of weather
each day (sunny, rainy, and so
on) and daily temperatures (day
and night for higher attaining
children); board or flip chart;
paper and writing materials.

WHAT TO DO

Talk to the children about
the chosen seaside destination.
Encourage discussion of their own
seaside experiences by asking what kinds
of things they like to do when they are at the
seaside. Support those who have never been to the
seaside by either organising a trip so that all of the
children are familiar with the context, or spend many
sessions prior to this lesson talking about what it
is like. Recreate a seaside area in the classroom if
possible and let the children paddle in water and walk
on sand. Listen to music and stories about seaside
features. Give the children some time to pretend they
are on holiday at the seaside by letting them use the
recreated seaside area or any areas you have created
during other work.

Talk about the kind of weather that can be
expected from a UK seaside holiday. Look on the
Internet to find weather statistics for a seaside place
near you for the current week. The BBC weather site

usually contains useful information (www.bbc.co.uk/
weather), as do newspapers and the local tourist
office. Get the children to interpret the weather
statistics you collect by making graphs and tables to
show how many sunny, wet, windy days there have
been and which days were the hottest and coolest.
Use the information to discuss which would have
been the best days to spend on the beach, and which
to spend on a visit to a local attraction or looking for
souvenirs to take home. Then talk about how long the
children would spend on each excursion.

Tell the children that they are going to write
postcards to people who have never visited this
seaside place. Ask, *What kind of things do you think
people will want to know about a visit here? Will they
want to know about the weather, attractions, things to
do, how easy it is to get to? What else can you think of
that will interest people at home?*

Show the children the postcards of the seaside
place and focus on the pictures. List on the board
some of the places and activities that the children
can see in the pictures.

Then ask the children to look at the
amount of space available to write
to friends and family about the
holiday. How much information
do the children think they
can squeeze into this small
space? Talk about the
importance of selecting
the most interesting and
relevant information,
perhaps a really exciting
event. Make a list of all
the things that could
be included, such as the
likely weather for the place,
activities that the children could
take part in and any special events.
Record these sentences as a bulleted
list. Do the children think the person they are
sending the postcard to will have a good idea of what
their holiday destination is like from the information
they have suggested?

Explain that often when writing a postcard we
abbreviate the sentences, and write a few examples,
such as *Having a lovely time; Went to the beach
Tuesday; Put lots of sun cream on – was so hot and
sunny.* Look at your list of sentences and ask the class
to suggest abbreviated versions, so that important
information is included but unnecessary words are
removed.

Model the writing for the children, showing them
how to organise their ideas so that they have room
to fit them all into the space. Then let them work

in groups to write their own postcards home, using the information they have collected about the weather and information about the seaside place. Let some work in the recreated beach area. Ask them to consider their audience: *Who are you writing the postcard to? How will this affect the things you write?* Share the final postcards with the class.

DIFFERENTIATION

Give lower attaining children a list of sentences about the holiday destination and work with them in a small group to help them choose three ideas they will use to write their postcards.

Higher attaining children can be given additional information to that used in the main lesson, including night time temperatures and information about the local cultures.

WHERE NEXT

Talk about the kinds of things you would write about on a holiday abroad, or on a holiday to different kinds of places. Show the children pictures of these destinations, from the Internet if available, to help them with their ideas.

ASSESSMENT

Note the children who are able to decide or evaluate for themselves which information to include in their postcards. Who can select the most interesting and relevant information for their recipient, which best describes the kind of holiday they would have? Organise another, similar activity for those who do not evaluate the information, and work with this group of children next time.

LEARNING OUTCOMES

The children will learn to evaluate, select and present the information that is most relevant for a particular audience; interpreting, using and presenting information appropriately.

FURTHER ENGLISH AND ICT CHALLENGES

Holiday world

The children can evaluate and use the information to make posters to attract visitors to the seaside destination. Tell them to select the most interesting pieces of information to attract visitors. Ask, *What would people most want to know about this destination? What is its most attractive feature?* Talk about the size, colour and clarity of text on the poster, whether to include a picture, comic illustration or symbols. Do they need quotes from previous visitors to persuade others to come? Use the computer for this work if possible, to help the children to change and modify their work without

having to start again. It is an ideal activity for two children to work on together throughout a half-term unit of work.

Postcards from Fiji

Ask the children to evaluate the sort of information they would include in postcards sent from these paradise islands. Ask them to research the flora and fauna of Fiji, the beaches and weather before writing postcards home.

SOUVENIR HUNTERS

SUBJECT: MATHS. NNS OBJECTIVE: TO RECOGNISE ALL COINS AND BEGIN TO USE £ AND P NOTATION FOR MONEY.

LEARNING OBJECTIVE

To write different amounts of money using £ and p notation.

THINKING OBJECTIVE

To evaluate information and judge monetary value.

THINKING SKILLS

The children will look at a range of mail order catalogues and evaluate what information is included and how it is presented to attract people to buy the items. They will collect and process the information and judge the usefulness and quality of it, before displaying their own ideas persuasively. During the activity they will continually evaluate and make suggestions for improvement in the content and layout of their entries, and use the information to decide how much to charge for each item in the catalogue. Finally, they will use their evaluation skills to interpret how much each item costs in terms of coinage and which coins to use to represent each amount.

WHAT YOU NEED

A large collection of items that would be found in a seaside souvenir shop, including buckets and spades, tea towels, beach balls, ornaments, sticks of rock, packets of fudge and biscuits, sun cream, beach toys and gear; photographs of each one, either from a magazine or taken with a digital camera; several mail order catalogues; sheets of paper in a range of colours; writing materials; coins (real or plastic); glue; scissors.

WHAT TO DO

Show the children the items you have in your collection. Ask them if they can think of other things to buy from a seaside souvenir shop. If possible ask them to lend items from home that are not too precious to use for the activity. Show the children the photographs you have of each item and explain that they are going to use the items to create a catalogue to sell things by mail order.

Look together at a page from a mail order catalogue and talk about how it is organised. Ask, What information is included? How are the sales items organised? How is the price written? Show the children the different coloured papers you have and decide which is the best one to show the pictures off to their best. Work with the children in smaller groups to plan where to put the photographs of each item, letting the children explain why they have decided to put them where they have. Then give each pair of children a different page to work on and get them to stick the pictures in a way that the observer can see the items clearly.

Tell the children to think about the price they will charge for each item. Consider first the actual prices usually charged for the items to make the activity realistic. Ask the children to write each price by the side of the pictures using the relevant £ or p signs. For example, if the price is 99 pence, they will write 99p, but if it is 4 pounds and 50 pence, they will write £4.50. Ask the children to use the coins to make the amounts they have found. Can they find more than one way to make the same amount, using different coins?

Finally, the children ask the children to write a description for each item, on the computer if possible, and glue this next to their items. If you have used a digital camera to photograph the items the photographs can be inserted directly onto the page of text.

DIFFERENTIATION

Use cheaper items, which require prices only in pence or that will require the children to choose one coin only, for example sweets, sticks of rock, postcards and comics. Prices which can be made using exact coins work well for lower attaining children to work with. For example, 22p, 15p, £1.50, and so on.

Consider post and packaging charges with higher attaining children. Provide parcels of different sizes and weights, and ask the children to find out how much it costs to send them through the post. You could make up a basic cost system for them, based on weight and size. Make sure that some parcels are light and heavy enough to invite amounts that are different. The children can make a list of costs to include in the catalogue, and to display in the post office role-play area.

WHERE NEXT

Use the mail order catalogue in a role-play for the children to solve problems using money. Invite the children to order and buy items form the catalogue, finding the coins they will need for each purchase, or purchases, if they buy more than one item. Develop a series of problems, matched to different ability groups, for the children to solve.

ASSESSMENT

Notice if the children can evaluate the information in the catalogues and comment on it. Note the children who can match the coins to the correct written amount. Make a list of those who are able to find totals using exact coinage and those that are able to find different coins for different amounts.

LEARNING OUTCOMES

The children will make judgements to decide which coins to use to make different amounts of money. They will be able to evaluate how to present the items in a catalogue format and judge the actual cost of the items.

FURTHER MATHS CHALLENGES

Parcel post
Ask the children to judge how much it will cost to send parcels with different weights through the post. Challenge the children to write the correct price in £ or p and to find the right stamps to stick on the parcels. Then let them weigh the parcels to find the correct value in stamps and coinage. Ask them to find out the least and/or greatest number of coins and stamps to use for each total.

All wrapped up
Ask the children to evaluate which paper is best from a weight point of view for wrapping parcels, but which will still give the parcel enough strength to protect the contents during the journey. Ask the children to give reasons for their choices. Extend this

into enquiry skills by asking them to say how they can find out whether they are right.

THE SEASIDE CAFÉ

SUBJECT: SCIENCE. QCA UNIT: 2D GROUPING AND CHANGING MATERIALS.

LEARNING OBJECTIVE
To learn that some materials change when heated.

THINKING OBJECTIVE
To predict outcomes, anticipate consequences and test conclusions.

THINKING SKILLS
The children will be investigating what happens to food if it is not kept cool. They will predict what will happen to different foods if heated and test out their ideas. They will have the opportunity to note the changes that occur at different stages of food being heated and will use this information to think of the best place to store the food.

WHAT YOU NEED
A slice of bread and some hard butter; a potato; different foods to heat up, such as cheese, jam, biscuits, ice cream, chocolate, cake; a microwave; a sharp knife and a butter knife; a potato peeler; board or flip chart.

WHAT TO DO
Make sure you choose items of food that will not go mouldy or turn sour during the investigation. Ask the children to suggest food items that a café is likely to sell, and make a list of these on the board. Make sure that you break this down into the original food produce if necessary, for example *chips* would be *potatoes*. Look at each of the food items and talk about what they look like. Are they hot or cold, soft or hard, crispy or smooth?

Make a sandwich and ask the class to watch. What do the children think will happen when you try to spread the butter onto the bread? Show the children how difficult it is to spread hard butter. Ask them, *How can I make it softer? Will this make it easier to spread? Why?*

Peel the potato and cut it into chips. Ask the children to suggest the best way to store these in a café to keep them fresh. What do they think will happen if the potato pieces are left outside on a hot summer's day? List their ideas and test each one out by simulating the heat in a microwave. Put each chip in the microwave for only a few seconds each time, noting the changes that take place. Each time

before you put the item back in the microwave, ask the children to say what they think will happen, to anticipate the consequences of heating up the food.

Heat up each of the other items of food for a short time in the microwave, and note with the children the changes that occur. Ask the children to use the information they find out to suggest how each food item should be stored in the café.

DIFFERENTIATION
Work only with the bread and butter with lower attaining children to note the changes that occur when the butter is warmed.

With higher attaining children investigate food items that return to their original state again when cooled, including jelly, chocolate, butter and cheese. Ask them to say first which items they think will return to their original state and those that will not, before testing out their ideas.

WHERE NEXT
Plan a picnic that builds on the children's conclusions. Choose items that will not change when exposed to heat, such as orange juice and Scotch eggs.

Talk about the different changes that occur to potatoes when they are cooked in different ways.

ASSESSMENT
Make a note of the children who anticipate what will happen to each food item when heated. Some may explain this through personal experience, while others may be using their scientific knowledge and understanding. Note the children who can test out their ideas and use the information to suggest improvements to the way that food should be stored in a café.

LEARNING OUTCOMES
Most children will be able to anticipate what will happen to certain foodswhen heated. Some children will be able to test out their ideas to find out which ones return to their original state when cooled.

FURTHER SCIENCE CHALLENGES
A cool picnic
Look at the range of ways that food is kept cool and set up an investigation for the children to find out

which is the most effective for keeping food cool when out on a picnic. Can they find a better way to keep the food cool? Measure the outcomes with a thermometer and make a table of the results. Use the results to draw conclusions with the higher attaining children.

Scrambled eggs on toast

Ask the children to anticipate or predict what changes they think will occur when you make scrambled eggs on toast for the seaside café in the classroom. Ask, *What will happen to the bread when toasted? What will happen to the butter when spread on the warm toast? What will happen to the beaten egg when heated in the microwave?* Carry out the investigation and ask the children to draw 'before' and 'after' pictures to show what they have found out. Discuss whether the changes are reversible.

SEASIDE TOYS

SUBJECT: HISTORY. QCA UNIT: 1 HOW ARE OUR TOYS DIFFERENT FROM THOSE IN THE PAST?

LEARNING OBJECTIVE

To note similarities and differences between seaside toys in the past and the present day.

THINKING OBJECTIVE

To ask and answer questions.

THINKING SKILLS

The children will ask questions to help them find out about how toys they use today are the same as and different from those used by their parents and grandparents. They will answer, or ask someone else to answer, the questions to find out about the past.

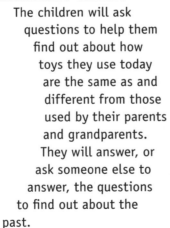

WHAT YOU NEED

Modern spades and beach toys; a collection of seaside toys, including spades, from the past, such as bats and balls, frisbees and kites (the local museum service may be able to help, or ask parents, grandparents and older members of staff for loaned items); the sandpit area; photographs of people playing games on the beach in the past, or an older adult for the children to interview; a camera; A3 paper and writing materials.

WHAT TO DO

Talk to the children about the kinds of things they like doing on the beach. Relate the activities to the games played in school for those who have never visited the seaside. Include playing with frisbees and balls, playing football.

Wonder with the children what people did at the seaside many years ago, when their grandparents were children. Model the language of the past, and include historical vocabulary, such as *modern, old fashioned, old, new* and *in earlier times*. Ask the children to find out how many of their parents and grandparents visited the seaside when they were young. Explain that this would have been possible for those living close to the sea, but for many, transport was more difficult as few families owned cars. It would have been a very special event for many children.

Show the children the old items in your collection. Choose one to talk about. What do the children want to know about it? What questions would they like to ask? Help them if they can't think of any. Questions could include, *What is it? How was it used? Is it, or one similar, still used today?*

Focus the children on using the old spades to play with in the sand at this point, and look at any used by their parents or grandparents if any have been brought in. As the children play, draw their attention to the materials from which the spades are made and ask them to think of a question to ask about them, such as *What is the spade made from? How is the handle attached?*

Explain that in the past the handle often fell off, or the spade bent because the materials were not strong enough to carry the weight of the sand. Tell the children that all the spades looked the same, although you could buy them in different sizes.

Look together at the different spades in your modern collection. Focus on the colours, shapes, sizes and designs. Which are the children's favourite and why? Ask, *What are these made from? Are they stronger than the old ones we have looked at? How else are they different?*

Get the children to sort the toys in your collection into two sets – those used today and those from the past. When they have done this ask them to think about which set contains the most items. Why? Is it because things have got lost over time, or is it because there is a greater range of beach toys today?

If possible invite someone in to talk to the children and to answer their questions. List the questions that the children would like to ask beforehand so that the visitor comes prepared and the children's questions are focused. Tape the conversation so the children can listen to the answers again at a later date and perhaps list further questions they might ask.

Photograph the two sets of toys that the children have made. Display these alongside two large sheets of paper, one for the children to note the similarities between the two sets of toys and the other one for the differences. They should focus on the range, colour, materials, size, design and shape of the toys.

DIFFERENTIATION

Model questions for lower attaining children to develop their enquiry skills. Start with things like, *I wonder how long this bucket and spade lasted? Do you think the children bought a new one every time they went to the seaside? Was going to the shop to buy your bucket and spade a big event in the 1950s?*

Explore with higher attaining children how the development of new materials, such as plastic, has increased the range of toys available today. Set up an enquiry for the children to find out if more people go to the seaside today. What questions would they like to ask? Questions such as *Is it because of better transport systems?* would be appropriate.

WHERE NEXT

Invite the children to think of questions to ask to find out what food items were available for children to eat at the seaside in the past. Start with the children's own exeriences of seaside food and use this as a starting point for developing questions. For example, *Were there places on the beach for people to buy burgers, hotdogs or chips in the past? Could people buy ice cream?*

ASSESSMENT

Note the children who ask relevant questions. How many think of a supplementary question to further their knowledge and understanding? Note any pertinent comments that individual children make which show they are developing an understanding of the passing of time. Note who uses suitable historical vocabulary in their questioning.

LEARNING OUTCOMES

The children will learn to ask questions about the past. They will listen to answers and note the relationship to the evidence in front of them. They will find out about the past from accounts, photographs and artefacts.

FURTHER HISTORY CHALLENGES

Deckchairs

Ask the children for questions which will help them to find out the similarities and differences between deckchairs from the past and those today. Also ask

them to suggest questions to help them find out what other things are used today which were not available a long time ago, such as windbreaks, beach umbrellas and beach balls.

Changing fashions

Ask the children to develop a list of questions to ask about bathing costumes when their parents or grandparents were young, following the same lines of enquiry. For example, *What materials were the costumes made from? What were the designs like? How were the straps attached? Did they wear out quickly, stretch or go out of shape?* Send the list of questions home with the children for them to put to an appropriate adult. They could record their answers onto a tape for other children to listen to back in school.

BEACHES

SUBJECT: GEOGRAPHY. QCA UNIT: 4 GOING TO THE SEASIDE.

LEARNING OBJECTIVE

To identify and describe what places are like and where they are.

THINKING OBJECTIVE

To locate and analyse information.

THINKING SKILLS

The children will develop their information-processing skills by locating and analysing information on maps, and using this information to describe what particular places are like.

WHAT YOU NEED

A map of the UK labelled with the names of places for which you have matching postcards and/or pictures (include different types of coastline, for example the sands around Morecambe, the ports of Dover and Birkenhead, the cliffs at Beachey Head and the Needles on the Isle of Wight); a map of a seaside area which shows the beaches, local attractions, transport routes and surrounding countryside (tourist maps are likely to be most suitable) and matching postcards; board or flip chart.

WHAT TO DO

Look at the map of the UK with the class and locate where the sea meets the land. Explain that this is called the coastline. Start from any point and follow the coastline with your finger. Ask, *Is it straight or curved? Does it go in and out? Does it go past any rivers?* Ask the children to describe the directions your finger travels in.

When you come to a section of the coastline that shows sand, stop and ask the children if they notice anything different about this part of the coastline. Ask, *Is it a different colour on the map? What do you think we might find in this place? What do we call an area covered in sand?*

Continue to follow the coastline with your finger, stopping at relevant points that show shingle beaches, cliffs, ports and river estuaries. Note human features as well as physical ones, such as lighthouses, buildings and picnic areas. Note the differences in the way they are represented on the map and name the different features. List on the board the physical and human features you have found.

Show the children the postcards and, by matching the pictures to the symbols on the map, get the children to place the postcards in the correct locations. Ask, *Do the places look different on the map? How do we know it is the same place?* To help them, draw attention to how the features are represented on the map.

Look for one of the places where there are lighthouses and ask the children to suggest why they think there is a lighthouse located in that particular place. Referring to the symbols and features, encourage the children to describe what that place is like. Prompt them with questions, such as *Are there cliffs at this place? Is there a beach? Why do ships need to stay away from the coast?*

In groups, get the children to look at a map of a seaside place and locate the features, activities and transport routes that they can find. (The south east of England has a variety of coastlines, places of interest, ferry and train routes.) Using the information they have collected, ask the children to describe what the place is like. Confirm the children's descriptions by looking at matching postcards of the same areas.

DIFFERENTIATION
Work from the postcards or pictures with lower attaining children in the group activities and develop their geographical vocabulary in locating and analysing the features. Give higher attaining children a map of a seaside area and ask them to find clues which tell them what the area is like, for example the White cliffs of Dover, Rye harbour, a marina.

WHERE NEXT
Ask the children to bring in postcards and photographs of seaside places they have visited and talk about what the places are like. Ask them to find them on a map and match symbols to the pictures on the postcards.

ASSESSMENT
Note the children who are able to locate the features on the map and use these to match the correct postcard to its position. Who can process the information to describe what the place is like?

LEARNING OUTCOMES
The children will be able to process the information found on pictures and maps in order to describe the physical and human features of different places and begin to identify what gives different places their character.

FURTHER GEOGRAPHY CHALLENGES
Where am I?
Give the children a picture of a chosen place and ask them to compare it with a map, noting the features on both. The Island of Coll is suitable for this activity (available through the Katie Morag stories). Set up a game for the children to play. Give them a picture of an individual feature or place, such as a lighthouse, café, car park or beach, and ask them to note on a map of the area where they could be standing to see these clearly. Higher attaining children should be challenged to find the correct perspective.
Where is it?
Using the children's knowledge and understanding of the place being studied, help them to glue the pictures and photographs of the chosen area onto a large wall map.

THE PUNCH AND JUDY SHOW

SUBJECT: DESIGN AND TECHNOLOGY. QCA UNIT: 2C WINDING UP.

LEARNING OBJECTIVE
To observe how winding and pulling mechanisms work, making their own mechanism based on their observations.

THINKING OBJECTIVE
To analyse mechanisms.

THINKING SKILLS

The children will be analysing how pulling mechanisms work. Some children will also evaluate which is the most effective mechanism to operate the curtains in a Punch and Judy theatre. The children will make their own mechanism to reinforce their anaysis, and will evaluate their finished models and mechanisms.

WHAT YOU NEED

Pre-made puppet theatres (one for each group); pieces of fabric; plastic, metal and cardboard tubes; wheels; dowelling; glue; scissors; rulers; a pair of small curtains attached to a rail with a pulling mechanism; a working roller blind and venetian blind; an example of a winding mechanism, such as an electrical extension lead, a tape measure or a hose on a reel; paper and drawing materials.

WHAT TO DO

Show the children the roller blind and the venetian blind, and talk about how they work. Do they both work in the same way? Repeat this with the curtains. Describe what happens to the curtains when the cord is pulled.

Talk to the children about how theatre curtains are operated. *Are they pulled up? Why not?* Explain that they are so big and heavy that they are too difficult to pull up. Explain that it is easier for people to wind them up.

Unwind the tape measure, extension lead or hose to its full length. Ask the children to take it in turns to wind it up. Did they find this easy or difficult? Ask the children to look carefully and say how the tape measure is put together. What happens inside as the handle is turned? Show this by unwinding and winding the equipment.

Explain to the children that you want them to make a curtain for the front of a Punch and Judy puppet theatre. Tell them that you want them to make a curtain or blind that will wind up. Leave the collection of tubing, wheels, dowelling, glue and fabric out for the children to explore. Ask them to design their curtain or blind first and to identify how they will make this. Tell them they should include joining ideas and the mechanism they intend to use to wind the curtain up. Challenge higher attaining children to make a curtain that works by pulling it across the front of the puppet theatre. Show them the curtain again to remind them how it works. Ask, *In which direction will you need to pull the curtain?*

Ask the children to work in groups, and as they work to make their curtain, ask them how the mechanism works. If any are struggling with the concept of making a mechanism, help them to focus,

by asking questions such as *How can you make the curtain go up so that the puppet show can begin? How will you let it down again? How will you make sure that the fabric is the correct length and width? What will you use to measure the opening? Will the fabric need to be the same size, smaller or bigger? How will you keep the fabric in place while you glue it into position?*

When the groups have finished, try out the children's designs and talk about how well they work. Talk about any difficulties, which could include questions such as, *Is it easy to turn the curtain rod? Does it need a handle? Is the handle too close to the edge of the theatre, making it difficult to operate? Does the curtain roll up tightly enough? Does the curtain stay rolled up or does the winding mechanism need something to lock it into place?*

Ask the children to evaluate their designs, discussing difficulties they encountered and what they did to overcome them. If they had another opportunity, what would they do differently? Would they plan the making process as well as the design?

DIFFERENTIATION

Ask higher attaining children to design and make a curtain which will move across a rod from side to side and ask them to evaluate whether this mechanism works better than one that moves up and down. As the children work, talk to lower attaining children individually and help them to evaluate the materials used in their designs and to analyse how their mechanism works.

WHERE NEXT

Ask the children to analyse the effectiveness of puppets that drop down onto the stage during a performance, such as spiders or ghosts, which are operated by a winding mechanism.

Look together at a range of items that work by winding up and encourage the children to analyse how easy it is to make them work.

ASSESSMENT
Note the children who can analyse how pulling and winding mechanisms work. Note those who evaluate their finished designs to make sure that they wind up and down effectively. Which children use their evaluations to make improvements to their work?

LEARNING OUTCOMES
Most children will be able to analyse how a pulley mechanism works and design one of their own. They should also be able to evaluate how effective their mechanisms are and to use this information to make adjustments or changes to their finished design. Some will also be able to evaluate whether a mechanism that pulls a curtain up or across is best.

FURTHER DESIGN AND TECHNOLOGY CHALLENGES
Wind it up!
Show the children a winding mechanism and help them analyse how it works. Then get them to use commercial construction kits to make cranes which are operated by winding-up mechanisms. Ask the children to try each other's out and to evaluate which is the best one and why.
Heavy weight
Set up a pulley system and a winding system for lifting a bucket of sand in the classroom. Ask the children to try out the two systems to analyse which is the easiest way to lift the bucket. Make sure that you use enough sand to enable them to find the answer, but not so much that it is too heavy for the children to pull or wind up.

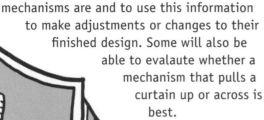

SANDCASTLE FLAGS
SUBJECT: ICT. QCA UNIT: 2C FINDING INFORMATION.

LEARNING OBJECTIVE
To use appropriate search techniques to find information about the flags of the UK and the world.

THINKING OBJECTIVES
To locate and collect information; to analyse flags.

THINKING SKILLS
The children will look closely at a number of different flags and analyse the patterns, colours and lines which are used to make each one. They will use the computer to collect other flags which represent different countries and organisations.

WHAT YOU NEED
Flags of St Patrick, St George, St Andrew, St David and the Union flag (small versions of these or pictures will do); the flags of St Patrick, St George and St Andrew copied onto OHT or for use on an interactive whiteboard; an OHP or interactive whiteboard; access to the Internet for three groups of children; CD-ROMs, encyclopaedias and reference books with information on flags; a colour printer; a large map of the United Kingdom; rectangles of card, straws and sticky tape; access to the sandpit area.

WHAT TO DO
As a whole class, look at a map of the United Kingdom and locate England, Wales, Scotland and Northern Ireland. Also locate where your school is. Ask the children to point to which country the school is located in.

Look together at the flags of St Patrick (Northern Ireland), St George (England) and St Andrew (Scotland). Label the map with the flags. Include the Welsh flag of St David. (Explain that when the Union flag was developed, Wales was part of England so was represented by the flag of St George.)

Ask the children to analyse what the flags look like. Talk about the colours and designs on them. Look at the crosses on each one and whether these have been created with vertical, horizontal or diagonal lines. Look at the Union flag and talk about the colours and designs on that. What do the children notice about the colours and lines of the Union flag and the colours in the flags of the separate countries? What about the shapes created by the lines. What can they see?

Begin to assemble the Union flag. Place the flags of England and Scotland on top of each other on the OHP or interactive whiteboard. Ask the children what they notice. Can they see any similarities with the Union flag at this point? Can they note any differences? Next place the flag of Northern Ireland on top of the half-made Union flag. What do the children notice now?

Tell the children that you want them to find information about flags around the world, and talk about where this information can be found. List the possible sources, including books, CD-ROMs, and the Internet.

Show the children how to search the Internet and CD-ROMs for information about the flags of different countries. Show them how to use key words, menus and hyperlinks to conduct searches to find different flags.

Organise the children into groups. Let a lower attaining group build a large sandcastle together in the sandpit while you start off the other research groups. Explain that the sandcastle will house the different flags when they have been found. Once the other groups are busy, focus on helping this group to locate and print flags from the Internet for them to add to their sandcastles.

Work with Group 1 to find the flags of St Patrick, St George and St Andrew. Go to the BBC website (www.bbc.co.uk) and get the children to search for the Union flag. Ask the children to print out the flags, cut around them and attach them to straw flag poles.

Group 2 can research the flags of the world and print out their favourites to make flags for the sandcastle activity. Encourge them to use the Internet and CD-ROMs primarily for this activity. Again, they should cut out and stick their flags onto straws.

Encourage children in Group 3 to use their own ideas to create imaginary flags. Perhaps a school logo, or seaside emblems could be used. They could use clip art for this or a computer program with a stamp facility, making their designs into flags using straws.

Look together at the range of different flags the children have collected. Talk to them about how they located the flags. Ask, *Did you use the Internet, a CD-ROM or a book? Which was the quickest way? What are the benefits of using a computer and printer? Did anyone use a hyperlink?*

Finish by allowing the children in the lower attaining group to add the flags on poles to their sandcastle.

DIFFERENTIATION

Expect higher attaining children to analyse the designs of different flags and to use this knowledge to reproduce them from memory.

WHERE NEXT

Look with the children at the emblems of England, Wales and Scotland and talk about the origins of these. Talk about where the children may see them. For example, on sports shirts, mugs, flags and banners.

Look at flags used at the seaside, particularly those which indicate when it is safe and not safe to swim. Help the children interpret the message they are giving by analysing the symbols and colours together. (Include flags which represent organisations such as the Blue Flag Campaign and the RNLI.)

ASSESSMENT

Keep the range of flags the children have made as evidence that they have analysed closely what each flag looks like, and that they have located and collected information successfully.

LEARNING OUTCOMES

Most children will be able to analyse the information on flags – the colours, lines, patterns, pictures and symbols – to help them remember the country they represent. They will also be able to use the computer to locate and collect a range of flags from around the world.

FURTHER ICT CHALLENGES

Flags of the world

Build on the children's research on flags from other countries in the main activity. In a class plenary and ongoing group activity, create a large display of a map of the world. Ask the children to find certain countries on the map and mark them with their flags. Look at the European Union flag and talk about what the stars signify. Ask the children to design a flag for the school if you do not already have one. Alternatively, they could design a banner to show a particular event, such as a birthday or national celebration.

Holiday destinations

Ask the children to find out six facts about a country of their choice and to present the information in a holiday brochure format. Make a class holiday brochure for a travel agent role-play area. My First Amazing World Explorer is a suitable computer program to use.

SAND SCULPTURES

SUBJECT: ART AND DESIGN. QCA UNIT: 1C WHAT IS SCULPTURE?

LEARNING OBJECTIVES
To explore from first-hand observation the materials used in making sculptures; to explore ideas for a design.

THINKING OBJECTIVE
To think imaginatively.

THINKING SKILLS
The children will be using their knowledge and understanding of line, shape and form in this lesson through an activity which challenges their imaginative thinking. They will use things found naturally on the seashore to create a picture or sculpture which will be given a title intended to make the observer think.

WHAT YOU NEED
A collection of shells, driftwood and pebbles (reinforcing to the children that we should never remove living material from an area); fish-shaped moulds or similar; small trays filled with silver sand; larger sand trays; spray bottles of water; a digital camera; sketchbooks and drawing materials.

WHAT TO DO
Let the children spend ten minutes handling and examining your collection of materials. Encourage them to talk about the lines, shapes and colours of the objects. Turn the shells, driftwood and pebbles around and ask the children to say whether one side is more interesting to look at than another? Ask, *Why do you like this side?* Allow the children another ten minutes to sketch some of the interesting lines, shapes and colours they have found among the objects.

Tell the children they will use these materials to make sand pictures or sculptures, which will reflect some of the interesting lines, shapes and colours they have found. Before they start, ask the children to close their eyes and try to imagine what their finished work will look like. Then ask them, *Which materials will you use? Will you use them to make a picture or a sculpture? Which of the interesting shapes and lines we have talked about will you include? How will you make sure that these can be clearly seen in your finished work?*

Let the children work individually if they wish, making pictures of fish or seaweed, for instance, in trays of silver sand. Alternatively, they could work in small groups to make a larger class collage picture or a 3-D sculpture from the materials in larger sand trays. Perhaps they can make a tower of shells and pebbles to show the interesting shapes and colours, decorate a sandcastle mould with shells and pebbles without knocking them down, or make sand towers of different heights. Show the children how to use a water spray to seal the moulded shapes. Ask them to remember to incorporate some of the interesting lines, shapes and colours they found in the materials earlier. Talk to the children as they work. Ask questions where necessary to focus them, such as *Can you make your sculpture or collage more interesting by building sand towers together in a small cluster? Can you arrange your shells and pebbles into the shape of an animal that lives in the sea, for example a starfish or an octopus?*

The children will come up with some imaginative ideas. Give them the freedom to do this. Use the digital camera to take photographs of the finished sculptures and seascapes. Invite the children to give their finished pictures and sculptures titles which reflect what they are depicting. Use these in a plenary session to review what they have done, and to say what they think and feel about each other's work.

DIFFERENTIATION
Help those children who require support with their ideas. Talk to them about what they are trying to create. Give them ideas for a title and question them to spark their imagination further.

Invite higher attaining children to work together as a group first so that they can bounce ideas off each other. Then allow them time to incorporate any new ideas in their own designs. Ask them to comment on the similarities and differences between their own and others' work.

WHERE NEXT

Make a display of the children's work, interspersed with the raw materials they used.

The children could use sewing techniques to create a fabric collage.

ASSESSMENT

Talk to the children as they work. Note those who describe the lines, shape and colour in their work, and those who have investigated the materials and are able to say why they have chosen a particular focus. Listen to the titles and note the children who have thought about the position and design of the materials to create a particular effect.

LEARNING OUTCOMES

The children will think about what they like about a particular material, and will have the opportunity to talk about how they created certain effects in their sculpture or picture. They will think imaginatively to make a creative picture or sculpture.

FURTHER ART AND DESIGN CHALLENGES

Table decorations

Ask the children to use the materials to create imaginative table decorations for the seaside café in the role-play area. Give them a selection of containers, sand and oasis to assemble the materials. Give them complete freedom to use their imagination to decide for themselves whether to create a pictoral theme or just a pretty decoration.

Fish tablecloths

Ask the children to use shells, seaweed and sea creature designs to create imaginative tablecloths for the seaside café. They can print their designs with string glued to blocks of wood, or use fabric crayons to draw their designs onto fabric. Tell them to plan their design first in their sketchbooks and think about where any patterns in their design will be placed. Is there an ordered pattern to the children's designs or are they spontaneous?

DONKEY RIDES

SUBJECT: MUSIC. QCA UNIT: 3 THE LONG AND THE SHORT OF IT.

LEARNING OBJECTIVE

To learn to identify how a composer uses short notes to create a certain effect.

THINKING OBJECTIVE

To evaluate rhythms (judging usefulness).

THINKING SKILLS

The children will evaluate how a quaver pattern creates a feeling of steady movement, before using this in their own composition and performance. They will select percussion instruments, supporting their evaluation skills through their choice of these, to create an aural picture of donkeys trotting. The

children will also use their evaluation skills through listening and appraising their own and others' performance.

WHAT YOU NEED

A copy of the song 'Donkey Rides' from *The Multicoloured Music Bus* by Peter Canwell (Collins); unpitched percussion instruments; a piano if appropriate.

WHAT TO DO

Teach the children the song 'Donkey Rides' and talk about the rhythm of the tune. Ask them, *How has the composer created the sound of donkeys trotting?*

Show the children an enlarged copy of the score. What do they notice about the quavers (or short or running notes) that are used in the tune and in the left-hand piano accompaniment? (They should notice that in the left-hand accompaniment (the bottom stave), the notes start at the end of the introduction and finish at the end of the song.) Explain how the quavers in the tune reinforce the syllables in the lyrics which describe the riding of the donkeys, and together paint a picture of donkeys trotting. For example, *riding on a donkey by the sea* and *sitting in the saddle I'm a cowboy on the prairie*. If you are able, play this part to the children on a piano. Get the class to sing the song through again, asking the children to listen to the quavers as they sing. Divide the class in half. Ask one half to clap the quaver rhythm throughout while the other half sings the song. Give both halves the opportunity to perform each part.

Divide the class into groups and let them explore a range of unpitched percussion instruments to add a suitable accompaniment to the song. Coconut shells, two-tone wood blocks, claves, castanets and bells are obvious choices for the children to choose, but allow them to decide for themselves whether to use these or cymbals!

Gather the children back together and ask each group to perform their accompaniment to the class, explaining why they chose the instruments they did. Prompt the groups with questions, such as *Why did you choose this instrument? What sort of sound does it make? How did you play the instrument to make that sound? How loud/fast did you play? What happens to the effect if you play the rhythm faster?* Ask the rest of the class to express an opinion about whether the accompaniment paints a picture of donkeys trotting along a beach.

Perform the song again, allowing each group to add their accompaniment.

DIFFERENTIATION

Put the higher attaining children into one group and work with these to evaluate the effect in the introduction to the song. Look at the rhythm of long and short notes and the way the song jumps down from top to bottom C. Listen to this and ask the children to evaluate whether the composer has created a picture of the donkeys braying. Ask, *What*

happens in the last bar of the introduction? What effect does the composer create by introducing the running notes or short notes here? Some children may be able to play the tune of the introduction on a xylophone, glockenspiel or keyboard.

WHERE NEXT

Play the children *La Mer* by Debussy, and evaluate how he uses long and short notes to create the picture of the sea moving.

ASSESSMENT

Assess the children's evaluation skills by noting those who understand that rhythm and melody can be used to create certain effects. See which children develop this further by choosing suitable instruments for the rhythms and giving pertinent reasons for their choices.

LEARNING OUTCOMES

The children will perform simple patterns and accompaniments, keeping a steady pulse. They will begin to evaluate how certain musical effects are created using rhythm. They will use this in creating accompaniments independently.

FURTHER MUSIC CHALLENGES
Café music
Put out a range of music for the children to listen to and ask them to evaluate its suitability to play in the seaside café. Include music from around the world, songs, instrumentals, pop and classical music. Ask the children to choose a piece and give suitable reasons why it would be relevant to include on a compilation to play in the café and seaside shop. Debate and discuss the 'fors' and 'againsts' of including each piece and then make a tape together to play in the café.

FRISBEE FROLICS

SUBJECT: PE. QCA UNIT: GAMES ACTIVITIES UNIT 2.

LEARNING OBJECTIVES
To explore and use skills, actions and ideas; to use information to improve their work.

THINKING OBJECTIVES
To think creatively; to evaluate performance (judging quality).

THINKING SKILLS
The activity starts with a creative thinking focus, and moves on to bring out the children's evaluation skills. The children will think creatively, considering

different ways to use familiar toys to create a new game. They will evaluate each other's games and suggest improvements to make the games more challenging or fun to play. They will learn to write precise rules and instructions to make sure that everyone can understand and follow their ideas.

WHAT YOU NEED

A collection of beach toys, including a beach ball, a fishing net, a frisbee, kites, bats and balls; a large space to explore and play with the toys; board or flip chart; paper and writing materials.

WHAT TO DO

Show the children the different beach toys in your collection. Allow them a few moments to explore different ways of playing with the toys. Make sure they swap the toys over so that the children have the opportunity to explore the range.

Then ask the children to work in small groups to choose a toy for a new game to play on the beach. Ask some questions to focus the children's thinking, such as *Does your game involve throwing and catching the toy? Do you send the toy in a different way? Is it a team game, or do individuals play it? Is there a scoring system?*

After ten minutes, ask the groups to demonstrate their games to each other. Ask the children to note two good things about each of the games they see. Next, invite them to offer suggestions to try to make the games more interesting or challenging. Ask the groups to practise the games again, trying out some of the suggestions offered by the rest of the class. See whether the children like the suggested improvements, or whether they have decided to keep their original ideas.

On returning to the classroom, make a list on the board of all the different ways that the toys were played with. Ask each group to make a list of rules on how to play their game.

Over the next few days, get the class to play each game in turn, following the written rules. Ask the writers to watch and evaluate whether their instructions are precise enough, or whether they need to give additional guidance or clearer directions.

DIFFERENTIATION

Work with lower attaining children in a small group, directing their ideas each step of the way by asking questions, such as *Why are you all standing in the same place? Why don't one of you stand there/here? Do you want to use more than one ball?* This will direct their evaluations towards thinking about tactics and strategies.

Ask higher attaining children to think about refining their game, but suggesting they think about the tactics they use to keep the toy in their possession, to intercept the other team or to improve upon the distance they can throw, for instance.

WHERE NEXT

Ask older children to play the games and to express opinions about their strengths and any developments they think could be made. Get the children to revise and improve their games in response to these evaluations.

ASSESSMENT

Note the children's level of skill in sending and receiving a range of equipment. Note those who make suitable suggestions about how to improve their throwing, for example by bending their knees and using this to help add power to the throw, or by following the throw through with the arm and hand. Note the level of evaluation of the class as a whole and develop this skill in the next PE lesson if necessary.

LEARNING OUTCOMES

The children will think creatively to develop their own games, before evaluating them and making improvements.

FURTHER PE CHALLENGES

Frisbee travels

The children could evaluate different frisbees judging the qualities of each. Which shaped frisbee travels the furthest? Which is the easiest frisbee to throw? Who is the class champion frisbee thrower? Ask the children to evaluate how to improve their throws and invite them to say what needs to be done to improve the throwing technique.

HANSEL AND GRETEL

Subject and QCA unit, NLS or NNS objective	Activity title	Thinking objective	Activity	Page
English NLS objective: To write sustained stories with a variety of story elements	And they all lived happily ever after	To think imaginatively and extend ideas	Writing an alternative ending to a story	148
Maths NNS objective: To sort shapes and describe their features	Sweets galore	To sort and analyse shapes	Sorting sweets to different criteria to decorate the witch's house	149
Science QCA unit: 1C Sorting and using materials	Trailblazers	To evaluate information (judging usefulness) and develop criteria for judging; to test conclusions	Evaluating which materials will make a good trail, and testing these predictions	150
History QCA unit: 4 Why od we remember Florence Nightingale? ICT QCA unit: 2C Finding information	Famous authors	To locate and collect information	Using search techniques on a computer to find information about famous authors	152
Geography QCA unit: 1 Around our school – the local area	Home at last	To make deductions	Plotting and describing a route to get from one point on a map to another	153
Design and technology QCA unit: 1C Eat more fruit and vegetables	A house made from cake	To think laterally and imaginatively	Selecting and using appropriately shaped cakes to make a model of a house	154
Music QCA unit: 2 Sounds interesting	Character music	To think imaginatively	Creating sounds and phrases to depict a character in a story	156
RE QCA unit: 2B Why did Jesus tell stories?	Feelings	To make inferences.	Identifying with the feelings of characters in stories	158
PE QCA unit: Dance activities unit 2	The witch's ride	To evaluate movements	Creating a dance to represent a character	159

AND THEY ALL LIVED HAPPILY EVER AFTER

SUBJECT: ENGLISH. NLS OBJECTIVE: TO WRITE SUSTAINED STORIES, USING THEIR KNOWLEDGE OF STORY ELEMENTS: NARRATIVE, SETTINGS, CHARACTERISATION, DIALOGUE AND THE LANGUAGE OF STORY.

LEARNING OBJECTIVE
To use interesting vocabulary and knowledge of story elements to write an alternative ending to a story.

THINKING OBJECTIVE
To think imaginatively and extend ideas.

THINKING SKILLS
The children will be thinking creatively by using their imagination to write an alternative ending to a familiar story. The activity is set within a precise structure focused on writing skills. The children will extend their own ideas by exploring their vocabulary choices to make the ending as interesting as possible to the reader.

WHAT YOU NEED
A version of the story 'Hansel and Gretel'; thesauruses; board or flip chart; paper and writing materials.

WHAT TO DO
Read 'Hansel and Gretel' to the children, finishing at the point where the witch is killed. Talk with the children about the ending of the story. Ask, *Was this a happy ending? Who was happy at the end of the story?*

Wonder with the children how else the story could end and write their ideas on the board. Choose one idea and expand it with the class. For example, the idea may be that the children decide to sell the witch's jewels and buy a big house for themselves and their father. Ask questions to help the children's creative thinking process, such as *Would they invite their stepmother? Where do you think they would buy the house? What would happen to the witch's house? How big do you think the new house will be? How will the children feel when they move in with their father?*

Write the new ending on the board, emphasising the importance of using interesting vocabulary. Invite the children to choose another idea and to write their new ending individually this time. Bring the children's attention to the thesaurus, which they may wish to use. Tell them their story only needs to be a few sentences, and this should motivate even the most reluctant to write. Before they start, focus them on the kind of things they might want to think about, such as *How will the children feel at the end of the story? Will your ending be a happy one?*

Read some of the children's story endings to the rest of the class. Choose those that use interesting vocabulary or are particularly well organised. Bring the children's attention to these elements as you read them.

DIFFERENTIATION
Act as scribe for lower attaining children so that their ideas are not stifled by their inability to write well. Choose a few words and ask them to think of substitutes that will make the story more interesting. Challenge higher attaining children to write an alternative ending, imagining what may happen if the children do not kill the witch.

WHERE NEXT
Look at a range of story endings with the class and think of alternative endings to them together. Identify which are happy endings and which are not.

ASSESSMENT
When you mark the children's work, look carefully to see whether they have used interesting vocabulary to extend their ideas.

LEARNING OUTCOMES
The children will write a piece which is relevant and clearly linked to the previous content in a story, thus developing their knowledge and understanding of story structure. They will think imaginatively to create a new ending based on their previous skills and knowledge of story elements and structure.

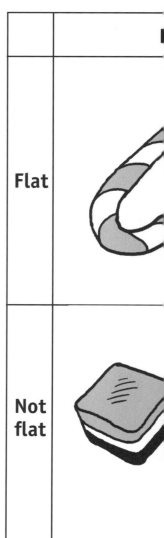

Further English challenges

Hansel, Gretel and another

Ask the children to think of another character to introduce into the story. This could be another person, a pet or a woodland animal. Ask them questions to focus their thinking, such as *Who is*

...gether	Do not fit together

Sweets galore

SUBJECT: MATHS. NNS OBJECTIVE: TO SORT SHAPES AND DESCRIBE SOME OF THEIR FEATURES.

Learning objective

To learn to sort (sweets) into sets according to observable attributes of size, shape and colour and using more than one criterion.

Thinking objective

To sort and analyse shapes.

Thinking skills

The children will use information-processing skills to help them decide which sweets are most suitable for decorating different parts of the witch's house in 'Hansel and Gretel'. The children will analyse and organise the different shapes, colours and types of sweets they have and use this information to reason which are the right size and shape to create the best effect when decorating the house. They will also evaluate the quality of the final result.

What you need

An illustrated version of 'Hansel and Gretel'; a collection of sweets including chocolate fingers or Matchmakers, Smarties, liquorice strips, lollipops, Dolly Mixtures and Liquorice Allsorts; sorting rings; large sheets of paper and drawing materials.

---

the character? What will he or she be like? Will he be friendly? What role will he play? Will he help Hansel and Gretel, or the witch? Ask the children to write a short part only for this character.

The kind witch

Ask the children to imagine that the witch is kind rather than wicked, and challenge them to rewrite the part of the story when the children come to the witch's cottage. Ask, *What sort of house does this witch live in? Is it made from fruit and vegetables to provide a healthy diet for the children who visit? How does she greet them? Does she help them to find their way home?* Talk about the dangers of talking to strangers and going into people's houses without a parent or carer.

What to do

As a whole class, look at a picture of the witch's house in 'Hansel and Gretel' and talk about the decoration. Ask, *What has the witch used? Why has she chosen the things that she has?* Discuss the colours, shapes and sizes of the sweets on her house. Are they arranged to make a pattern or just put in randomly over the house?

Show the children the sweets in your selection. Sort these together using Venn diagrams and, depending on the level of skill of the children in your class, Carroll diagrams (see the example above left). Look at the shape and colour before thinking about sorting them according to whether they would be suitable for decorating the roof, the windows and doors or for making a garden fence. Explain that the criterion for sorting should be whether the shapes will fit together without leaving any spaces. Can the children find anything that will reflect the trees and flowers in the garden?

In groups, ask the children to draw pictures of the witch's house, labelling the sweets used for decoration based on the previous sorting activities and decisions made about the suitability of each sweet. Ask them to say whether each sweet is suitable for the use they have allocated to it because of its shape, size, colour or some other reason.

Bring the class back together and discuss which sweets the children have decided to use. Expect them to give reasons for their choices. Can any of the children in other groups suggest additional reasons for the use of sweets, for example a lollipop looks like the shape of a tree because of the long stick and the big, roundish top part.

DIFFERENTIATION

Limit the range of sweets with lower attaining children so that they do not have too many things to consider. Also limit the sorting to observable attributes only. Ask higher attaining children to think about two criteria for sorting, for example a suitable colour and shape for roofing tiles. Ask them to use Carroll diagrams to note these.

WHERE NEXT

Ask the children to find strategies for sorting the sweets into sets so that they can count the number and types of sweets used.

ASSESSMENT

Check the children use mathematical language and the correct names for the 3-D shapes of the sweets when talking about their work. Note those who can sort using more than one criterion, and who can use this to analyse which are the best shapes to cover or make features for the house.

LEARNING OUTCOMES

The children will learn to analyse and then organise information according to certain criteria. They will also learn to evaluate information.

FURTHER MATHS CHALLENGES
Two colours

Tell the children that Hansel and Gretel decide to build their own house, but they only have sweets of two colours. Ask the children to sort sweets by colour and to choose two sets to create as many designs as they can. Ask, *How have you found using only two colours? Does your design have a pattern? Have you grouped the colours together to make a block of colour?*

Square corners

Give the children a shape problem. Explain that the witch has only square sweets with which to decorate her house. Tell the children that you want them to find all the square sweets from a selection that you give them and find out how many different ways the witch can fit the squares together to make different patterns. Then tell them that she has decided to cut the squares in half to make triangles so that she can make more designs. Encourage the children to find some of the patterns the witch might make.

TRAILBLAZERS

SUBJECT: SCIENCE. QCA UNIT: 1C SORTING AND USING MATERIALS.

LEARNING OBJECTIVES

To understand that materials are chosen for specific purposes; to test ideas about whether materials are suitable for a particular purpose.

THINKING OBJECTIVES

To evaluate information (judging usefulness) and develop criteria for judging; to test conclusions.

THINKING SKILLS

The context here is scientific enquiry, as the children will be involved in planning and carrying out a group investigation. They will be required to test materials and record their results in a table. They will use some evaluative thinking skills when judgng the usefulness of the results and criteria for which materials make good trail indicators.

WHAT YOU NEED

A collection of items that will and will not make good trail markers, such as white and green stones, marbles, paper bits, leaves and breadcrumbs; board or flip chart; paper and writing materials.

WHAT TO DO

Some children will want to test their predictions outside, so arrange a suitable area and adult help as necessary.

Give the children the question you want them to investigate in the lesson: *Which materials are most suitable for Hansel and Gretel to use to make a trail with?* Show the children the collection of materials and items you have. Ask them to say which they think will not make good trails and to give reasons why. Look at the attributes of the items in your collection to inform questions to ask the children about their

Item or mater
Will creatures them?
Will they roll a
Will they blow
Are they light enough to car
Are they readi available?
Can they be se grass?
Can they be se earth?

choices, or to help them make choices. For example, *Is it because they will roll away? What will happen to the item if it rains, or the wind blows? Which items will be seen clearly? Does this depend on the colour of the ground at different times? Which items can we see clearly on earth or on grass?*

Ask the children what they think would, therefore, make good trails. Agree with them the criteria by which the items will be compared. List a set of questions they suggest, which may include: *Will creatures eat them? Will they roll away? Will they blow away? Are they light enough to carry? Are they readily*

White stones	Green stones	Marbles	Paper bits	Breadcrumbs	Leaves
N	N	N	N	Y	Y
Y	Y	Y	N	N	N
N	N	N	Y	Y	Y
Y	Y	Y	Y	Y	Y
Y	N	N	Y	Y	N
Y	N	N	Y	Y	N
N	Y	N	Y	Y	N

available? Can they be seen on grass? Can they be seen on earth? Organise the items into two lists, according to whether the children think they will make good trails or not.

Tell the children you want them to test their predictions in groups of about four. Ask what resources they think they will need, how they are going to test each item, where they will carry out their investigation, who will do what in their groups. Give them time to organise the resources needed to carry out the investigation and to test their predictions.

Tell the groups to use a table to record their results and to evaluate against each of the earlier criteria questions how each item performed as a trail indicator (see the table above left as an example).

Ask the children to use their information to evaluate which material makes the best trail from the collection. How do they know? Ask them to say whether what they found out was what they

expected. Based on what they have found out, can the children suggest additional items which may be suitable?

DIFFERENTIATION
Talk to higher attaining children about how they are recording their information. Is it clear enough for them to use to put the items in order from best to worst?

Organise lower attaining children into small groups so that you can interact with them individually to make sure they understand why they are carrying out the investigation as well as understanding what they have to do to find answers to the questions.

WHERE NEXT
Investigate further items which the children think will make good trail indicators.

ASSESSMENT
Note the children who can plan their investigation and test out their ideas. Who approaches the task systematically and completes a table unaided?

LEARNING OUTCOMES
The children will, with help, make their own suggestions about how to develop criteria to judge the usefulness of materials for a specific purpose. They will go through the process of planning, predicting, testing and saying whether what happened was what they thought would happen.

FURTHER SCIENCE CHALLENGES
Pathways
Ask the children, in groups, to make a pathway around the school for their friends to follow. Tell them they can choose any natural items they like, but they must show the start and finish very clearly. Ask, *Would it be best either to break the branches off trees or make marks on the trees? Which would do least damage and keep the environment looking good?* Give the children a plan of the school and the grounds so that they can plan their route. After they have completed their trails, ask them to evaluate them all, saying which were better than others and why. They can use this information to improve their ideas or create new trails.
Night trails
Set up an investigation to find out which items can be seen in the dark (think about using a dark place, a torch and a collection of items, some of which do and do not glow in the dark). Before carrying out the test, the children should predict which items they will be able to see. Get them to plan and carry the investigation out independently to test their ideas.

FAMOUS AUTHORS

SUBJECT: HISTORY. QCA UNIT: 4 WHY DO WE REMEMBER
FLORENCE NIGHTINGALE?
SUBJECT: ICT. QCA UNIT: 2C FINDING INFORMATION.

LEARNING OBJECTIVES
To ask and answer questions about the life of a
famous person; to use appropriate search techniques
to find information.

THINKING OBJECTIVE
To locate and collect information.

THINKING SKILLS
The children will develop their information-processing
skills by locating and collecting information from
the Internet to find out about the lives and works of
the Brothers Grimm. They will suggest questions to
identify what information they wish to find out about
the Brothers Grimm. They will extend their thinking
by identifying other stories written by the same
authors.

WHAT YOU NEED
Access to the Internet; board or flip chart.

WHAT TO DO
Please follow the school's policy on Internet safety
when carrying out this activity. Use the Internet
prior to teaching the activity and set up a search for
authors. Vet the web pages you find and save them as
favourites, or list those which will prove useful.

Explain to the children that you want
them to find out some things about
the Brothers Grimm, the authors
of 'Hansel and Gretel', using the
Internet. Ask them what kind
of things they could try to
find out. Make a list of these,
and any other of the children's
questions, on the board. Possible
questions could include, *When did
the Brothers Grimm live? How long
ago was that? Where did they come
from? Did they write any other stories?
What were they called?* Then together suggest key
words which can be used in searches on the Internet.
For example, *Wilhelm Grimm, Jacob Grimm, Hansel,
Gretel.*

Model to the class how to find one piece of
information on the Internet. Go to a web page
you have chosen and use *Edit* and *Find* to look for
information based on one of the questions. Print the
information out. Let the children work individually,

in pairs or in small groups to find the answers to the
questions on the Internet.

At some point during the lesson, work with higher
attaining children to make sure they have answered
the questions, and ask them to feed back what they
have found out to the whole class. Invite
additional information from the other
children to add to the list. Record what the
children have found out next to the original
list of questions.

DIFFERENTIATION
Find another story written by the same
authors for lower attaining children to enjoy
with an adult. Read the blurb on the back
cover of the book with them to see what it
tells them about the authors. Allow higher
attaining children free reign to set up their
own searches to locate information on an
Internet site you have chosen.

WHERE NEXT
Ask higher attaining children to identify the
search words needed to locate and collect
information about other fairy tale authors,
such as Hans Christian Anderson. Carry out
one of the searches together so that you can
monitor the children's Internet use.

Show the children stories by more modern
authors and get them to ask questions to
find out about the plot. Can they locate
where to find the answers to their questions
in the story? Make sure
they think of looking
in the text, at the
illustrations and
on the book
cover.

ASSESSMENT
Note the children who
understand how to locate
information using the
resource available to them.
Note those who can search
for information on the Internet,
and plan additional tasks for this group to
do independently at another time to extend this skill.

LEARNING OUTCOMES
Most children will begin to understand that they can
find out about famous people from the past and how
to locate information using the Internet. They will
learn to use ICT to locate and collect information
using straightforward lines of enquiry.

FURTHER HISTORY AND ICT CHALLENGES
Books old and new
Set up an enquiry for the children to ask questions which will help them identify the similarities and differences between modern books and those

belonging to their parents and grandparents (comic books and the characters in them are good for assessing this). Where did the children locate the information they needed to answer their questions? Ask them to list the sources of information they used. These could include text, pictures and information on the covers.

HOME AT LAST

SUBJECT: GEOGRAPHY. QCA UNIT: 1 AROUND OUR SCHOOL – THE LOCAL AREA.

LEARNING OBJECTIVE
To recognise physical and human features, and to describe a route.

THINKING OBJECTIVE
To make deductions.

THINKING SKILLS
The children will deduce how to get from one place to another using co-ordinates on a simple map. This is essentially a self-directed activity, which is guided by your questions. There is also a strong locating element in the activity, requiring the children to find different physical and human features. This activity can be adapted for a map of any story, such as 'Jack and the Beanstalk', 'Snow White' or 'Little Red Riding Hood'.

WHAT YOU NEED
A copy of a map (see illustration, left) showing features in the world of 'Hansel and Gretel', divided into 16 squares labelled A, B, C, D along the bottom and 1, 2, 3, 4 up the side to provide a grid reference; paper and writing materials.

WHAT TO DO
Show the children the map and talk about the features on it. Identify the physical features and those that are made by humans, such as bridges and paths. Talk about the grids that are drawn on the map, too. Ask, *Why does the map have lines drawn on it? Who can tell me the directions that the lines are drawn in? Why are there numbers and letters written across the bottom and up the side?* Explain that this is to help locate exactly where features are on the map.

Ask the children to name the feature that can be found, for example in square B4, D4 or C2, and so on. When you are sure that the children understand how to use the co-ordinates, proceed with the next part of the activity.

Tell the children that you want them to find the way home for Hansel and Gretel from the witch's house. Explain that they need to find a route for the children from the witch's house in D1 to their own home in A4. Let the children work in pairs to find a suitable route. If they get stuck or are not finding a suitable route, ask them: *How will you get over the river? How will you make sure that you do not go too close to the cave where the forest wolf lives? Can you find a different way so that you don't go too near the dragon's lair?*

Ask the children to list the co-ordinates of the route they intend to take, such as D1 to D2 to C2, and so on, and when they have all finished share some of the routes with the class. Check to make sure that they all cross the river safely, do not go too near the cave and find their way home.

DIFFERENTIATION

Divide the map into more than 16 squares for those who are more able. Give them a blank version and ask them to add the grid references themselves.

Make a large floor version of the map for lower attaining children so they can walk through the route. Transfer the activity to a paper copy when you are sure they understand.

WHERE NEXT

Look at a road map of the local area which has gride references on it. Give the children a starting and finishing point and ask them to find a way from one place to another. Can they work out what physical and human features they will pass on the way?

Give the children a road map – this could be the role-play road mats usually found in most Reception classes, a picture map of the Isle of Struay or a large map you have made yourself – and ask them to locate the feature in a particular square. Then ask them to write down the co-ordinates for certain features and to locate the human and physical features they can see on the map.

ASSESSMENT

Note the children who are able to follow the map and find a suitable route to get Hansel and Gretel safely home. Note those who can locate the different features on the map and deduce the positions by using co-ordinates. Who can reason sufficiently to find a safe route home for Hansel and Gretel?

LEARNING OUTCOMES

Most children will be able to locate the physical and human features on a map, using suitable geographical vocabulary. Some will locate these using simple co-ordinates and be able to plot a route between two points. Many will use their reasoning skills and think creatively to decide which is the most suitable route to take to get the children home safely.

FURTHER GEOGRAPHY CHALLENGES

Co-ordinated maps

Challenge the children to add a grid to a map of the school grounds, the local area or local playground. Challenge them to use the co-ordinates to locate different features and objects such as the swings, pedestrian crossing or school pond. Ask them to think of questions to ask their friends so they can deduce in which squares certain things are.

Find me

Add pictoral evidence of animal life to the map in the main activity. For example, deer prints, birds' nests, rabbit droppings, feathers, wool, butterfly cocoons, leaves and scratched bark. Challenge the children to find all the signs of animal life in the forest. Can they deduce which animals are present in the forest from the clues they have left behind?

A HOUSE MADE FROM CAKE

SUBJECT: DESIGN AND TECHNOLOGY. QCA UNIT: 1C EAT MORE FRUIT AND VEGETABLES.

LEARNING OBJECTIVE

To develop design ideas, and to select and use appropriate cakes to make a model.

THINKING OBJECTIVE

To think laterally and imaginatively.

THINKING SKILLS

The children will draw upon their creative skills to design and decorate model houses made from cakes. They will think laterally to work out how to cut and place the shapes together to make the different areas of the house, before using their imagination to decorate the finished house with sweets. They will evaluate how successfully their model has been created and make suggestions on how to make improvements.

WHAT YOU NEED

A design for a decorated cake made in a previous lesson (see What to do); play dough; cakes in cuboid shapes, both large and small, such as Battenburg or Jamaican ginger cake; small Swiss rolls; icing sugar; water; bowls; plastic knives; palette knives; sweets for decoration; a camera; paper and drawing materials.

WHAT TO DO

In a previous lesson, get the children to design a cake model of the witch's house in 'Hansel and Gretel'. Use pictures of the witch's house from a copy of the story to inspire them. Make sure they focus on what shape the roof, bottom of the house and chimney are.

Share their designs. Then shape some of the play dough into cuboid and cylindrical shapes. Fix the cylinder onto the cuboid and ask the children if this looks like a house. Explore with them which shape is missing. Identify that it is the triangular prism shape that makes the roof.

Show the children the cakes. Ask, *Do we have a cake which is a triangular prism shape? How can we change a cuboid into a triangular prism shape?* Invite some children to show how this can be done by asking them to reshape a cuboid-shaped piece of play dough. Explain that the cake cannot be reshaped in the same way because it cannot be moulded. Suggest to the children that they may wish to use an item in your set of resources to convert the cuboid cake into

a triangular shape. If no one suggests it, show the children the plastic knife and suggest that they may wish to cut the cuboid. Let a few children experiment with this and if they do not solve the problem themselves, show them how to cut the cuboid diagonally from corner to corner and either use one half to make the roof shape or reposition the two parts to make a triangular prism shape. You may wish to do this as a maths problem-solving activity earlier in the week.

Show the children the larger cuboid and small cylindrical cakes. Ask, *Do you have cakes of the matching shapes to make the different parts of your model? Which shape is missing?* Note again that the missing shape is the triangular prism to make the roof shape. Cut the cakes in the same way as the earlier explorations.

Next, explore with the children how they can join the cakes together. Ask, *How can we stop the cakes coming apart? How can we get the sweet decorations to stick to the cake house?*

Again, your set of resources can act as tips if no one comes up with a suitable suggestion. Show them how to mix the icing sugar and spread some onto the cakes, joining them together to make the shape of a house. Agree with the children that it does look like a house.

Either let the children make small cake houses individually from the smaller cakes, or let them make one large house in groups, using larger cakes. Allow them to spread icing over the outside and to decorate the house with sweets. Tell the children to follow their original design to decorate their houses.

Either ask the children to draw pictures of their finished houses or take photographs. Ask the children to list the tools they used and to say what they did to join the materials together. They could also write a short evaluation of their models and suggest improvements that could be made to them.

Enjoy the cakes after lunch, being careful not to damage teeth or trigger allergies. Perhaps a tooth brushing activity can follow this. Alternatively, let the children take the cakes home to share with their families.

DIFFERENTIATION

Give the children who cannot 'see' where to place the cake shapes, 3-D shapes to work with. When they have put the shapes into the correct position to make a triangular prism, let them copy the design with the cakes.

Higher attaining children should be encouraged to design their cake house first, labelling which shapes and cakes they need and listing the sweets for the decoration.

WHERE NEXT

Plan additional cooking activities for the children to create imaginary creatures or real animals that live in the wood. For example, use chocolate, shredded wheat and puffed rice cereal to model creatures with fine hair, or chocolate and cornflakes to make hedgehogs.

ASSESSMENT

Note which children were thinking laterally to work out how to make the triangular prism shape of the roof from the cuboid-shaped cake. Note those children who use their imaginations well in decorating the house with suitable shaped and coloured sweets.

LEARNING OUTCOMES

The children will learn to select relevant tools and components and use a range of techniques to create models from different shapes and sizes of cake. They will think laterally to solve the problem of making shapes from other shapes, and use their imagination to decorate their finished models. Their evaluation of their finished models will lead to consideration of techniques and design, and any improvements that need to be made.

FURTHER DESIGN AND TECHNOLOGY CHALLENGES

3-D characters

Give the children nets of a pyramid, cone, cylinder and cuboid and a range of materials to use in making those shapes. Help the children to fold and glue the nets into the relevant shapes. Then let them choose from a range of items to add features to their shapes in order to make different characters. Let the children's imaginations run wild. Remind them that you want characters rather than people, and that these can include animals, robots or even imaginary beings from outer space! They could include characters from the 'Hansel and Gretel' story, too. You could also challenge the children to make their characters with limbs and other features that move if appropriate.

Cake magic

Let the children think imaginatively to come up with other models that can be made from cake. Let them design and label the shapes they will need before making their models. Compare these to pictures in a recipe book to see whether they have thought of anything unique. Get them to write instructions in a recipe format outlining how to make their models, before choosing different ones to make as group activities.

CHARACTER MUSIC

SUBJECT: MUSIC. QCA OBJECTIVE: 2 SOUNDS INTERESTING.

LEARNING OBJECTIVES

To explore expressive use of sounds; to explore instruments.

THINKING OBJECTIVE

To think imaginatively.

THINKING SKILLS

The children will work together as a class to think about the character of the witch in 'Hansel and Gretel'. They will begin to consider the sounds they could use to paint a picture of the witch before working in small groups to compose their own piece of music. The questions will direct their thinking to consider several musical elements, such as pitch, tempo and dynamics. They will evaluate each other's work to select the bits they like in order to make a class composition.

WHAT YOU NEED

A range of pitched and unpitched instruments, including a xylophone; a tape recorder; board or flip chart.

WHAT TO DO

Ask the children to think about the characters in the story 'Hansel and Gretel' and list them on the board. Concentrate on the witch with the class, as this is probably the most vivid character to compose a musical picture of. Encourage the children to talk about her character. Ask, *What is she like? What does her voice sound like? How do you think she moves? Does she like the children in the story?*

Together, choose an instrument that the children think would be good to depict the witch's character, such as a cymbal or drum. Ask, *How should we play this instrument to represent the witch? Do we need a loud or a quiet sound? A fast or slow beat?*

Develop the character sound by adding a tune on a xylophone. Ask, *Do we need a tune that goes up or down? Can you create a repeating pattern with long and short notes? Can we play several instruments together to make the character sound more dramatic and scary?*

Divide the class into groups and ask them to come up with a composition for the witch's character, using their own choice of instruments and how to play them to create the sounds they want.

Then ask the class to evaluate each group composition and to pick out the bits they like best from each to make one overall performance. Record this on tape for use later.

DIFFERENTIATION
Challenge higher attaining children to compose music for the characters of the step mother and the father in the story, and to evaluate each other's work. Ask lower attaining children to think about the sounds of the animals that Hansel and Gretel may have heard when they were lost in the forest. Ask them to compose sound effects for the animals they

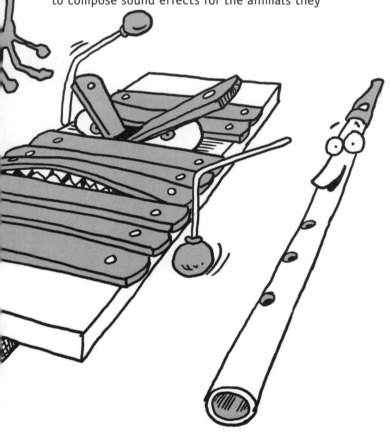

want to include. Extend the learning by suggesting they combine more than one musical element to improve the texture of their pieces. Ask, *How can the sounds be changed to alter the timbre?* If the children struggle with this ask them to compose rhythmic accompaniments to their piece with a repeating pattern. This will begin to extend their learning beyond the average.

WHERE NEXT
Divide the class into groups to make music for all the characters in 'Hansel and Gretel'. Put the compositions together and read the story with the sound effects added. Use the children's compositions to accompany a series of dance lessons. Get the class to perform their finished dance to another class and ask them to evaluate it.

ASSESSMENT
Monitor the children's group work and ask questions to get them talking about their imaginative thinking processes. Questions will also encourage them to evaluate how they have used the elements in their compositions and to consider how effectively they have used them.

LEARNING OUTCOMES
The children will think imaginatively to use musical elements to represent a character from a story. They will think about the effects that the combination of different musical elements have. They will evaluate the performances of themselves and others and note how the evaluation process can be used to make improvements to their own work.

FURTHER MUSIC CHALLENGES
Story extracts
Choose different parts of 'Hansel and Gretel' and ask the children to compose sound effects to reflect what is happening. They will need to use their imaginations to consider sounds that may help to show this, such as the roaring fire as the witch cooks the bread for dinner, the bird song as Gretel collects wood to feed the fire. Evaluate the elements the children have used and ask them to think about how these can be developed further, by playing instruments in different ways to create different timbres, for instance.
Sweet delight
Ask the children to think about the feelings of Hansel and Gretel when they start to eat the house. Tell them to use their imaginations to compose music to depict these feelings in groups. Ask, *What sort of music would show their delight?* Invite the children to use body percussion as well as traditional instruments. Suggest they include some short sequences and sound effects which show that the children shouldn't be doing this, because they don't know who lives in the house. Listen to the sounds the groups have composed and ask the children to evaluate whether they effectively paint a picture of the children's feelings. Gather the children's ideas about the feelings that the different sounds evoke.

FEELINGS

SUBJECT: RE. QCA UNIT: 2B WHY DID JESUS TELL STORIES?

LEARNING OBJECTIVE
To identify with feelings and understand that feelings are important emotions.

THINKING OBJECTIVE
To make inferences.

THINKING SKILLS
The children will look closely at part of 'Hansel and Gretel', and will begin to infer how the characters are feeling at different points. They will be able to identify the author's use of a number of feelings and emotions in the story which help to keep the reader's attention. They will also need to think imaginatively and to extend ideas in this activity.

WHAT YOU NEED
Four large sheets of paper; A4 paper and writing materials; board or flip chart.

WHAT TO DO
Remind the children of the story. Divide an area of the board into four parts, writing one of the following four sections of the story in each:
1. The children hear their stepmother plotting to leave them in the forest.
2. The children are lost in the forest.
3. The children kill the witch.
4. The children find their way home and are greeted by their father.

Talk to the whole class about the first section, and how the children must have felt when they heard their stepmother talking about leaving them in the forest. Suggest they probably felt sad and frightened, but can the children think of other feelings they may have felt? Ideas could include angry, confused, upset, disbelieving and determined. Record the children's ideas in the first section on the board and ask a few volunteers to act out each part to add first-hand experience to the discussion.

Organise the children into four groups and allocate each group a section of the story. Give them a large sheet of paper on which to record their ideas about the feelings the children may have had in their part of the story. Let a lower attaining group work with an adult to act out the first part of the story. Reinforce with them how they can infer the way Hansel and

Gretel must have felt when they overheard their stepmother plotting.

Give the children about ten minutes to talk and record their ideas before gathering them back together to listen to each other's ideas. List their ideas on the master copy on the board. When each group has finished relating their list of feelings, invite the other groups to add some more of their own. Question them to prompt additional feelings. For example, *When the children were lost in the wood, were they brave in trying to find their way home?* This will steer the children away from thinking about negative feelings.

Take one positive emotion and one negative one from those listed and explore with the children one or two of their own experiences both at home and at school. Can the children think of a time when they forgot to consider the feelings of others? Can they remember an occasion when they were very considerate? Can they remember an occasion when their feelings were not considered, when someone was unkind or unthoughtful towards them? What could that person have done to make things better?

Finish by asking the children to draw a picture of one positive and one negative occasion, and to indicate their feelings by drawing a happy or sad face next to it.

DIFFERENTIATION
Ask an adult to work with lower attaining children to talk about how they know how the characters are feeling. Ask the adult to question the children in order to prompt their ideas. Allocate the third section to the higher attaining children and expect them to think carefully about the rights and wrongs of killing the witch.

WHERE NEXT
Tell the children some of the stories that Jesus told, and ask them to infer from the events how the different characters must have felt, and what messages the stories are giving.

Read the story of Joseph to the children and discuss the many feelings he, his brothers and his father may have felt as the story unfolds. Repeat the activity with the story of Rama and Sita.

ASSESSMENT
Note the children who understand how they can infer how characters are feeling from the events in a story and can say how people's behaviour and attitudes can have an impact on the feelings of others.

LEARNING OUTCOMES
The children will learn to empathise with the central feelings and responses of the characters in a story by inferring what they must be feeling.

FURTHER RE CHALLENGES
Wet Mondays
Read a poem to the children about wet weather. 'A Dibble-dubble Day' by Joan Poulson, in *Twinkle Twinkle Chocolate Bar* compiled by John Foster (Oxford University Press), is suitable. Develop the children's inference skills by asking them to list all the emotions and feelings they might have on such a day. Prompt them with questions, such as *Do you like wearing your wellingtons, splashing in puddles and getting wet? Do you have a favourite umbrella or raincoat which you like to carry or wear? Who might be happy about the rain? Who will not like the rain?*
People who help us
List all the people the children can think of who they might go to for help if they have a problem. Develop

the children's inference skills by asking them to say how they know they can trust these people. Ask them, *Is it because they wear a uniform? Is it because you know them? Is it because your parents know them?* Reinforce the rule that the children should never go off with anyone, not even the people they have listed, unless their parents know.

THE WITCH'S RIDE

SUBJECT: PE. QCA UNIT: DANCE ACTIVITIES UNIT 2.

LEARNING OBJECTIVE
To compose and perform dance phrases which express and communicate ideas.

THINKING OBJECTIVE
To evaluate movements.

THINKING SKILLS
Using a piece of music for inspiration, the children will think about the character of the witch in 'Hansel and Gretel' and create a dance to represent what the music suggests she is doing. The children will think about how she looks, what she is doing and the reasons for the flight. They will look at the movements in the dance, evaluating them and suggesting improvements by adding interest in dynamics, direction, rhythm and speed. They will also need to think imaginatively to conjure up a picture in their heads of the witch flying over the treetops in the forest.

WHAT YOU NEED
The four minute extract 'Witch's Ride' from the opera *Hansel and Gretel* by Engelbert Humperdinck.

WHAT TO DO
Play the children the opening 12 bars of the music and talk about what the witch may be doing. Has she started to fly yet or is she preparing to fly?

Ask the children to develop an opening to a dance to this part of the music. Depending on the children's ideas this could include the witch walking purposefully towards where she has left her broomstick, climbing on her broomstick and holding tight, or standing and looking around to see where she will fly.

Listen to the next part and decide together all the different directions the witch may travel in. As the music is playing ask the children, *Will she move straight forwards to this part? Will she go backwards? Will she go round in circles? Will she zig-zag? Will she go fast, slow or a mixture of the two? Will she stop and look around at all?*

As a class, develop a sequence of movements which show the witch flying in different directions, in different patterns and at different speeds. Develop some of the actions she may be doing, such as looking for food or someone to talk to – perhaps another, friendly witch.

Invite the children to describe which movements they like and why. Encourage them to describe the shape of the movements, how the space is used, the speed and rhythm employed. Ask questions to encourage the children to start evaluating the movements, such as *Can you suggest any improvements to make the dance more dramatic? Do the movements show a variety of flying moves? Do they show the character of the witch? Is she enjoying the flight? How do you know?*

Play some more of the music and ask the children to listen for the clue which tells them that she has started to slow down and look for her house in order to land (it's about two minutes into the music and is symbolised by a large chord). Then listen to the last two minutes and ask the children to think about what her landing looks like. Ask, *How does she land – gently and smoothly, or with a bump?*

Agree at which part of the music you will create the ending to the dance. Ask, *How will you make sure that the audience knows it is the end of the dance? Will you change the direction and speed of the movements? Will they become simpler?* Suggest they consider using a balance or representing the witch walking into her house and replacing her broom before making breakfast.

DIFFERENTIATION

Retell the story to individual children to help them think about the character of the witch and the things she may be doing. Reinforce the beginning, middle and end of the dance by reminding the children when to change the dynamics and levels of their movements. Involve the children in the evalalution so that they can hear for themselves when to make changes in response to the music.

WHERE NEXT

Incorporate the children's character compositions to build an imaginative dance to tell the whole story of 'Hansel and Gretel'. Get the children to perform the dance to another class, without telling them which part of the story it represents. Invite the children to guess which character the dance depicts and what is happening. Afterwards, ask your class to consider why the audience said what they did.

ASSESSMENT

Note the children who are beginning to understand how to use other people's ideas and suggestions to improve the interest of their movements. Which children co-operate and develop ideas together before thinking about individual sequences and movements?

LEARNING OUTCOMES

Most children will be able to explore and select suitable movements and evaluate these, developing them to add interest to their work. They will work together to select those movements they like and develop these in response to the needs of the music. They will also develop their creative thinking by responding to musical stimuli and use their enquiry skills to make improvements to their work.

FURTHER PE CHALLENGES

Visiting places

Extend the story 'Hansel and Gretel' by pretending that the witch has gone somewhere else to visit. Can the children imagine what sort of places she has visited? Choose pieces of music to match the children's suggestions and get them to build a longer dance sequence for the witch's travels. Ask the children in groups to develop a different scene to show the rest of the class. They should evaluate and help each other improve the movements, changes of direction, speed and rhythm before performing the whole dance.

Treetops

Ask the children to imagine the things which the witch might see on her journey. Suggest characters, like small animals and birds, to prompt the children's imaginations. Organise the class into pairs, and ask one child to act out the part of the witch and the other the part of an animal. Ask the 'witches' to identify the things which they may find interesting and may want to linger to look more closely at during their journeys. Tell them to think about these things in their movements and to incorporate changes in speed and direction as they fly around the forest. Ask the 'animals' to evaluate their movements by getting them to think about what they are feeling, and whether they will want to stay and look at the witch or dive for cover to hide from her.